WORLD CROP PROTECTION

Volume 2

PESTICIDES

WORLD CROP PROTECTION

Volume 2

PESTICIDES

K. A. HASSALL, PH.D., B.SC., F.R.I.C.

Senior Lecturer in Crop Protection and Biochemistry
University of Reading

LONDON   ILIFFE BOOKS LTD

ILIFFE BOOKS LTD
42 RUSSELL SQUARE
LONDON, W.C.1

© K. A. Hassall 1969

First published in 1969

592 00031 1

Filmset by Photoprint Plates Ltd
Wickford, Essex
Printed in England by
J. W. Arrowsmith Ltd., Bristol

CONTENTS

PREFACE

Few subjects, even within the rapidly expanding discipline of biological chemistry, have catalysed so much controversy as has the use of chemicals for crop protection. The present volume is intended as an introduction to this important subject—one which is likely to become both more fundamentally based and more controversial as the areas of monoculture enlarge to match increasing world population. In general, the subject matter should be readily intelligible to any reader with the equivalent of advanced level chemistry, especially if this knowledge is associated with some wider reading in applied biology or biochemistry. It should therefore be of interest to the educated layman who is dissatisfied with the emotive and incomplete accounts which occur only too frequently in the popular press, as well as to farmers, undergraduates and advisory officers of many kinds. I should like to stress in this respect that, after half a lifetime studying the effects of toxic substances, I no more condone the haphazard use of toxic substances without prior consideration of possible alternatives, than I can accept the view that, in a world in which man has deliberately opted out of the usual mechanisms leading to species equilibration, poisons should in no circumstances be applied to edible crops. Imperfect though chemical control often is, it is a valuable method for buying time for the nations of the world to put their social and political houses in order by methods leading directly or indirectly to birth control.

It is apparent to those concerned with the teaching of the chemistry of crop protection that, while the substances used in the field vary from year to year, and while the relative importance of various groups of compounds at any one time may not be the same in different countries, there is nevertheless a dimension in which the subject is evolving much more slowly. The principles governing the formulation, method of application, metabolism and potential toxic hazard of crop protection chemicals are, within limits, applicable to most insecticides, fungicides and herbicides; (the unsatisfactory, but only general term, pesticide, from '*pest :* anything noxious, mischievous or destructive' will be used to cover these and other crop protection chemicals). Thus phase distribution phenomena of various types, together with chemical stability in a variety of circumstances, are of overall importance for many types of compounds with many different uses, while the biological problems associated with the use of toxic chemicals on, in, or near edible crops present few problems which are unknown in other branches of toxicology. Surprises and new problems will inevitably turn up, especially when entirely new groups of compounds are introduced or when well known substances are applied in some novel way, but the difficulty is mitigated at the present time by the fact that the great post-war explosion in new *types* of pesticides appears to be subsiding. Nevertheless, the important metabolic contribution made by microsomal enzymes has for some years interested workers in many branches of toxicology and there is considerable evidence that fundamentally similar mechanisms may lead to the detoxication of pesticides belonging to quite different chemical classes.

These scientific principles which relate to the formulation, persistance, degradation, synergism, toxicology and side effects of pesticides form much of the subject matter of this book. Individual compounds are used to illustrate how these principles work out in practice when applied to substances of different types but, for the reasons outlined above, the title 'World Crop Protection—Pesticides' does not imply that every compound of local importance in crop protection has been mentioned by name. Indeed, whatever the objections which may be levelled at a necessarily subjective choice of examples, the inclusion of all crop protection substances which are in use at the time of writing (and dozens more will be in use by next year) would lead either to an unreadable catalogue or to a voluminous text quite unsuited to the needs of those who wish to see the wood rather than the trees. It is also probably true that no book which merely catalogued the many hundreds of chemicals in use at any one time would be of practical relevance a decade later, whereas the underlying principles are likely to be as enduring as the subject itself.

Nor is this book concerned with the individual practical uses of particular chemicals for the control of infestations or infections of particular crops. The latter task has been undertaken by Dr. Gayner and Mr. Stapley in a companion volume in this series (World Crop Protection, Volume 1, Pests and Diseases). Conversely, those who wish to know more about the materials referred to by these authors will find that most of the major groups they mention are discussed in this book from the chemical, biochemical and toxicological point of view.

1969   K.A.H.

1

SOME GENERAL CONSIDERATIONS

THE HISTORICAL SETTING

The use of toxic chemicals to combat pests is by no means new, for Homer mentioned the fumigant value of burning sulphur, and Pliny (AD 79) advocated the insecticidal use of arsenic. By the sixteenth century, the Chinese were employing moderate amounts of arsenical compounds as insecticides, and at least 300 years ago the first natural insecticide—the nicotine in extracts of tobacco—was in use against the plum curculio and the lace bug. By 1828, another plant, pyrethrum, was providing a second natural insecticide and in the middle of the nineteenth century, soap was added to the list of insecticides, for it was being used to kill aphids, and sulphur had been advocated as a fungicide on peach trees. A treatise by Forsyth published over 150 years ago described clearly the preparation of a combined wash to combat insects and fungi:

'Take tobacco one pound, sulphur two pounds, unslaked lime one peck . . . pour on the above ingredients ten gallons of boiling water . . .' (See Horsfall, 1956).

The discovery of these pesticides can probably be attributed, like many quasi-medical remedies of early times, to an admixture of acute observation following trial and error application, with undertones of superstition. But by the middle of the nineteenth century the first scientific and systematic studies were appearing. The range of materials used for pest control widened somewhat, but the materials remained of simple chemical composition. Experimentation with new arsenical compounds led, for example, to the introduction in 1867 of an impure copper arsenite called Paris Green, in an attempt to check the serious spread of the Colorado beetle in the State of Mississippi. Its use had become so widespread by 1900 against

I

both the Colorado beetle and the codlin moth, that, according to De Ong (1956), it occasioned the introduction of the first State legislation governing the use of insecticides in the United States of America. In the meantime, Bordeaux mixture (comprising copper sulphate, lime and water) was introduced as a fungicide in 1885 for the control of downy mildew of vine (Horsfall, 1956), while, by the turn of the century, lime sulphur was well established in both Europe and California as a fungicide against diseases of fruit trees. These inorganic fungicides are still of importance, and are discussed in Chapter 7.

In 1896 a French grape grower, who was applying Bordeaux mixture to his vines, noticed that the fungicide caused the leaves of yellow charlock growing nearby to turn black. It was probably from this chance observation that the idea of selective herbicidal action originated. Shortly afterwards, it was observed that iron sulphate, when sprayed on to a mixture of cereal and dicotyledonous weeds, killed the weeds but left the cereal undamaged. Within the next decade, many other simple inorganic substances, including sodium nitrate, ammonium sulphate and sulphuric acid, were found to have selective properties when applied at suitable concentrations. Ordish (1963, 1964) has referred to several interesting examples of the early use of various types of pesticides.

The use of pesticides accelerated during the inter-war years, and the number and complexity of the materials employed increased simultaneously. In particular, organic substances began to replace certain of the inorganic compounds. Amongst the relatively simple organic materials introduced during this period were tar oil, petroleum oil and dinitro-ortho-cresol. The latter substance eventually replaced tar oil for the control of eggs of aphids, and a few years later, in 1932, its use as a selective herbicide was recognised by the filing of a French patent covering its use for the control of weeds in cereals. It is probable that the increased use of pesticides during the period 1925–45 was one of several factors contributing to the greatly increased farming efficiency which was a striking feature of that time.

Two further advances of note occurred during the second world war. One of these, the discovery of DDT, dichlorodiphenyl trichloroethane, was made in Switzerland and the second, the introduction of insecticidal organophosphorus compounds, was a German success. Although discovered in 1942, the great insecticidal potential of DDT was not fully appreciated until 1944, when it enabled a severe typhus epidemic in Italy to be brought under control. Its introduction led naturally to the mass screening of thousands of organochlorine compounds (or chlorinated hydrocarbons, as they were at first called), with the result that, in 1942, benzene hexachloride, BHC, was discovered in the biological laboratories of Imperial Chemical Industries Ltd. This search was also partly occasioned by the need to find an alternative to derris powder, when, because of the war, supplies ceased to arrive from Malaya. Meanwhile, in Germany, the insecticidal value of organophosphorus compounds had been discovered by a team, under Schrader, which had been searching not only for a nicotine substitute, but also for new poisonous gases for use in warfare. Further information about the organochlorine insecticides is to be found in Chapter 4, while Chapter 5 describes the chemistry and toxicology of organophosphorus compounds.

Several organic substances had found rather restricted use as fungicides long before the successes of the organochlorine and organophosphorus insecticides gave additional impetus to the search for new materials. Organomercury compounds, for example, had been marketed as seed dressings before the beginning of the first world war, and salicylanilide, first introduced for the control of mould on textiles, was used successfully against the tomato leaf mould in 1931. In the same year a patent was issued to an American firm covering the fungicidal uses of the dithiocarbamates, a group of poisons which has proved to be one of the most valuable introduced so far (Chapter 8).

Chloranil was available as a seed dressing by 1940. Since then, the impact of the development of many organic insecticides has stimulated a flood of new fungicides—derivatives of phthalimide, glyoxalidine, guanidine, nitrobenzene, and many others. In recent years, much work has also been directed towards finding an efficient systemic fungicide, that is, one which will penetrate into and persist within a plant for a limited period of time. The success of the new protective fungicides, and the disappointments which have attended work on systemic fungicides, are described in Chapter 8.

Organic herbicides of a more or less selective nature, such as hydrocarbon oils and dinitro-ortho-cresol, assumed increasing importance in the years just before the second world war, but it was back-room investigations during this period that were to revolutionise weed control. Observations by Zimmermann in 1935 suggested that certain synthetic substances could produce effects upon plant growth which resembled those caused by natural growth regulators. A continuation of this work led Slade, Templeman and Sexton (1945) to observe that yellow charlock was killed by a concentration of α-naphthylacetic acid which had no deleterious effects on oats. Further studies led to the introduction of the phenoxyacetic acid group of herbicides, typical members of which are dichlorophenoxyacetic acid, 2,4-D, and methylchlorophenoxyacetic acid, MCPA. These, and

3

higher homologues which have more specialised uses, are described in Chapter 9.

As with fungicides and insecticides, the usage, as well as the number, of organic herbicides increased enormously in the period 1945–55. In 1946, Templeman and Sexton pioneered work on the herbicidal uses of the esters of carbamic acid. It was at first hoped that these would be complementary in action to the phenoxycarboxylic acid herbicides, and would control grasses growing in dicotyledonous crops. Their early promise was, in this respect, hardly fulfilled; but the pure and applied research which followed their introduction catalysed a chain reaction which was to lead to the discovery, development and marketing of herbicidal derivatives of urea, triazole and triazine. It also led to the development of pre-emergence techniques, in which the chemical is applied directly to the soil before the crop emerges. As will be seen in Chapter 2, substitution of the essentially hydrophilic surface of soil for the lipophilic surface of a leaf enables different chemical and physical attributes of both toxicant and its carrier to be exploited, and so widens the range and versatility of materials available for crop protection. These soil-directed herbicides, as well as quaternary ammonium and other new foliage poisons, are described in Chapter 9.

PRODUCTION AND UTILISATION OF PESTICIDES

Surprisingly little reliable information exists about world statistics on pesticides, or indeed, about the form such information should take to facilitate its interpretation. According to Holmes (1960), perhaps the best single measure of world dependence on these materials would be an assessment of the total arable acreage sprayed, and a comparison of these figures as they change from year to year. Unfortunately, such data are seldom available except for a few specialised areas, and it is therefore necessary to resort to less adequate methods of representation, which include estimates of the total tonnage of pesticides in use at a given time, or the total financial outlay on them. It should be remembered, however, that different pesticides differ both in cost and in potency, and therefore the changing pattern of pesticide utilisation from year to year might well be hidden behind gross statistics of this sort.

World sales of pesticides are probably of the order of £200 million p.a. In the United States of America, sales amounted to about £95 million in 1957–8, and it has been estimated that this annual figure may well quadruple within seventeen years (Vernon, 1958). In Britain, according to Edson (1963), the farming community was spending approximately

4

£25 million annually on pesticides—or approximately 1·4% of the total estimated annual value of British agricultural produce—to purchase some 150 different active spray ingredients made up in over 750 different formulations.

So far as tonnage is concerned, the most complete figures are probably those compiled by the Food and Agriculture Organisation (F.A.O.) of the United Nations. Even these, however, are not always easy to interpret, for some of the member nations have provided data based upon tonnage of active ingredient while others have given figures which refer to diluted trade products. Of the insecticides, the organochlorine compounds are still the most widely employed; according to F.A.O. figures for 1962, the world utilisation was then about 170,000 metric tons. If the pattern of earlier years (Gunther and Jeppson, 1960) has been retained, the tonnage of DDT is likely to account for rather over half of this figure. On the other hand, the organophosphorus compounds have assumed greatly increased importance in recent years. In 1954 parathion and TEPP (tetraethyl pyrophosphate) together accounted for almost all the organophosphorus insecticides produced in the United States of America, and their combined tonnage was less than one-twentieth of that of DDT. Yet estimates made from F.A.O. data for 1962 suggest that by then the world utilisation of organophosphorus compounds had risen to over 100,000 metric tons—approximately 60% of the organochlorine insecticide production for that year.

According to Gayner (1961), the world expenditure in 1958 on agricultural fungicides, expressed in terms of wholesale prices, was of the order of £40 million. In terms of tonnage of active ingredient, sulphur was the most widely used material. Even excluding sulphur employed in the form of lime sulphur, some 275,000 tons were then employed in world agriculture. In comparison, 56,000 tons of copper (corresponding to about 224,000 tons of hydrated copper sulphate) were employed in various formulations, while the combined tonnage of all organic fungicides (expressed as active ingredients) amounted at that time to only 12,000 tons. Since then, the production of organic fungicides has probably risen considerably and the use of copper compounds may well have declined.

Shaw (1963) reported that approximately 90,000 tons of herbicides were being employed annually on 90 million acres in the United States of America. This corresponds to the use of 2·2 lb herbicides for every acre under cultivation. Nearly the whole of the tonnage of weedkillers now in use comprises the 'hormone' type of compounds, of which 2,4-D and MCPA are the best known. The importance of these materials rests in the fact that they control weeds in cereal crops, and since these crops tend to be grown in vast areas of monoculture, chemical control is frequently the only practicable solution to the weed problem. In contrast, in many parts of the world where money is short but labour is cheap, and where factors such as quality of soil and low rainfall severely limit food production, it is not unusual to find that negligible amounts of weedkillers are employed at the present time.

ECONOMIC ASPECTS OF PESTS AND THEIR CONTROL

The food losses attributable to all forms of pests, including for this purpose pathogens and weeds as well as arthropods, are very difficult to estimate, and to a certain extent the estimates are subjective in nature—it is not easy to say with certainty what the yield of a crop might have been in some hypothetical, disease-free circumstance. Nevertheless, farmers are usually shrewd business men, and the remarkable increase in utilisation of pesticides implies that they recognise that a problem exists and that it can in part be mitigated by the use of these substances.

The losses which can be attributed to pests are of several kinds. Sometimes, losses occur as a result of direct reduction of growth with concomitant reduction of yield; such reduction results both from competition of weeds and from damage caused by insects and pathogens. Frequently, a loss of quality is also evident; deformed, discoloured or small-sized produce often carries small market value. A third type of loss relates to costs incurred by the farmer in attempts, successful or otherwise, to reduce damage caused by pests; in addition to the cost of chemicals and their application, there may be costs arising from additional cultivations or from the need to purchase more expensive, resistant varieties of crop. Furthermore, resistant varieties are sometimes less productive than susceptible ones, and indirect costs are incurred this way, as they may be when the farmer resorts to crop rotation for the purpose of crop hygiene.

As has been mentioned, it is difficult to quantify losses although figures of the order of a 10 to 20% loss of useful crop are frequently quoted both in the United States of America and in Britain. Assuming prices would not fall if crop losses were suddenly eliminated—itself a rather dubious assumption, at least for some types of crops, as Ordish (1963) has pointed out—the annual loss to British agriculture can be calculated to be about £150 million to £300 million, inclusive of the cost of control measures. Gunther and Jeppson (1960) have quoted estimates of losses in America; excluding the cost of control measures, the annual loss to American agriculture could well exceed £3,000 million. Clearly, even allowing for gross

6

inaccuracy and for disagreement about various terms of reference, pests of all kinds lead to great financial losses, wastage of produce and also of land (since more land is needed to grow unit amount of food if the yield per acre is lowered by pests). To these losses must be added any losses taking place during storage and transport, for insects, rodents and fungi may destroy 10% or more of all stored produce in the absence of control measures. In human terms, as well as in financial ones, the bill is a heavy one and any method of control would seem desirable—even though solutions to problems in science have an embarrassing habit of throwing up new problems at the same time. Chemicals have been, on the whole, of great value, but as will be shown, they have created a number of difficulties of their own.

ACUTE AND CHRONIC TOXICITY

Two distinct types of toxic effects can be observed for many poisons. Since, for any one poison, there may be little or no relation between either the mechanism of these two kinds of toxic action or the magnitude of the concentrations which evoke them, the two effects must be carefully distinguished. An acute toxic response is one which occurs shortly after application of a single dose of the poison. It is determined by the intrinsic toxicity of the substance to the organism and can often be traced to some specific disruptive effect at the biochemical level. A chronic effect, on the other hand, is one which sometimes occurs when an organism is exposed to repeated small and non-lethal doses of a poison over a considerable period of time.

The appearance of acute toxic symptoms may be sudden and dramatic. These symptoms are usually readily detected and, being attributable to some definite biochemical effect, will often respond to emergency action such as the administration of an antidote. Similarly, since the acute toxic hazard can be recognised in fairly precise scientific terms, it is possible to take common sense precautions in the handling and use of the poisons.

The commonly accepted measure of acute toxicity is the 50% lethal dose, or LD_{50}. This is the amount of poison which can kill half the organisms in a batch of named experimental animals when applied to them in a particular way and under particular experimental conditions. To determine the LD_{50}, batches of the animals are exposed to doses of the toxicant, and the numbers of organisms dying in each batch recorded, together with the magnitude of the concentration which brought about that response. From these data, the LD_{50} and its standard error can be calculated by statistical analysis.

If, for the experiments just described, the concentrations used, or preferably, their logarithms, are plotted against the observed percentage kills, a sigmoid curve is obtained (Fig. 1.1). The reason for this relationship will be explained in the next section. The sigmoid curve is steepest in the region of 50% response, so that, over this region of the curve, a small change in

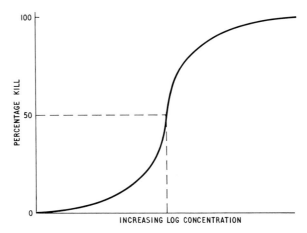

Fig.1.1. Relation of percentage response to the logarithm of the toxic concentration

concentration produces a large change in percentage kill. Conversely, the curve is flattest as it approaches concentrations causing zero and total kill. The dose which kills half the organisms in a random sample and hence, by implication, in the total population—is thus a more sensitive index of toxicity than any other, and the LD_{50} is for this reason usually adopted as the standard for comparing the relative toxicities of two or more substances (compare Tables 1.1, 4.1, 7.1). It should be observed that the LD_{99} is an extremely unreliable estimate of toxicity.

The LD_{50} is usually expressed in terms of mg toxicant per kg body weight of the experimental animal. This expedient partly eliminates complications inherent in the fact that many different types of organisms, of greatly differing body weight, have been chosen in different laboratories as test organisms. Such LD_{50}s also provide a rough but useful indication of what the toxicity of the poison might have been if administered to man, to a domestic animal or to livestock.

Acute toxicity data for numerous pesticides have been provided by many authors, including Gunther and Jeppson (1960), Gaines (1960) and Edson, Sanderson and Noakes (1966). Some selected examples are given in Table 1.1. It will be noticed that the toxicity of any one substance is lower when applied to the skin than when it is administered as a single dose by mouth.

Since the toxicity increases as the toxic dose falls, compounds with *small* LD_{50}s present the greatest potential acute hazard.

An empirical definition of levels of toxicity has been used by Frazer (1963). It gives some practical meaning to the magnitude of the LD_{50} per unit body weight. According to this definition, an extremely toxic substance is one with an LD_{50} of less than 1, while a highly toxic substance is one with an LD_{50} lying between 1 and 50. The corresponding range for a moderately toxic material is 50 to 500 and for a slightly toxic substance, 500 to 5,000 mg per kg body weight.

In contrast to acute toxic effects following accidental ingestion or contact with a single large dose of poison, the steady accumulation of poison over the years in a living organism may eventually lead to the development of chronic or long term symptoms. This is most likely to occur when a substance has physical properties and chemical stability that

Table 1.1 ACUTE TOXICITY TO THE RAT OF SOME PESTICIDES APPLIED ORALLY OR BY 24 HOUR DERMAL CONTACT (AFTER EDSON, SANDERSON AND NOAKES, 1966)

Substance	LD_5 as mg/kg body weight		Use
	Oral dose	Dermal application	
Aldrin	40*	> 200	Insecticide
BHC	200	500*	Insecticide
Chlorbenside	2000*	—	Acaricide
Copper salts	700*	—	Fungicides
DDT	300*	2500	Insecticide
Dimefox	2	2*	Insecticide
Diquat	400	—	Herbicide
DNOC	25*	200*	Herbicide, Ovicide
Ethyl mercury chloride	30	200	Fungicide
Malathion	1400*	>4000	Insecticide
MCPA	800	>1000	Herbicide
Mevinphos	3*	90	Insecticide
Monuron	3500	>2500	Herbicide
Nicotine	70	140	Insecticide
Schradan	5	50*	Insecticide
Thiram	375*	—	Fungicide

*signifies that, of a range of reported values, the lowest is given here.
>signifies that the highest dose tested failed to kill 50% of the organisms.

enable the substance to persist in food and then perhaps to accumulate in certain tissues of the consumer. Such chronic effects often occasion symptoms which are incapable of ready scientific measurement or precise definition and are often brought about by physiological malfunctioning not obviously related to the biochemical action responsible for the acute toxic response. Thus, as will be seen in Chapter 4, it is the relatively safe DDT and BHC, when toxicity is judged by the values of their dermal or oral LD_{50}s, which have aroused public concern.

Unlike acute toxic effects which are obvious externally, chronic toxicity may be caused by gradual histological changes in tissues which are in continuous contact with small amounts of a poison. Necrotic changes in liver and kidneys can, for example, be induced experimentally by long term application of small doses of certain poisons; these changes may not be suspected prior to autopsy, death apparently being due to natural causes. Chronic effects are often indeterminate in nature, and are frequently of such a type that it is difficult to assess their significance by statistical methods. They therefore present a baffling problem to those responsible for the marketing and control of pesticides, for it is often impossible to know in advance whether or not prolonged contact with traces of a poison will have some insidious irreversible effect upon the general body structure.

PROBIT METHOD OF EXPRESSING ACUTE TOXICITY DATA

The probit method of Bliss, later extended by Finney (1952) is one of several techniques for analysing acute toxicity data. Of the other methods, the use of logits or angles instead of probits occasionally has some advantages (McIntosh, 1961). A brief account is given in this section of some of the background information upon which the probit method is based, but for mathematical details Finney's book should be consulted.

In common with many other variable factors of a biological nature, the susceptibility to poisons of individuals in a population of organisms approximates to a normal distribution (Fig. 1.2) if the variable—in this case the

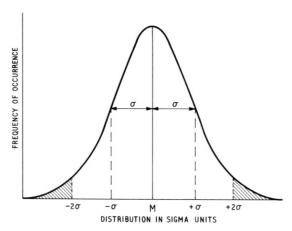

Fig. 1.2. The normal curve; 4·5% of individuals lie in the
shaded 'tails' of the curve, 2·25% in each

applied concentration—is plotted on a logarithmic scale. (The mathematical features characterising normal distribution are considered in texts of elementary statistics.) In particular, all such curves belong to a family and can be standardised by considering the 'spread' of the curve as divided into units of sigma, σ, measured out from the mean point, M. Sigma is called the standard deviation; its geometric significance is shown in the figure. The probability of any member of the population being more extremely situated from the mean than any stated value of σ is then readily determined by reference to a table, the figures of the table being calculated from the equation for the normal curve. For example, it is known that 95·5% of the values lie within the limits $\pm 2\sigma$, and therefore only 4·5% lie in the shaded parts of the curve in Fig. 1.2. Clearly, this is another way of saying that the ratio of the shaded area under the curve to the total area is 0·045.

When the special case of a population of organisms varying in their susceptibility to a poison is considered, the x-axis then represents the dose of poison applied and only one of the two shaded areas is important (Fig. 1.3). Since any (logarithmic) concentration, c, kills all organisms with lower

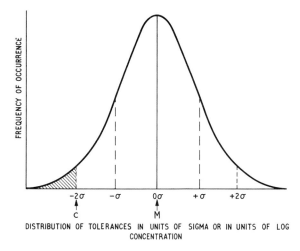

DISTRIBUTION OF TOLERANCES IN UNITS OF SIGMA OR IN UNITS OF LOG CONCENTRATION

Fig. 1.3. Ratio of killed to surviving organisms on applying a dose such that its logarithm, c, induces a response in organisms lying 2σ or more below the mean. M is the log LD$_{50}$; 2·25% respond to log dose, c

tolerances, c represents a position on the x-axis which divides the curve into two sections; organisms in the population lying to the left of c will be killed while those lying to the right of it will survive this dose. As c—the logarithm of a lethal dose for some level of kill, small or large—increases towards M (the logarithm of the LD$_{50}$) the percentage kill rises, at first slowly, but then rapidly as M is approached; when c is greater than M, the reverse occurs, the percentage kill rising more slowly as c becomes more extreme. This is the justification for the assertion made earlier that a sigmoid relation exists between logarithms of dose and percentage response (Fig. 1.1). Such a curve represents the summation of the areas under the normal curve for each concentration as c increases progressively from zero to infinity; it is thus in the first instance an integrated normal curve, being only secondarily an expression of a dosage-response relationship.

In an idealised experiment involving *large numbers* of organisms at each concentration tested, and batches of organisms which are *perfect sub-samples* of the original population, experimental results would in theory lead to a set of data fitting exactly a sigmoid curve (Fig. 1.4a), but in any actual experiment a scatter of points, more or less profound, is to be anticipated (Fig. 1.4b). The larger the scatter, the more difficult it becomes

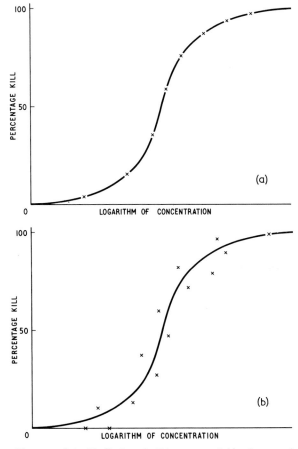

Fig. 1.4. (a) Idealised and (b) more probable fitment of toxicity data to a sigmoid curve

to estimate with accuracy the LD_{50}—the concentration which would cause the death of half the organisms of the population if it could in some way be applied to all the organisms of that sort in the world.

In effect, the probit method of analysis 'straightens out' the sigmoid curve by providing in its place a line which on theoretical grounds should be linear; the justification of the probit method rests in the fact that it is much easier to calculate the position of the line of best fit if that line is straight, rather than if it is curved. In practice, unless the scatter of points is very great or unless standard errors are required, it is often sufficient to plot the data in the form of a probit graph and then to fit the line by inspection.

The principle of the probit method is as follows. As has been shown, the x-axis of the normal curve can be expressed alternatively in two forms of units, namely, in units of logarithmic concentration or in units of standard deviation. The logarithmic concentrations are experimental in origin and for each of these, the percentage kill of the organisms in the sample is known. But the other experimental quantity, the percentage kill, can (for the reasons given above (Fig. 1.3), and subject to certain statistical considerations relating to size and randomness of sample), be expressed readily in terms of the standard deviation, σ. For example, it was shown earlier that 2·25% of organisms lie in the tail to the left of -2σ from the mean. These are the organisms which would be killed if a poison were applied at a concentration, the logarithm of which is c, to an idealised batch of test organisms (Fig. 1.3). By the use of a table of σ, each observed percentage kill can similarly be expressed in units of sigma.

If, then, the alternative units for the x-axis of the normal curve are plotted against one another, the converted percentage kills forming the

Table 1.2 TRANSFORMATION OF PERCENTAGES TO PROBITS
(SIMPLIFIED; FOR THE FULL TABLE, SEE FINNEY, 1952)

Percentage	Probit	Percentage	Probit	Percentage	Probit
14	3·92	38	4·69	62	5·31
16	4·01	40	4·75	64	5·36
18	4·08	42	4·80	66	5·41
20	4·16	44	4·85	68	5·47
22	4·23	46	4·90	70	5·52
24	4·29	48	4·95	72	5·58
26	4·36	50	5·00	74	5.64
28	4·42	52	5·05	76	5·71
30	4·48	54	5·10	78	5·77
32	4·53	56	5·15	80	5·84
34	4·59	58	5·20	82	5·92
36	4·64	60	5·25	84	5·99

y-axis of the new graph, a linear function is to be expected. In practice, and to avoid the use of negative values of σ, probits are used instead of σ, but a probit, or *probability unit,* is merely the σ value plus five. Thus the logarithm of the LD_{50} is the value on the x-axis when the probit value is 5·0. Table 1.2 shows the probit values for percentage kills varying from 14 to 84%, and Fig. 1.5 shows a typical probit-log concentration graph plotted from experimental results.

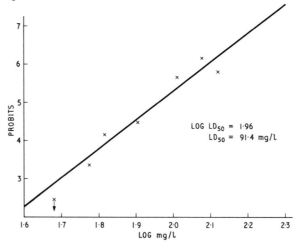

LOG LD_{50} = 1·96
LD_{50} = 91·4 mg/L

Fig. 1.5. Dosage—response data for n–amyl chloride applied as a fumigant to the grain weevil

Concentration mg/l	Log concentration	Percentage kill	Probit
47·5	1·677	0·0	$-\infty$
59·2	1·772	4·8	3·34
64·9	1·812	20·0	4·16
80·2	1·904	30·0	4·48
101·9	2·008	75·4	5·69
119·1	2·076	87·0	6·13
131·8	2·120	77·7	5·76

MORTALITIES FROM PESTICIDES

The Public Health Service of the United States Department of Health, Education and Public Welfare has for many years issued figures showing the number of people killed by poisons. De Ong (1956) tabulated some of the figures for the years 1933 to 1950; more recent data have been examined by Hayes (1963). From such information, an interesting and somewhat unexpected pattern emerges. In America, deaths each year from all causes,

14

per 100,000 of the population, total about 935. Of these, only 2, on average, represent deaths arising from accidental poisoning. This incidence— 2 per 100,000 per year—has remained almost constant for the years between 1939 and 1963. Earlier records show that at the turn of the century, and long before pesticides were used extensively, figures twice this magnitude were not infrequent.

Of deaths from accidental poisoning, about 10% can be attributed to pesticides, so some three or four hundred Americans are likely to die accidentally from acute pesticide poisoning in the coming year. Such figures are no cause for complacency, especially when it is recognised that nearly every one of them occurs through a human failing of some sort, but in order that both their magnitude and their tragic impact should be viewed in perspective, it should be recalled that American road casualties for a one day national holiday in 1965 included 393 deaths. Nevertheless, it is particularly relevant to the question of human failing that children are the victims in some 60% of all fatal casualties involving pesticides.

One interesting aspect of the statistics quoted above is that, even as recently as 1956, nearly 70% of all accidental deaths from pesticides were caused by poisons which were well established as pesticides before the introduction of DDT. Thus, the evidence does not support the widely held view that the introduction of modern organic pesticides has increased the risk of death from accidental acute poisoning. It should be added, however, that there are probably about one hundred moderately serious incidents involving poisoning by pesticides for each fatality, and it is impossible to over-emphasise the need for more care, more thought and, above all, for a greater exercise of common sense. It is especially important to ensure that concentrates are stored and handled in such a way as to minimise the risk to young children.

Mortality statistics do not describe fully the effect of pesticides on the probability of human survival for, thanks to better nutrition and to the rapid advances in medical science, the expectation of life nowadays is higher nearly everywhere than it has ever been before. In this respect, it must be recalled that pesticides have contributed to increased food production, so these and many other types of toxic chemicals have greatly reduced risk of early death from disease. Certain aspects of these inter-related factors have been discussed by Brown (1962) and Pal (1962). In India, for example, the death rate has been halved since 1947, while in Ceylon it fell by 34% in one year. It is no coincidence that this rapid improvement in health in many developing countries has occurred during a period of rapid expansion in the use of pesticides; the fall in the death rate in Ceylon can be ascribed very largely to the spraying of houses with DDT.

15

Furthermore, as the following extract from a pamphlet issued by the World Council for the Welfare of the Blind so poignantly illustrates, health is an essential prerequisite to adequate, let alone efficient, farming:

In certain parts of Africa 'near streams, in heavily infested areas, we find villages in which every adult is blind. In these villages, children are precious things, for they alone can see to lead about their elders for a few years until they themselves turn blind'.

The simulium fly, which carries the organism responsible for river-blindness, like the mosquitoes, tse-tse flies and other insect vectors of debilitating diseases, is readily controlled by insecticides. Since such diseases sap men's strength and destroy both their will to work efficiently and their desire to plan for the future, the use of pesticides for medical purposes may, in some areas, contribute as much to agricultural efficiency (and hence to yield per acre) as their use to protect crops from the predations of insects. This indirect contribution of pesticides to agriculture has often been given too little attention, perhaps because most authors do not come from countries infested with the insect vectors of extremely unpleasant diseases.

THE DEVELOPMENT AND MARKETING OF NEW PESTICIDES

SOME PRECAUTIONS AND PROBLEMS

It is to the credit of the majority of manufacturers of pesticides throughout the world that a keen awareness exists of the urgency of the problems posed in the preceding sections. Enlightened self-interest, as well as moral responsibility, demands that no reputable manufacturer releases a new material on the market before it has been adequately tested for both potential toxic hazard and pesticidal efficiency. Sometimes, in the light of new experience or unforeseen mishaps, it has been found necessary to modify or extend the preliminary testing procedure, but at any one time the tests performed have usually been those demanded by the whole fund of experience and foresight available at that time. It would be quite erroneous to imagine that new materials are marketed in an irresponsible manner, with the profit motive as the only objective; if such a policy were, indeed, pursued, it would be rapidly self-defeating for the offending manufacturer.

Optional or compulsory clearance schemes operate in many countries.

These ensure that the merits of potential pesticides are assessed by independent bodies. When the schemes are optional, as in Britain, most manufacturers welcome their existence and willingly co-operate with those who run them. In fact, in a circular issued by the Association of British Manufacturers of Agricultural Chemicals (Anon, 1965a) it is reported that a demand for the compulsory registration of all pesticides was conveyed by the Association to the Ministry of Agriculture in March, 1964. Such is the importance attached by the manufacturer to having official sanction in the form of clearance by an independent body, that 98·5% of the agricultural chemicals supplied by the Association's members to British farmers are approved under the Voluntary Approval Scheme at the present time.

The development and manufacture of a new substance is a complex process which has been discussed in detail by Edson (1964) with particular regard to the responsibility of the manufacturer for the safety precautions which must be taken at each stage of development. After the synthesis and screening of numerous related substances, the vast majority are eliminated from further study because they are unsuitable in some way. The remainder undergo a rigorous series of toxicity tests. Amongst the many possible risks that are investigated are those which could arise from absorption through the skin, from the breathing of vapour, from cumulative effects and from delayed action. The risks to users, the public and to consumers of food—as well as to farm stock, bees, fish, wild life and game—can all be assessed in advance with an accuracy limited only by the scientific know-how of the time (Anon, 1965b). A promising compound which is likely to be used on food crops also undergoes exhaustive residue tests.

Before any pesticide is marketed it has, in many countries, to comply with the requirements of some voluntary or compulsory notification, registration or approval scheme. Broadly speaking, the data of the manufacturer are vetted by an independent body to confirm that tests establishing the level of safety and field efficiency of the new material have been adequately performed and that the results of those tests are such as to merit the appearance of a new toxicant.

In the case of the present voluntary system operating in Britain, the independent body which investigates the *toxicological* aspects of a new pesticide is the Scientific Sub-Committee of the Ministry of Agriculture's Advisory Committee on Poisonous Substances. There are no representatives of the pesticide manufacturers on this Committee. Its recommendations for the safe use of each approved pesticide are published in a loose leaf dossier entitled *Chemical Compounds used in Agriculture and Food Storage in Great Britain—User and Consumer Safety—Advice of Government Departments;* they also appear on the label of the pesticide container.

If and when clearance is given by the toxicological Committee mentioned above, the product passes to a second Committee, the task of which is to ascertain that the biological or *field efficiency* of the substance merits its appearance on the market. This second Committee operates under another official scheme, which is termed the Agricultural Chemicals Approval Scheme. The object of this Committee, which again consists of independent experts, is to ensure that the user is safeguarded against the purchase of useless or inferior materials.

Research on a new substance, however, does not end once clearance has been obtained; it tends to spread from the research laboratories of the manufacturers to those of many other interested organisations. Such research consists of investigations into the mode of action of the poison and into long term ecological and residue problems. It should not be forgotten that post-clearance work acts in the nature of a feedback mechanism; if it reveals any new hazard or any shortcoming in the original testing technique, the tendency will be for the requirements of one of the official Committees to be altered so that the appropriate tests in future become part of the pre-clearance investigations. In Britain, additional research is undertaken in universities, by the Nature Conservancy, by wild life interests and by many Government establishments.

To ensure that research work on problems of special importance to wild life interests is used to best advantage, two joint working Committees were established in October, 1963, consisting of representatives of manufacturers and of all the major wild life interests. One of these Committees exchanges information and ideas on the character and the results of research work, while the other is concerned with educational aspects of the safe use of toxic chemicals (Anon, 1965b). It cannot, therefore, be said that manufacturers wash their hands of all responsibility once a pesticide has gained official acceptance. The main question is, perhaps, whether they contribute enough money, as a social duty or business requirement, rather than as an act of largess, in support of the various institutes and organisations whose research activities remove in part the financial burden of these long term projects from their shoulders.

The manufacturer also has an important responsibility in seeing that his products are adequately labelled and packed in containers which neither leak nor corrode. Great improvements in all of these matters have occurred in the last few years so far as British products are concerned, but, in the opinion of the writer, some countries have not always faced their problems and responsibilities. It is desirable—and this indeed now happens in Great Britain—that each label should carry the chemical name as well as the trade name of the product; perhaps it should also carry in bold type an assessment of its acute oral toxicity on the Frazer scale (page 9). In addition, many people feel that containers above some agreed size should be returnable, and a fee should be charged as a dis-incentive to the indiscriminate dumping of empty cans and drums in sheds, fields, ponds and streams, where they are a potential hazard to children, wild life and fish. The individual farmer, despite educational publicity and warnings on labels, very often does not appreciate the very great danger of local water pollution; this is a hazard not only to swimmers and fish but also, through percolation into the soil, to the micro-organisms upon which the fertility of his land may depend.

All these considerations—the need for toxicological studies; for laboratories specialising in synthesis and analysis; for land and labour to enable extensive field trials to be carried out; and for supporting post-clearance research—lead to the conclusion that only very large companies with vast financial resources can in future hope to develop pesticides in a manner which will fulfil all the developmental, safety and other requirements now essential for the launching of a successful new pesticide.

SAFETY PRECAUTIONS MEASURES

Great Britain

A Notification of Pesticides Scheme was first operated in 1954, but formal documents were not completed until 1957 (Moore, 1964). It was to this scheme that reference was made in the previous section. Its primary aim is to obtain from the manufacturer sufficient information about the product before it is marketed to enable the Government to issue recommendations about its *safe use*. The Ministry of Agriculture Advisory Committee of the scheme works in conjunction with a scientific Sub-Committee of seventeen scientists which meets monthly. The administration of the Notification Scheme is facilitated by the issue of technical documents informing firms what types of information the Sub-Committee will require, and by four appendices which give guidance on the data required in relation to toxicological studies, food residues, wild life toxicity and the labelling of products.

The original scheme has now been extended to include materials used for the protection of food in storage, in addition to those applied to growing crops. It is now called the Pesticides Safety Precautions Scheme and works side by side with a very similar scheme which was recently introduced to cover veterinary products; this is termed the Veterinary Products Safety

Precautions Scheme. In this case the Ministry of Agriculture Advisory Committee on Poisonous Substances receives advice from a veterinary Sub-Committee.

The schemes mentioned above are voluntary, but they are nevertheless associated closely with legislative measures. The Agriculture (Poisonous Substances) Act, 1952, was introduced to protect agricultural workers by ensuring that, where necessary, they are provided with sufficient protective clothing when working with dangerous substances. Many pesticides are excluded from the regulations (e.g. DDT, MCPA) and the remainder are divided into three categories called Part 1, Part 2 and Part 3, in which the requirements vary according to the hazard which the substances present when handled.

Another scheme, the Agricultural Chemicals Approval Scheme, allows official approval to be given to proprietary brands of pesticides. The Organisation of the scheme operates on behalf of the Agriculture Departments of the United Kingdom and a list of approved products is published in February each year in a booklet entitled *Agricultural Chemicals Approval Scheme—List of Approved Products for Farmers and Growers*. The booklet also names the materials in the three categories referred to in the previous paragraph. Approved products are marketed in containers which carry a mark consisting of a capital 'A' surmounted by a crown. The presence of such a mark confirms that the product fulfils the claims made on the label so far as practical efficiency is concerned.

United States

The principal United States legislation has aimed at controlling the level of residues on or in the crop at the time of harvesting, and is embodied in Public Law 518—the Miller Amendment—which was enacted in 1954. Briefly, this law requires that any person who has registered a pesticide under the Federal Insecticide, Fungicide and Rodenticide Act must lodge with the Secretary of Health, Education and Welfare a petition for the establishment of a tolerance for the new compound. To succeed with the petition—to obtain what amounts to clearance—information must be provided covering the composition and proposed use of the substance, together with data on the acute oral and chronic toxicity of the compound and the proposed analytical procedure whereby the magnitude of any residue on the crop may be determined. The law is quoted and discussed in detail by Gunther and Jeppson (1960).

If the United States Food and Drug Administration concludes that the substance is innocuous, the material is exempted from a tolerance limit. In all other cases, a tolerance is ascribed which may vary with the manner in which the substance is used and with the crop to which it is applied. The tolerance, as parts per million fresh weight (i.e., mg per kg) represents a residue limit which must not be exceeded in the harvested food material.

The Federal Department of Agriculture has compiled a *Federal Register* of official tolerances, the magnitudes of which give some indication of those substances the Department regards as most hazardous. Some two thousand tolerances have now been issued for numerous materials on various crops; a list is reprinted annually by the National Agricultural Chemicals Association (Anon, 1968). The validity of such tolerance limits has been assessed by Schechter (1963), who concluded that the system was of doubtful value when the tolerance limits were extremely low. In addition, the method of assessment of residues (ppm fresh weight) has been criticised by Gunther and Jeppson (1960) who consider that some form of assessment based upon dry weight would be scientifically more satisfactory.

Gunther (1962) described the analytical methods used to ensure that legal requirements are met; many modern methods measure down to tenths or even hundredths of a part per million. Carson (1962) has, however, questioned the practicability of a Federal tolerance system. She pointed out that the activities of the Food and Drug Administration in the field of consumer protection were limited by the fact that the Administration 'only had jurisdiction over foods shipped in inter-state commerce; foods grown and marketed within a state are entirely outside its sphere of authority'. She further claimed that the laws of most of the individual States concerning pesticide residues were 'woefully inadequate'.

A short account of the present arrangements for controlling residues in foodstuffs made by Australia, Denmark, France, West Germany and the Netherlands is to be found in an official publication issued by the Department of Education and Science (Anon, 1967).

GENERAL LITERATURE ON PESTICIDES

The reader whose work brings him into occasional contact with pesticides will need to know where to look for general information. Some of the more valuable sources of information are provided in the list immediately below. In addition, however, individual workers will need more detailed information on specialist topics. Such information is to be found in the references at the end of this and subsequent chapters. These references in turn will usually lead to wider reading for those who need it.

1. Ministry of Agriculture, Fisheries and Food, *Agricultural Chemicals Approval Scheme. List of Approved Products for Farmers and Growers.* (A yearly publication obtainable from H.M.S.O.).

2. Ministry of Agriculture, Fisheries and Food (Safety, Health and Welfare Branch, Great Westminster House, Horseferry Road, London, S.W.1). A loose leaf dossier with sheets provided periodically and entitled *Chemical Compounds used in Agriculture and Food Storage : Recommendations for Safe Use in Great Britain.*

3. *Insecticide and Fungicide Handbook for Crop Protection,* (2nd Ed.) (1965). Edited by Martin, H., on behalf of the British Insecticide and Fungicide Council, Blackwell Scientific Publications, Oxford.

4. *Handbook of Toxicology; Volume 3, Insecticides* (1959), edited by Negherbon, W. O.; prepared for the Division of Biology and Agriculture, National Academy of Sciences. Published by W. B. Saunders Co., Philadelphia. A valuable compendium of data, such as the physical and chemical properties of insecticides, their toxicity to insects and to animals.

5. *Weed Control Handbook* (1968) Vols. 1 and 2, (5th Ed.). Edited by Fryer, J. D. and Evans, S. A. and issued by the British Crop Protection Council. Blackwell Scientific Publications, Oxford.

6. Martin, H. (1964), *The Scientific Principles of Crop Protection,* (5th Ed.), E. Arnold, Ltd., London.

7. Gunther, F. A. and Jeppson, L. R. (1960), *Modern Insecticides and World Food Production,* Chapman and Hall, London.

8. Audus, L. J. (1964), *Physiology and Biochemistry of Herbicides,* Academic Press, London.

9. *World Review of Pest Control,* a quarterly journal. In addition to general information and reviews, this journal carries a Supplement which lists the chemical and biological characteristics of newly introduced compounds.

10. *Advances in Pest Control Research,* a series of volumes edited by Metcalf, R. L., and published by Interscience Publishers, London. Additional volumes are added from time to time—Volumes 1–7 have appeared so far—and thus it is in some ways like an expanding textbook, in some ways like a journal.

11. *Analytical Methods for Pesticides,* edited by Zweig, G., and published by Academic Press, New York. This series of volumes started to appear in 1963 and five volumes have so far been published. They provide valuable information about the qualitative and quantitative determination of pesticides.

References 3, 4 and 5 include tables giving the common names of pesticides with their chemical formulae and full chemical names. References 1 and 3 relate common names to trade names for some of the more important products and formulations marketed in the United Kingdom. In order that the above list should not be unwieldy, several important text-books and many journals have been omitted; most of these, however, have been mentioned in one or more of the nine Chapter References.

REFERENCES

Anon (1968), *Natn. agric. Chem. Ass. News,* **26,** (3), 3

Anon (1965a), Press release by the Assoc. British Manufacturers of Agric. Chemicals, entitled *Agricultural Chemicals—Pattern for the Future.* Release N.1600/IS/P. 14/8

Anon (1965b), Press release as above but numbered N.1158/IS/P. 14/8

Anon (1967), Dept. Education and Science publication, *Review of the Present Safety Arrangements for the Use of Toxic Chemicals in Agriculture and Food Storage,* H.M.S.O., London

BROWN, A. W. A. (1962), *Wld Rev. Pest Control,* **1,** (3), 6

CARSON, R. (1962), *Silent Spring.* Hamish Hamilton and Co., London

DE ONG, E. R. (1956), *Chemistry and Uses of Pesticides* (2nd Ed.), Rheinhold Publ. Corpn., New York

EDSON, E. F. (1963), *Food Supply and Nature Conservation—A Symposium.* Held at the Cambridgeshire College of Arts and Technology

EDSON, E. F. (1964), Symposium entitled *Agricultural Chemicals—Progress in Safe Use,* organised by the Assoc. British Manufacturers of Agric. Chemicals, the Nature Conservancy and other conservation interests, 16th March, 1964

EDSON, E. F., SANDERSON, D. M. and NOAKES, D. N. (1966), *Wld Rev. Pest Control,* **5,** 143

FINNEY, D. J. (1952), *Probit Analysis,* (2nd Ed.), Cambridge Univ. Press

FRAZER, A. C. (1963), An address entitled *Balance of Pesticides: the Benefits and Risks.* (Professor of Medical Biochemistry, The University, Birmingham)

GAINES, T. B. (1960), *Toxic. appl. Pharmac.,* **2,** 88

GAYNER, F. C. H. (1961), *Soc. Chem. Ind. Monogr.,* **15,** 23

GUNTHER, F. A. (1962), *Adv. Pest Control Res.,* **5,** 191

GUNTHER, F. A. and JEPPSON, L. R. (1960) *Modern Insecticides and World Food Production* (pp. 90–103). Chapman and Hall, London

HAYES, W. J. (1963), *Natn. agric. Chem. Ass. News,* **22,** (1), 3

HOLMES, E. (1960), *Outl. Agric.,* **3,** 23

HORSFALL, J. G. (1956), *Principles of Fungicidal Action.* Chronica Botanica Co., Waltham, Mass., U.S.A., (References to Forsyth, see Frontispiece and p. 159; reference to Bordeaux mixture, see p. 4)

MCINTOSH, A. H. (1961), *J. Sci. Fd Agric.,* **12,** 312

MINISTRY OF AGRICULTURE (1966 and each year), see General Literature list on p. 22

MOORE, W. C. (1964), *Food Supply and Nature Conservation—A Symposium.* Held at the Cambridgeshire College of Arts and Technology

ORDISH, G. (1963), *Wld Crops,* **15,** 254

ORDISH, G. (1964), *J. Inst. Corn agric. Merch.,* **12,** (1), 23

PAL, R. (1962), *Wld Rev. Pest Control,* **1,** (2), 6

SCHECHTER, M. S. (1963), *J. Ass. off. agric. Chem.,* **46,** 1063

SHAW, W. (1963), *Natn. agric. Chem. Ass. News,* **21,** (2), 14

SLADE, R. E., TEMPLEMAN, W. G. and SEXTON, W. A. (1945) *Nature, Lond.,* **155,** 497

VERNON, J. (1958), *J. agric. Fd Chem.,* **6,** 886

2

PHYSICO-CHEMICAL FACTORS

A number of physical and chemical attributes, not only of a poisonous substance but of any other substances applied with it, interact to determine the overall characteristics of a mixture applied to control pests. This interplay is of such complexity that the precise conditions needed to secure that optimal balance of properties which leads to the best results in any particular set of circumstances still has to be determined empirically. Nevertheless, it is first clearly necessary to be aware of the nature of the interacting factors and why they are important, for it is then possible to predict the policy most likely to give good results. The problem can in some ways be compared to a game of chess, for in each case the combination of the effects of a number of simple rules results in an extremely complex interaction of factors or moves and in a system of infinite variability.

Before a substance can be applied satisfactorily, with maximal efficiency and safety, it is necessary to know where, how, and why it is being applied, for the combination of chemical and physical characteristics which leads to the best results is not an absolute thing; on the contrary, it will vary with the *nature of the surface* to which the application is made, the *state* of the substance or mixture of substances applied to that surface, and upon the *biological purpose* the application is intended to achieve. In addition, chemical factors specific to each particular chemical used as a poison, and biological factors characteristic of each particular species of organism being poisoned, must usually be superimposed.

SURFACES TO WHICH PESTICIDES MAY BE APPLIED

Agricultural pesticides are normally directed at one or other of two types of surface. They may be directed at *foliage,* either to kill it, as when herbicides are being used, or to deposit a substance upon it that will protect crop plants against the predations of insects or the attack of fungi. Alternatively, pesticides may be applied to the surface of the *soil,* to control organisms crawling upon it or living beneath it. A number of other possibilities exists, including the use of poisons for the treatment of seeds prior to planting, the incorporation of the material into the bulk of the soil, and the use of the poison as a fumigant by allowing it to operate in a bulk gas phase.

Since soil and waxy surfaces such as leaves and insect cuticles are very different in their physical and chemical characteristics, the conditions needed to ensure that a substance is deposited in adequate amount and persists for a sufficient period of time to achieve its purpose, may be very different when the same toxic substance is applied to these contrasting targets.

A typical soil, rich in silicate minerals, may be compared to an ion exchange column in which, by successive adsorption and elution, polar substances are leached downwards at different rates. This action is accelerated by rain and is countered by factors which include upward capillary action and fixation by organic colloids. Since a typical soil contains a continuous aqueous phase, the persistence in soil of a pesticide of low aqueous solubility is likely, in the simplest case, to be greater than that of a highly soluble substance. Several complicating factors, however, are frequently superimposed, important amongst them being the stability of the substance in water and the action of soil micro-organisms. In addition, volatility, which not only contributes to loss by evaporation but also frequently influences toxic effectiveness, may play a significant role, as may physical or chemical inactivation following reaction with, or sorption on, the organic and silicaceous colloids of the soil. The interaction of factors affecting the usefulness of soil fungicides has been described by Vaartaja (1964).

The entire surface of a plant above ground level is covered with, and protected by, a waxy cuticle which diminishes water loss. Deposited outside and merging into the cellulose walls of epidermal cells, the cuticle varies in thickness and in composition in different plants and in different parts of the same plant. Thus, unlike soil, the most obvious physical characteristic of the surface of foliage (and also insect cuticle) is the existence of a more or less substantial lipid, and therefore hydrophobic, barrier, which restricts access of aqueous solutions to the cells beneath.

Ordinary parenchymatous cells are initially separated by a middle lamella composed of salts of pectic acid, a polymerised galacturonic acid. The primary cell wall is thin and consists largely of cellulose and pectin, a methyl ester of pectic acid. The thicker secondary wall assumes increasing importance as the cell ages; although variable in composition, it contains cellulose, polysaccharides other than cellulose, pectins and hemicelluloses. The complexity of cell walls has been portrayed in the monograph by Siegel (1962), but the significant fact so far as the chemistry of crop protection is concerned is that, unless they are protected or 'waterproofed' in some way, cell walls of parenchymatous cells are probably permeable to water and to substances dissolved in it. Inside the cell wall lies the delicate but relatively impermeable plasmalemma, which is the outer layer of the protoplast. According to some authors it exudes into some of the interstices of the wall.

The non-polar hydrophobic cuticular layer protecting the exposed side of epidermal cells is not an amorphous layer of wax but consists of several components arranged in a reticulum or lattice of considerable structural complexity, the nature of which is still not fully known. The major component of the non-polar region is cutin; it forms a sponge-like framework, within the compartments of which waxy material is deposited (Fig. 2.1).

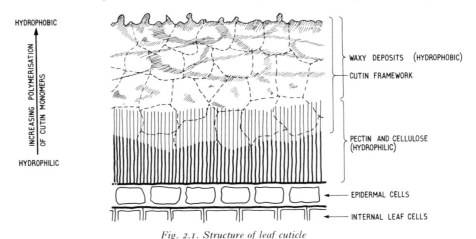

Fig. 2.1. Structure of leaf cuticle

Cutin consists of polymerised hydroxy- and di-carboxylic acids, the degree of polymerisation being highest towards the outside and least towards the inside where the cuticle merges with the cell wall. The permeability to water is inversely correlated with the degree of polymerisation, so the internal cutin probably offers less resistance to the movement of aqueous solution than does cutin of the external region (Mitchell, Smale and Metcalf, 1960). The waxy material embedded in the outer region of the cutin is deposited in the form of interconnected platelets. It probably consists of alcohols and paraffin hydrocarbons with molecules which con-

26

tain some twenty to forty carbon atoms. The cutin framework swells in contact with water, probably moving the extremely hydrophobic wax platelets further apart, with the result that permeability increases.

The cuticular layer is of considerable significance in crop protection, for there is much evidence that it normally presents a formidable barrier to the ready ingress of ions and of highly polar molecules. Conversely, some sorts of non-polar molecules might be expected to gain access to the cuticular wax but to meet with increasing resistance to diffusion as they move through the lower hydrophilic layers of cuticle to the living tissue beneath. Pesticides of different kinds are applied to achieve many different ends, and the degree of penetration which is desired, or is desirable, will vary; nevertheless, for all of them the importance of the cuticle in determining the pattern of uptake and distribution cannot be over-estimated.

It should be added, however, that knowledge concerning the precise contribution of the cuticle to rate and extent of uptake of external molecules or ions is far from complete. Some workers, for example, are not convinced that all ionic substances have difficulty in penetrating through leaf cuticle to the cells beneath. Furthermore, cuticular penetration may be facilitated if the outermost waxy layers have been damaged prior to application of the pesticide, or if they are attacked by some other component of the mixture, such as an oily carrier or surfactant. Nor must it be forgotten that the main barrier of the cuticle can sometimes be by-passed, penetration occurring through the epidermal cells overlying the veins of the leaf, or through stomatal pores. Although the latter offer an alternative means of access, the internal cavities of stomata are themselves lined with a thin cuticular layer (Currier and Dybing, 1959).

Substances used in crop protection are not always applied with the intention of getting them inside the plant, for the target may well be organisms established on, rather than in, its leaves. However, apart from the assessment of factors leading to selective uptake by different types of organisms, few new problems are presented by the existence of these alternative targets, for the insect cuticle shares with the plant cuticle the property of being primarily hydrophobic; the same may well be true of the walls of fungal spores.

Finally, it should be recalled that the plasmalemma and the intracellular membranes are typical lipoprotein double layers with negative fixed sites. These probably behave at the molecular level in somewhat the same way as the cuticle does at the macroscopic level. Thus, Wain (1961) regarded the behaviour of the protoplasmic membranes, when confronted with herbicides which are weak acids, as being the key to the different physiological activities of the molecules and ions of these substances.

PHYSICAL STATE OF A TOXICANT

1. FUMIGATION

Any pesticide may be applied in one or more of four physical states—
as a gas, solid, liquid or as a solution. When applied as a vapour, the
process is termed *fumigation*. Since this technique requires the existence
of an enclosed space, it might seem to be of limited application in crop
protection. However, soil restricts the diffusion of toxicants within it,
and many materials applied to the soil as solids and liquids probably act
partly or principally as fumigants. Even compounds of low volatility such as
BHC and aldrin probably possess a fumigant action in soils, and the
superior performance of aldrin over BHC for the control of wireworms
and leatherjackets has been attributed to its higher vapour pressure at
ordinary soil temperatures. When very volatile substances such as carbon
disulphide and chloropicrin are used as soil fumigants, it may be necessary
to place gas-impermeable drag sheets on the surface of the ground to
prevent the escape of the vapour from the soil surface. Several factors other
than vapour pressure may contribute to the relative efficiency of different
substances as soil fumigants under different conditions. Amongst these
factors are the level of soil moisture and the soil texture (Hollis, 1962).

Fumigation of greenhouses is of considerable value to the horticulturist
and the erection of gas-proof tents has enabled the method to be applied to
individual trees in orchards. Another notable use of fumigants is to protect
food material during storage and transit. Warehouses, holds of ships and
freight trains can be readily sealed, so fumigation often presents an ideal
method of pest control in such cases (Monro, 1961). Furthermore, since an
(unabsorbed) vapour rapidly disperses when the area under fumigation is
opened up, it is found that if the poison is carefully chosen, fumigation
presents a lesser residue hazard to the consumer than would occur if
liquids or solids were employed. Methyl bromide, ethylene dibromide and
other halogenated hydrocarbons have been used extensively for this purpose. There is evidence that the more specialised technique of vacuum
fumigation reduces the residue hazard still further (Bhambhani, 1964).
As well as gases and liquids, certain slightly volatile solids (e.g., BHC)
can be used as fumigants in soil and for the protection of stored produce.

2. DUSTING

For many years it was popular to *dust* solid, finely ground pesticides on to
foliage (Ripper, 1955), but except in regions where water is scarce the

method is not now frequently employed on a large scale. It suffers from the serious disadvantage of being wasteful, for not more than 10–15% of the applied material normally adheres to the leaf surface. Other difficulties relate to the danger confronting the operator and the hazard to neighbouring crops which can arise if a dust is applied when even a gentle breeze is blowing. The vulnerability of dusts to rain falling shortly after application is a further disadvantage. Solids are, however, frequently spread on or incorporated into soil, sometimes in the form of dusts and, more recently, in granular form. The use of granules is worthy of note, for it is a method which is likely to increase in importance in the next decade, but it is a process distinct from dusting, being similar to it only in that it involves the application of a solid.

Only small quantities of highly toxic substances need be present on unit area of leaf or in unit volume of soil to achieve the desired degree of pest control. For this reason and with few exceptions, uniform application of a poison in solid form is usually difficult to achieve unless it is diluted with some inactive diluent or filler prior to the application. The organochlorine insecticides such as DDT and BHC are, for example, somewhat waxy solids and are diluted by the manufacturers with a variable percentage of a silicaceous mineral when they are to be applied in the solid state. The method of formulation of a particular pesticidal dust may profoundly influence the effectiveness of the substance in the field; in general, a finely ground and intimate mixture of toxicant with diluent operates more efficiently than one which, though cheaper to buy, is less finely ground or less well mixed. Nevertheless, the situation is complex, for even preparations that are uniformly ground may possess a wide distribution of settling characteristics. This is due to the fact that dust particles tend to cluster into agglomerates which may contain as many as 300 separate particles.

A generalisation which is often true for a wide range of rates of application is that the number of particles of toxicant per unit area of foliage is more important than the weight deposited per unit area. David (1959) has, however, pointed out that on warm days convection currents are able to prevent particles smaller than about 20μ diameter from settling out. Another complication is that electrical forces may influence, favourably or adversely, both the deposition of particles on the surface of leaves and the degree of retention of the particles once they are there. The magnitude of these electrical forces is often a function of particle size.

Particle size may also be significant when pesticidal dusts are applied to soils, for the rate of volatilisation of a substance with an appreciable vapour pressure increases with the degree of dispersion. This is important, for many materials applied to the soil as solids are believed to owe some part of their toxicity to their activity in the vapour phase. When granular solids, as distinct from dusts, are applied to soil, the principles involved are somewhat different, for random distribution on, or intimate admixture with, soil is no longer a requirement for their mode of action; in certain cases it is deliberately avoided by placement of the pesticide near the crop to be protected. In such cases, the active ingredient gradually passes into solution, though not necessarily by a straightforward physical dissolving process. The advantage of formulating materials as granules is that it facilitates distribution by aircraft or fertiliser drills, reduces problems associated with wind and air currents and at the same time enables the material to be placed rapidly but accurately on the chosen target (Ripper, 1955). Furthermore, some types of compounds (e.g., organophosphorus insecticides), originally employed mainly as foliage sprays, can now sometimes be formulated in granular form. Where such a change in the technique of application is possible, so that entry is through the roots, an obvious advantage would seem to be a substantial reduction in the risk to beneficial organisms.

3. SPRAYING

The commonest method of applying a pesticidal substance is to *spray* it as a solution or suspension, or, much more rarely, as a pure liquid. The principles underlying spray chemistry are complex, for numerous factors interact to determine how effective an application will be. As well as the properties of the sprayed surface it is necessary to take into consideration the properties of the liquid carrier and of any substances added to ensure that the best use is made of the active ingredient. External factors such as weather may add further complication. Some of the factors influencing the distribution and deposition of the material and others influencing adhesion to the sprayed surface, are outlined below.

A mixture of a pesticide and its carrier liquid may be either homogeneous or heterogeneous. In the former case the toxicant is sufficiently soluble in the liquid to form a solution at the required spray tank concentration and problems prior to spraying are trivial. If, however, the solute is insoluble in the liquid continuous phase, the bi-phasal system will tend to separate out under gravitational forces. Since the continuous phase is almost always water, oil droplets will float and most solid particles will settle. This tendency must be countered in some way, for separation would have serious consequences owing to uneven distribution of pesticide; some plants would be damaged by receiving too much deposit and others left open to attack by the pest by receiving too little. Separation can be hindered by physical agitation of the mixture in the spray tank or by adding a special substance to the mixture. A substance which stabilises a suspension (a mixture with a solid disperse phase) is termed a dispersing agent; an emulsifier, on the other hand, stabilises a mixture with a liquid disperse phase.

For reasons relating to cheapness and general availability, water is the only liquid normally used as the solvent, or continuous phase, in a spray mixture. Furthermore, when leaves—or the insects upon them—are the target, it is usually essential to use water as a carrier if damage to the crop plant is to be avoided, for most other liquids are toxic. A material, or mixture of materials, which causes damage to the crop plant is said to be *phytotoxic*; note that by definition a weedkiller would not be described as phytotoxic unless it damaged the crop as well as destroying the weeds.

It is an unfortunate fact that water, despite the economic advantages mentioned above, is, from the physico-chemical viewpoint, almost the worst material that could be chosen to deposit a pesticide on a lipophilic surface, for water has a very low affinity for waxy or greasy surfaces. In addition, many of the more complex organic pesticides are almost insoluble in water, and if dispersed in water would cause serious difficulties, especially when applied as a low-volume wash. Moreover, water also possesses a very high surface tension (78 dynes per cm) and this, as will soon be evident, is frequently disadvantageous.

In consequence, these adverse physical characteristics have to be circumvented. This is done by addition of *spray supplements* which minimise the disadvantages mentioned above and so allow the active ingredient(s) of the spray mixture to be used as effectively as possible. Two types of supplements—dispersing agents and emulsifiers—have been mentioned so far. Another type, termed a spreading agent, increases the contact between spray droplets and the sprayed surface, so reducing wastage due to run-off. These three types of supplements have surfactant properties, but several other types of spray supplements also exist (Fig. 2.2, p. 33).

Some of the factors determining the deposition on, adherence to, and penetration of a leaf surface by a poison applied in water are similar to those relating to dusts. But for sprays it is even harder to attempt to consider the physico-chemical characteristics of the toxicant independently of those of its carrier and of such supplements and other ingredients as may be present. The situation is at once both more versatile and more complex.

As well as quantity of material deposited per unit area, the operator of a modern spraying machine is able to control, within limits, the average size of the droplets which are delivered and the pattern they make as they fall from the jets to the sprayed surface. This is done by adjustment of the height and angle of the spray beam, by using different sorts of nozzles, by regulating the pressure driving the liquid out of the jets and, finally, by using different amounts and types of spray supplements.

The first difficulty to overcome arises at the moment of spraying and before the droplets reach their destination, for they have to be *driven through the air* with sufficient force to get them to the more remote foliage. In high volume spraying, 40–150 gal liquid are applied per acre. The energy which drives the spray droplets is derived largely from the mass of the water impelled, for orchard spraying, by piston pumps, but for ground spraying, where a lower pressure suffices, by cheaper rotodynamic pumps. In low volume ground spraying the pressure driving the liquid through the nozzles is even less, and usually originates from a tractor-driven gear pump. The latter is sometimes supplemented by an airblast which blows the spray over the crop, thus fulfilling the same role as water mass in high volume spraying.

The retention of a droplet once it reaches a leaf or other lipophilic surface and the ultimate fate of the toxicant are likewise influenced by several interacting physico-chemical factors, including droplet size, surface tension and volatility of carrier; if, as sometimes happens, an electrostatic charge is present on the droplets, this may also make an important contribution. David (1959) pointed out that if the percentage retention of water droplets is plotted against decreasing droplet size, the percentage retention is seen to increase suddenly as the size of the water droplets falls below approximately 100μ.

The retention of spray fluid by the target is also greatly influenced by the surface tension of the carrier, being least for aqueous media when the surface tension is high (p. 31). If little or no spreader is present, the contact between droplets and a lipid surface is so poor that most of the droplets bounce off. On the other hand, if too much spreader is present, the deposited droplets flatten and coalesce, with the result that the liquid tends to run off a sloping surface, leaving only a thin film of active ingredient. Brunskill (1956) considered that the first of these, the 'reflection' of droplets, was usually the situation of greater practical importance, and his experimental work leads to the conclusion that the surface tension of aqueous sprays should not exceed 50 dynes per cm if adequate retention is to be assured.

After deposition on the leaf (or on the insects present there), the pesticide eventually *separates from its carrier*; the rate of this separation may influence both its toxicity to the pest and its phytotoxicity—the damage it does to the crop. The simplest possibility is the evaporation of solvent from a true solution, leaving a deposit of pesticide together with any spray supplements which were present. In such a case, over-spraying, which causes much of the applied material to run off the leaf, will naturally result in a loss of active material and reduction in overall retention.

For suspensions and emulsions the situation is more complex, but in general, there is little evidence that the disperse phase is held preferentially by the leaf if the surface is sprayed beyond the point of run-off. Emulsions of oil in water may sometimes be exceptions, for should they break quickly enough, the chemical affinity of oil for cuticular wax may result in rapid absorption and reduced run-off of the disperse phase. Since the stability of an emulsion is determined by the nature and the amount of the various spray supplements present, yet another interaction of physical factors is evident here.

The deposition of the toxicant may therefore occur by evaporation of the carrier, as, for example, in low volume sprays when water evaporates to leave an oily or solid deposit; or it may be due to absorption of the disperse phase into the sprayed surface. When oil is the disperse phase it should be noted that, as well as being a potential toxicant in its own right, it may be acting as a solvent and carrier for an oil-soluble pesticide. Thus oil may enter through stomata or through the cuticle, taking the dissolved substance with it, and in the latter case the absorption may result in a distortion of cuticular structure which in turn enables both oil and dissolved pesticide to penetrate further. Liquid surfactants combine oily solvent characteristics with surface activity and can be used instead of hydrocarbon oils as carriers or co-solvents (Fig. 2.2).

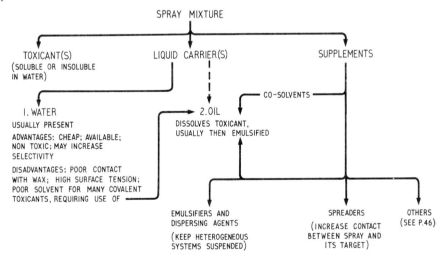

Fig. 2.2. Possible components of a mixture used for spraying

The length of time after deposition that a sprayed substance will remain on a surface is a complex function of the chemistry of the toxicant, the nature of the sprayed surface and of the physico-chemical properties of the spray mixture which usually comprises water, toxicant and supplements. Unless the toxicant rapidly enters the plant or the pest, its *persistence on the surface* may also be limited by loss or decomposition resulting from the action of wind and rain. Stickers or adhering agents are spray supplements which are employed to increase the persistence of certain types of pesticides. Unlike the supplements mentioned earlier, adhering agents do not necessarily possess surface active properties. Casein, gums, molasses, flour, gelatin and oils have all been employed as adhering agents from time to time. This additional use of oil is worthy of note; very little is normally required, and its sticking power is presumably due to a softening of the cuticle, which causes the active ingredient to become embedded in the surface instead of being merely deposited upon it. Rather similarly, perhaps, airblast (p. 32) used in conjunction with low volume applications may propel droplets so vigorously that they are forced into the surface. Park and Burdekin (1964) have found that initial decomposition of a fungicide (cuprous oxide) was unaffected by volume of application, but that low volume application gave deposits which were more resistant to weathering; the reason for this superior persistence is still uncertain.

CONTACT AND SYSTEMIC POISONS

A pesticide may be applied in order to control, by direct and immediate contact, a pest already on or amongst the crop. Rather similarly, it may be applied so that a deposit, persisting upon the surface, later kills a pest not present at the time of application. Alternatively, it may be applied to the crop in such a way that it enters the crop plant, and its point of contact with an insect or fungus is some distance from the place where it was originally deposited on the plant.

1. CONTACT POISONS

Contact poisons may conveniently be divided into two groups, non-persistent and persistent, according to the way their chemical stability or physical properties determine the principal practical use of the substances, though the dividing line between the two groups is an indefinite one. If, for any reason, the material is non-persistent, its use is necessarily limited to the control of an already established pest; this use is roughly analogous to the medical use of an unstable drug to cure an illness from which the patient is already suffering—except, of course, that medical use normally requires an internal distribution of the poison.

Unless the pest lives exclusively on one surface of a leaf, the complete destruction of a population of a susceptible pest already established on foliage ideally requires complete coverage of the infested surface, and complete coverage of foliage implies that both the upper and lower surfaces of all the leaves should be wetted. To achieve this objective, it was for a long time recommended that the coarse jet of spray machines should be used in conjunction with an excess of spreading agent, but, for the reasons mentioned earlier, such a method is necessarily wasteful; in practice, therefore, a compromise is often desirable. With the advent of more advanced spray machinery, the introduction of low volume spraying, the use of a wider range of spreading agents and of more versatile toxicants, such a compromise is generally feasible. Technical details relating to droplet sizes, spray pressures and the types of machinery suitable for application of contact pesticides have been provided by Ripper (1955). Examples of contact poisons possessing ephemeral action are (unionised) nicotine and pyrethrins for the control of insects, and diquat and sulphuric acid for weed control. It is noteworthy that, because of the host-parasite relationship which exists between a fungus and its host plant, there are few, if any, examples of successful non-persistent contact fungicides.

Non-persistent contact poisons

The advantage of contact poisons of low or limited persistence is that they usually present little residue hazard to man and to wild life. Furthermore, their toxic action can be made rather more selective with respect to other organisms in the environment than is usually possible when the material is persistent. For example, it is possible to select the time of application so that beneficial insects (e.g. bees) are unlikely to be present in the neighbourhood at the time. Moreover, while many predators and competitors of the pest species may still be destroyed, low persistence will allow recolonisation by beneficial insects shortly after application. Again, for reasons which will be described elsewhere (p. 84), a non-persistent material with a 'once and for all' action usually generates less pest resistance than a substance that persists in the environment, maintaining its lethal potential perhaps for weeks after the initial application. The disadvantage of the non-persistent contact poison is that while it may reduce more or less successfully the population of pest present at the time of spraying, it provides no protection against multiplication of surviving organisms or re-infestation from outside. It is therefore of value when a species has become a menace by getting locally out of control; and it is valuable for reducing numbers from epidemic to normal levels, with the implied hope that thereafter the natural equilibrium between pests and their competitors and predators will be re-established.

Persistent contact poisons

The second type of contact poison is one which is able to persist on the sprayed surface for a significant period of time after application. Such a use is roughly analogous to the medical use of an antiseptic ointment to minimise the risk, over a period of time, of an external infection entering the wound. Such pesticides are sometimes just called 'persistent' or 'protective' poisons. Most of these substances have an immediate contact action at the time of application upon organisms there at the time, but, in addition, because they persist on the surface, they are able to destroy at a later stage organisms which were not present on the surface when it was first sprayed or, if present, were not then in a susceptible stage of their life cycle. Certain persistent poisons are lipid-soluble and are absorbed by the wax of the leaf cuticle; such substances are often termed 'quasi-systemic'. Their use will be described in relation to the organophosphorus insecticides.

When long term protective action is the main objective, uniformity of application is of more importance than the deposition of a thin continuous film and to achieve this uniformity, the spray is applied so that small discrete droplets of sprayed solution or suspension dry *in situ*. Sufficient spreader is required to ensure contact of droplets with the sprayed surface, but not enough to cause them to flatten so much that they coalesce and run off. Furthermore, reasonable persistence requires that the dusted particles or deposit from evaporated spray droplets, should adhere firmly to the leaf surface, that the toxicant should be stable to hydrolysis, and that it should not be readily inactivated by oxidation or other effects of weathering. It must sometimes also be resistant to the action of certain enzymes.

A typical persistent fungicide remains on the leaf surface, destroying fungal spores by contact action when they begin to germinate. A persistent herbicide necessarily remains in the soil until it has an opportunity to enter the roots of a susceptible weed. For a persistent insecticide, however, the situation is more complex, for not only may a newly arrived insect walk on, or brush against, a protected surface, but it may also ingest the poison if it happens to feed on such a surface.

36

When a persistent poison enters the invading insect through the aliment-ary canal rather than by penetrating through the cuticle, it is customary to describe it as a stomach poison. This mode of entry introduces a number of new considerations, for a substance which is sufficiently stable to remain on the plant until the invader arrives may need to be 'solubilised', by the action of digestive enzymes or by other means, during the very few hours that the contaminated food material is within the gut. The mobilisation by caterpillars of the arsenate ions of lead arsenate is such a case. However, such materials can still be regarded as contact poisons, for the alimentary cavity is technically 'outside' the organism, and metabolic changes upon entry are in no way a prerogative of stomach poisons.

The advantage of persistent poisons is clearly that they introduce the parameter of time; pests arriving on the scene days or even weeks after the initial application can be controlled, thus reducing the risk of re-infestation. Most of the important persistent pesticides, and especially the insecticides, tend to be broad spectrum materials—i.e., they are indescriminate in their action, often killing beneficial organisms with the same facility as they destroy the pests. This has the serious disadvantage of removing biological control for a considerable period of time and may thereby occasion a later outbreak as severe as the original one. In addition, the continued presence of a poison in the environment may lead to the development of resistant strains of the pest which are both more difficult and more costly to control than were the organisms of the original population. Moreover, higher appli-cation rates as the control cycle is repeated increases the residue hazard in the environment. The organochlorine compounds such as DDT and the cyclodienes are notorious in these respects and the problems of insect resistance and of toxic residues are considered in more detail in Chapter 4.

Before leaving the subject of persistent contact poisons, it should be added that certain persistent materials are being investigated which do not have a contact action, nor are poisons in the usual sense, and hence do not belong to this group of compounds. Certain substances, for example, deter insects from laying their eggs, or from feeding, while yet others act as repellants (Martin, 1964; Ascher, 1964). Such substances are not so far used on a large scale in practical agriculture, but their development opens up interesting prospects in chemical and integrated pest control (p. 145).

2. SYSTEMIC POISONS

The practical use in agriculture of systemic poisons in some ways resembles the medical use of vaccines, for, upon application, the chemical

37

enters the plant and is carried around in the translocation or transpiration stream, or both. If it is a herbicide, the material has the advantage of being able to reach and to destroy parts of the plant not readily accessible to direct contact sprays. The importance of this will be appreciated if it is recognised that some of the most recalcitrant weeds are those with ramifying underground shoot or root systems, any part of which is capable of re-generating a new plant. Somewhat similarly, the systemic insecticide must persist within crop plants in an active, though not necessarily in an unchanged condition, until the contaminated material is sucked or eaten by insect pests. Work on systemic fungicides is still in its infancy, but some encouraging progress has been made (Chapter 8). In the case of herbicides, it is customary to speak of translocated rather than systemic substances, though the difference seems to be based more on historical accident than upon a real scientific distinction. The herbicides of the plant growth regulator group are particularly valuable systemic herbicides.

The most important advantage of the systemic insecticide is that it introduces two parameters, space and time, into the overall control system. The persistent contact insecticide enables control to be exercised at a time distant from the moment of application. The systemic poison achieves this same end, but in addition allows control in space distant from the point or area of application. It is possible, for example, to protect foliage formed by meristematic activity after the time the spray was applied. A second advantage possessed by some systemic insecticides is that systemic activity may be coupled with low contact action, and when this occurs a measure of selectivity between pest and beneficial insects can sometimes be achieved.

Unlike a material which persists on the surface, the systemic poison does not present problems so far as adhesion and weathering are concerned, but it must penetrate into and persist within the plant. Consequently, it must have sufficient solubility in lipid to enable it to pass through the cuticle (in the case of foliage-applied substances) yet sufficient solubility in water to enable it to move around in the aqueous fluids of phloem or xylem once the waxy barrier has been surmounted. This requires a very subtle balance between lipophilic and hydrophilic properties and greatly restricts both the type and number of candidate systemic poisons. Furthermore, it must resist hydrolysis and the action of enzymes within the plant for a sufficient length of time to make its use an economic proposition. The systemic insecticide must, in addition, be rapidly toxic to the insect if the plant is not to suffer considerable and irreversible damage before the insects are killed, while at the same time it must be non-phytotoxic at the insecticidal concentration.

When a substance enters a plant through the roots, it is not always clear whether it should be called systemic or not. Part of the difficulty relates to quantity and is reminiscent of the problem of defining what is meant by an 'insoluble' substance. But, in addition, some authors regard all substances moving within the plant as systemic while others confine the term to those which tend to escape from the xylem into other tissues of both root and stem. Yet others seem to use the term vicariously, regarding root uptake as systemic when the same substance is known to be systemic when applied to leaves. Perhaps all substances which gain entry via the root are systemic, some being 'more systemic than others'; if so, factors such as solubility, selectivity of uptake, and the extent to which the compound is bound to constituents of the root and the vascular system determine the magnitude of the systemic action.

SURFACTANTS AND OTHER SPRAY SUPPLEMENTS

From the discussion in earlier sections it will be apparent that it is often essential for substances other than the active ingredient and its carrier to be present in an applied mixture if the full toxic potential of the pesticide is to be realised. Such supplementary materials may exert their effect before the material leaves the spray tank (dispersing agents and emulsifiers), at the moment of impact with the sprayed surface (spreaders or wetters) or they may only become effective after impact. The last group includes materials which increase the persistence of a substance on the leaf surface (adhering agents or stickers), substances which assist penetration through a cuticular barrier (oils and co-solvents) and substances which appear to activate the toxicant.

Most dispersing agents, emulsifiers and spreaders are related in the sense that they share the physico-chemical attribute of being able to separate preferentially at a phase boundary. For electrical reasons, such separation leads directly to the stabilisation of suspensions and emulsions. But their presence at an aqueous interface also has the consequence of markedly reducing the surface tension, a property which enables surfactants to function as spreaders. In addition, the affinity of a portion of their molecules for wax and oil is sometimes responsible for sticking and co-solvent properties.

Surfactants fall into several chemical groups, but the general characteristics outlined above are best illustrated by first considering those of one molecular type. This is the type to which soap, the best known of all surfactants, belongs. Such a molecule consists of two ions, and is represented diagrammatically in Fig. 2.3.

The covalent portion of the negative ion consists typically of a long chain of carbon atoms, while the ionising group, in the case of soap, is a carboxyl group. This negative ion is the active ion of the ion pair so far as surfactant

Fig. 2.3. General structure of a typical anionic surfactant

properties are concerned, and since it carries a negative charge, compounds with ionised molecules of this type are called anionic surfactants. The anion is balanced by a suitable cation, X^+, which is usually an ion of sodium or potassium. The covalent part of the anion is lipophilic and non-polar in character (*similia similibus solvuntur*—like tends to dissolve like— is still a fair maxim for assessing dissolving characteristics) and the charged end of the negative ion is hydrophilic. The term *amphipathic* is applied to an ion with both lipophilic and hydrophilic portions (Pankhurst, 1953) while the balancing ion is termed a gegenion (from the German, *gegen,* against, counter).

On adding such a substance to a suspension of solid particles or of oil droplets in water, the amphipathic ions orientate themselves with their covalent portions directed away from the water (Fig. 2.4).

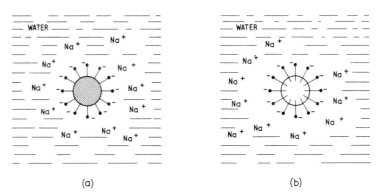

(a)   (b)

Fig. 2.4. How a surfactant stabilises suspensions and emulsions : (a) Solid particle with covalent chains adsorbed on to it; (b) Oil droplet with covalent carbon chains dissolved in it

The phase distribution of the opposing parts of the amphipathic ion can be pictured more readily in the case where the suspended material is a covalent solvent such as oil (Fig. 2.4(b)), but it must be remembered that when molecular films are being considered, the customary distinction between the meanings of such words as 'adsorbed' and 'dissolved' tends to disappear. The gegenions, for present purposes, can be imagined as being dissolved in the bulk phase and they need be considered no further. Since each suspended particle of solid becomes surrounded, in effect, by a sphere of negative electricity, the tendency of the particles to sediment out under the influence of gravity is opposed by the electrical charges upon them (Fig. 2.5). Similarly, emulsions normally tend first to cream and then

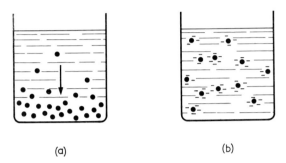

(a)   (b)

Fig. 2.5. Stabilisation of a suspension: (a) Without surfactant: solid particles sediment; (b) With surfactant: solid particles remain suspended since particles carrying similar electrical charges repel each other

to break—that is, for the adjacent droplets of creamed disperse phase to coalesce. The rate at which these undesirable effects take place can be reduced by the use of emulsifiers.

For the reasons given above, the presence of a surfactant in the spray tank reduces the rate at which a heterogeneous mixture separates out. In conjunction with mechanical agitation, the surface active substance helps to prevent non-uniform application of pesticide, a situation which would be economically damaging and possibly medically dangerous. Nowadays, many crop protection chemicals are formulated as oil in water emulsions, the pesticide being dissolved in the oil (Furmidge, 1959a), so the importance of emulsifiers in spray chemistry cannot be over-estimated.

One important practical difference exists between suspensions and emulsions, for whereas particles of solid normally remain their formulated size, the average size of droplets of oil in an emulsion tends to diminish as agitation is increased. If an emulsifier is present, the small droplets obtained by increasing agitation have difficulty in coalescing—that is, the emulsion is stabilised. It should be noted that the presence of the dispersing agent or emulsifier confers upon a suspension or emulsion electrical properties characteristic of the colloidal state although the particles themselves are well above colloidal dimensions.

It might perhaps be imagined that the procedure likely to ensure best use of a water-insoluble toxicant would be to add excess stabiliser. This, however, is not necessarily the case, for the surfactant properties of stabilisers still need to be taken into consideration after the stabilised heterogeneous systems have left the spray tank. For example, the amount of emulsifier in an insecticidal wash will determine the stability of the emulsion after the spray lands on the target surface and such stability may be inversely related both to contact toxicity to insects and to phytotoxicity. In addition, an emulsifier may well contribute both to the extent of spreading of spray droplets on the target surface and to the adherence of the toxicant. Thus the amount of surfactant of each type to add is an optimal amount— a compromise reached after each advantageous and disadvantageous factor has been assessed carefully.

The spreaders are surfactants which so modify the surface properties of water droplets that the optimal contact of the spray with the target surface is achieved at the moment of impact. As has been seen, what constitutes optimal contact will vary somewhat with the type of spray machinery employed and with whether the spray is acting primarily as a non-persistent, a persistent or a systemic poison.

The compactness and stereochemistry of water molecules enables them to approach one another very closely. This has two important consequences. First, the molecular geometry is such that hydrogen bonding can operate. This explains why water is a polar solvent despite the fact that it is only ionised slightly. Secondly, the close proximity of the molecules causes enormous forces of cohesion to be generated between adjacent water molecules. The magnitude of these forces is manifest at the surface as a high surface tension. So far as an individual droplet of water is concerned, surface tension may be regarded as creating an elastic surface film which, by contracting, causes the droplet to assume as nearly spherical a shape as its size and environment will allow. If such a droplet is placed upon a surface such as wax, for which water has no chemical affinity, the contact between it and the surface will be very small.

When a spreading agent is added to water, the molecules separate preferentially at the surface, forcing the water molecules apart, thus replacing high forces of cohesion of water molecules by either lower forces of adhesion between water and surfactant molecules, or low forces of cohesion between two molecules of surfactant (Fig. 2.6).

If, then, two droplets of the same size are placed on a waxy surface, one of which consists of pure water and the other of a solution of surfactant, the droplet containing surfactant will be the one which flattens out and makes the better contact with the surface. By analogy with the example above, it is as though the surface elastic had been weakened (Fig. 2.6b).

If little or no surfactant is present, limited contact of droplet with the surface will result in poor deposition on impact since the droplets will tend to bounce off. If the surface energy of the droplet (which is a function of its surface tension and surface area) is very low, i.e. if much spreader is present, the droplet will disintegrate on impact, or, if the kinetic energy of impact is not enough for this to happen, the droplet will spread till it coalesces with other droplets, when most of the liquid will run off. Thus

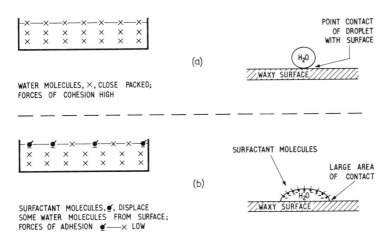

Fig. 2.6. Effect of surfactants on surface tension

in either case, wastage occurs. There is, in fact, an interplay between the opposing forces of kinetic energy and of (high) surface energy; the former tends to make the droplet flatten at the moment of impact, while surface energy tends to keep the droplet spherical. It is clearly desirable that the amount of spreader present should be such as to ensure the optimal interplay of these two factors for whatever purpose the spray is being applied. Except, perhaps, for certain types of contact spray, the optimum will be such that maximal deposition of material on the leaf surface is achieved.

Surfactants are specialist materials, some being better for one purpose (e.g. for stabilising emulsions) than for another (e.g. acting as spreaders), but all possess general surface active potential. Occasionally, the same material may be employed for more than one purpose, but frequently separate emulsifiers, spreaders and co-solvents are present in the same spray mixture. If more than one supplement is to be used, it is essential to ensure that those chosen are mutually compatible.

When surfactants are used as adhering agents to increase retention, or as co-solvents to ensure cuticular penetration, their effectiveness depends not only on their surface active properties but upon their solubility in lipid. The softening of cuticular wax and distortion of cuticular structure may enable the pesticide present to penetrate the surface layers of the cuticles of both plants and insects. Several other subsidiary functions of surfactants in spray chemistry have been mentioned by Currier and Dybing (1959).

TYPES OF SURFACTANTS

Surfactants are now being manufactured under thousands of trade names, but the majority fall into one of three groups, called respectively the anionic, cationic and non-ionic detergents.

Anionic surfactants are of the type already discussed, and possess a negative charge on the amphipathic ion. Considerable variability is possible with regard to both the detailed structure of the covalent part of the molecule and the nature of the ionising group. Typical examples, other than soap, are sulphated alcohols and sulphonated hydrocarbons:

Sulphated alcohols, e.g. $C_{12}H_{25}-O-SO_3^-Na^+$ Sodium dodecyl sulphate

Sulphonated hydrocarbons, e.g. $C_3H_7-(C_{10}H_6)-SO_3^-Na^+$ Propyl naphthalene sulphonate (sodium salt)

Such materials are often superior to soap for spraying purposes, partly because of the individual specialisation of surfactants and partly because the calcium and magnesium salts of many members of these two groups are soluble in water. As a result, they can often be used in hard water and in the presence of pesticides (such as lime sulphur) which contain cations of calcium or the heavy metals, whereas soap in such circumstances would undergo double decomposition. Insoluble materials such as free higher fatty acids and their heavy metal salts have no surface active properties.

Cationic surfactants carry a positive charge upon the amphipathic ion and a negative charge on the gegenion. Representative examples are quaternary ammonium and pyridinium salts (Fig. 2.7).

The advantage of cationic surfactants in spray chemistry is that they

(a) 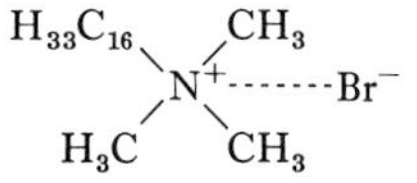 $H_{33}C_{16}$ \ CH_3
$>N^+\cdots\cdots Br^-$
H_3C / \ CH_3

(b) $C_{16}H_{33}(C_5H_5N^+)Br^-$

Fig. 2.7. (a) A quaternary ammonium salt, cetyl trimethyl ammonium bromide; (b) A pyridinium salt, cetyl pyridinium bromide

44

cannot react with ions of heavy metals. Their cost is sometimes a disadvantage, and the incompatibility of anionic and cationic surfactants must always be borne in mind if it is necessary to add more than one type of spray supplement to a spray mixture.

Compounds belonging to the third group of surfactants are not dissociated into ions and are therefore termed *non-ionic* detergents. Their surface activity depends on a balance of hydrophilic and lipophilic properties throughout the molecule. Condensates of polyethylene oxide and phenol are finding increasing use in spray chemistry; their hydrophilic

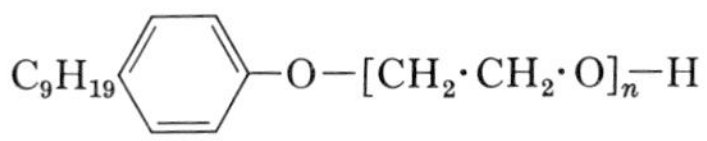

$$C_9H_{19}\langle\bigcirc\rangle - O - [CH_2 \cdot CH_2 \cdot O]_n - H$$

Fig. 2.8. Ethylene oxide-phenol condensates ; n equals from 9 to 30

activity is due to hydrogen bonding between oxygen atoms of the polyethylene oxide and water of the solution (Fig. 2.8) (McWhorter, 1963).

Their advantages include the fact that they are incapable of reacting with cations or anions present in other spray components or in hard water, and that they are not subject to hydrolysis by acidic or alkaline solutions. For many spray purposes they have the added advantage of low phytotoxicity, whereas the phytotoxicity of anionic and cationic surfactants is variable (Furmidge, 1959b). Phytotoxicity of supplements must always be taken into account, although it does not follow that for all purposes it is the least toxic which is the most suitable. For herbicidal purposes especially, some phytotoxicity of surfactant may be an advantage in that it assists the toxicant to do its allotted task. The lethal levels of certain surfactants to leaves were determined by Temple and Hilton (1963) and found to vary approximately tenfold, most of the cationic compounds tending to be rather phytotoxic.

For detailed information on the chemistry and uses of surfactants the following references should be consulted. Pankhurst (1953) has discussed the physical chemistry of surfactants, and especially the part played in the control of their physical characteristics by the tendency of their amphipathic ions to form micelles. The significance of the contact angle in the measurement of surface wetting properties has been described by Furmidge (1962) and by Yakowitz and Eisenberg (1964). Many techniques have been developed for evaluating and comparing the properties of different surfactants; some of them, and the apparatus employed for the purpose, have been described by Thompson (1958), Ashworth and Lloyd (1961) and by Yakowitz and Eisenberg (1964). The tendency for different detergents to specialise in different directions has been discussed by Foy (1963) and by Temple and Hilton (1963).

OTHER TYPES OF SPRAY SUPPLEMENTS

In addition to surfactants there are several other types of spray supplements, but since their uses are less general ones, or are mentioned elsewhere, they need not be discussed in detail.

Adhering or sticking agents are of greatest importance when persistent poisons are being used, for they help to bind the deposited toxicant more firmly to the leaf surface. Their use in increasing the retention of fungicides has been considered by Somers (1956).

Humectants are materials which increase the length of time between the application of the spray and the evaporation to dryness of the deposited droplets. This greater time interval sometimes facilitates better penetration into leaf (or other) cuticle. Glycerol, propylene glycol and polyethylene glycol have all been used for this purpose as adjuncts to herbicidal materials.

Propellants are materials which are vapours at room temperature and pressure, but are readily liquefied by compression. In the aerosol technique they serve a dual function, since their vapour pressure acts as the force driving a toxic mixture out of a pressure chamber, and their presence indirectly assists in the production of a mist of very small droplets. The case of DDT, which is frequently formulated as an aerosol for domestic purposes, may be taken as an example. In the pressure chamber, the DDT is dissolved in a small percentage of an involatile solvent such as oil and a large excess of a miscible volatile solvent such as methyl bromide. On releasing the pressure, the mixture is driven out through a jet by the vapour pressure of the propellant. As the volatile solvent evaporates, a very fine mist is left containing the DDT dissolved in the oil (Fig. 2.9).

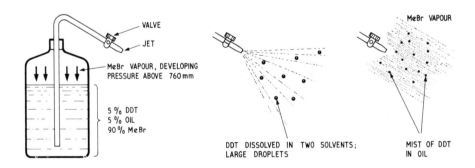

Fig. 2.9. Principle of the aerosol : DDT–oil–methyl bromide

46

Synergists and *activators* are substances which enable a fixed amount of toxicant, applied under otherwise identical and optimal conditions, to have a greater killing power. The way synergists operate is not always certain but the majority probably act at the biochemical level. Many, for example, inhibit microsomal oxidases and other enzyme systems which would otherwise rapidly destroy the toxicant (Sun and Johnson, 1960). An example is piperonyl butoxide, which increases the apparent effectiveness of pyrethrins and of certain carbamates. Suitable pairs of organophosphorus insecticides also have a mutually synergistic action (Dubois, 1961). Synergism (or potentiation,* as it is often termed in American literature) is important not only because it can enable better use to be made of an expensive toxicant by the addition of a cheaper synergist, but because its unsuspected occurrence when traces of several poisons are present in the diet could conceivably be a health hazard to man (Dubois, 1960, 1961).

The inhibition of the action of microsomal oxidases is of considerable interest and can have some curious consequences. Normally, these oxidases can be regarded as providing built-in detoxifying mechanisms for dealing with foreign molecules. Thus, they metabolise and eventually degrade heptachlor, chlordene and other organochlorine compounds. However, there is a certain inevitability about their action; they are not apparently very specific enzymes and should they be presented with a relatively non-toxic molecule which happens to oxidise to a more toxic one, they nevertheless act upon the substance, rendering the situation worse, at least for a period of time. This is what happens in the case of chlordene (p. 98), which is temporarily 'activated' to chlordene epoxide before further oxidation leads to inactivation. When the substance sesamex, which inhibits this oxidase, is administered together with chlordene, it is found that the appearance of toxic symptoms is delayed (since the formation of the epoxide is retarded) but that at a later stage synergism is apparent because the degradation of chlordene via the epoxide proceeds at a slower rate (Brooks, 1966).

Activators, in general, alter the physical state of a poison, allowing it better access to its site of action. The commonest case is that of an activator which alters the degree of ionisation of certain toxicants which are weak electrolytes. It will be recalled that ionised particles and unionised molecules often penetrate at different rates and perhaps by different routes through a barrier of lipid. The principle underlying the use of such activators is

---

*These words tend to be used synonymously; synergism, strictly speaking, should be confined to the case where the second substance, or synergist, is inactive when used alone, whereas, in potentiation, both may have a measure of toxicity when used separately.

illustrated below for the case of a weak acid, HX, for which the equilibrium equation is

$$HX \rightleftharpoons H^+ + X^-$$

If K is the dissociation constant of the acid (its value is known for all marketed pesticides), and if brackets represent concentrations in the usual way, the equilibrium can be represented by the equation

$$K = \frac{[H^+][X^-]}{[HX]}$$

Then
$$-\text{Log K} = -\text{Log}[H^+] - \text{Log}\left(\frac{[X^-]}{[HX]}\right)$$

Since
$$-\text{Log K} = \text{pK}$$

$$-\text{Log}[H^+] = \text{pH}$$

And for any term A
$$-\text{Log A} = +\text{Log}\frac{1}{A}$$

$$\text{pK} - \text{pH} = \text{Log}\frac{[\text{unionised molecules}]}{[\text{ionised particles}]}$$

For a given toxicant, pK is constant but the pH of the medium can often be varied within certain limits. Clearly, it is the difference between these two quantities, not their absolute values, which alone determines what proportion of the toxicant molecules is ionised. An activator is a substance which can increase or decrease this difference, at least until constituents of the droplets begin to penetrate into the sprayed surface. For a toxicant which is a weak acid (pK usually between 3 and 6) the proportion of unionised molecules rises as the pH falls. Albert (1960) has drawn up a table which relates the percentage ionisation to the difference between the pH of the medium and pK value of any weak acid, but the reader can readily calculate such values from the equation given above.

REFERENCES

ALBERT, A. (1960), *Selective Toxicity,* Methuen and Co., London (pp. 119, 209)
ASCHER, K. R. C. (1964), *Wld Rev. Pest Control,* **3,** (1), 7
ASHWORTH, R. DE B. and LLOYD, G. A. (1961), *J. Sci. Fd Agric.,* **12,** 234
BHAMBHANI, H. J. (1964), *Wld Rev. Pest Control,* **3,** (1), 53
BROOKS, G. T. (1966), *Wld Rev. Pest Control,* **5,** (2), 62
BRUNSKILL, R. T. (1956), *Proc. 3rd Brit. Weed Control Conf.,* **2,** 593
CURRIER, H. B. and DYBING, C. D. (1959), *Weeds,* **7,** 195
DAVID, W. A. L. (1959), *Outl. Agric.,* **2,** 127
DUBOIS, K. P. (1960), *J. agric. Fd Chem.,* **8,** 36
DUBOIS, K. P. (1961), *Adv. Pest Control Res.,* **4,** 117
FOY, C. L. (1963–4), *Hilgardia,* **35,** 125
FURMIDGE, C. G. L. (1959a), *J. Sci. Fd Agric.,* **10,** 267
FURMIDGE, C. G. L. (1959b), *J. Sci. Fd Agric.,* **10,** 419
FURMIDGE, C. G. L. (1962), *J. Sci. Fd Agric.,* **13,** 127

HOLLIS, J. P. (1962), *Pl. Prot. Bull., F.A.O.,* **10,** 97

MCWHORTER, C. G. (1963), *Weeds,* **11,** 265

MARTIN, H. (1964), *Scientific Principles of Crop Protection,* (5th Ed.) Edward Arnold Ltd., London (Chapter 5)

MITCHELL, J. W., SMALE, B. C. and METCALF, R. L. (1960), *Adv. Pest Control Res.,* **3,** 359

MONRO, H. A. U. (1947), *Scient. Agric.,* **27,** 269

MONRO, H. A. U. (1961), *Manual of Fumigation for Insect Control,* F.A.O. Agricultural Studies No. 56 H.M.S.O.

PANKHURST, K. G. A. (1953), *Lect. Monogr. Rep. R. Inst. Chem.,* No. 5

PARK, P. O. and BURDEKIN, D. A. (1964), *Ann. appl. Biol.,* **53,** 133

RIPPER, W. E. (1955), *Ann. appl. Biol.,* **42,** 288

SIEGEL, S. M. (1962), *The Plant Cell Wall,* Pergamon Press, Oxford

SOMERS, E. (1956), *J. Sci. Fd Agric.,* **7,** 160

SUN, Y. and JOHNSON, E. R. (1960), *J. agric. Fd Chem.,* **8,** 261

TEMPLE, R. E. and HILTON, H. W. (1963), *Weeds,* **11,** 297

THOMPSON, C. C. (1958), *J. Sci. Fd Agric.,* **9,** 650

VAARTAJA, O. (1964), *Bot. Rev.,* **30,** 1

WAIN, R. L. (1961), *Span,* **4,** 177

YAKOWITZ, M. G. and EISENBERG, W. V. (1964), *J. Ass. off. agric. Chem.,* **47,** 520

3
BARRIERS AND TARGETS
IN INSECTS

The cuticle of plants, discussed in the previous chapter, is frequently the target at which a pesticide is aimed. Sometimes it is a target by proxy, and is sprayed in order to hit insects living upon it, while sometimes it is a surface upon which a persistent insecticide or fungicide must be deposited or into which a systemic insecticide can diffuse. On other occasions, however, as when the foliage concerned belongs to weeds, the cuticle presents an *external* target, or barrier, through which a herbicide must penetrate if it is to reach its real target, its site of action within the plant. The present chapter deals firstly with the properties of external barriers in insects—a subject of great practical importance, since the structure and phase distribution characteristics of insect cuticle naturally determine how easily an insecticide can reach its site of action in any particular species of insect. Afterwards, a short account is given of the changes which occur when impulses are transmitted along nerves, for the nervous system is a vulnerable *internal* target, the principal site of action of the two most important groups of insecticides currently in use.

THE INSECT INTEGUMENT

THE NATURE AND IMPORTANCE OF THE INTEGUMENT

The outermost layer of cells of the insect is termed the epidermis or hypodermis. It secretes an organic, non-living, but by no means amorphous layer on its outer surface. This secretion has a protective function, and is called the cuticle. The cuticle and the epidermis—together with such modified epidermal regions as sensory or nerve cells—provide the boundary layer, or integument, of the insect. It should be noted that the insect *cuticle,* the part of the integument with which we are principally concerned, shares with a leaf surface and a fungal spore wall the property of presenting a lipophilic barrier to a sprayed toxicant. Webb (1949) rated the permeability of the insect cuticle to a potential poison as the most important factor, other than intrinsic toxicity, determining the practical value of an insecticide. The cuticle not only covers the whole exterior of the insect body, thereby offering some protection to the sensory cells (p. 54), at least against certain types of poisons, but it also lines the gut and extends in a more or less modified form into the cavities of the spiracles. The cuticle thus presents a potential barrier between a poison and its site of action, whether the insect comes into direct contact with poison, ingests it, or breathes it in.

The cuticle varies in thickness and in hardness in different areas of the insect body. Since such differences probably affect penetrability, it is not surprising that the relation of cuticle structure to susceptibility to insecticides is a subject of extreme complexity and one which is still imperfectly understood.

STRUCTURE OF THE INSECT CUTICLE

Wigglesworth (1947) and Richards (1951) have given general accounts of the structure of the insect integument and the chemistry of the various layers of the cuticle. Its physiology has been described by Wigglesworth (1957), its biochemistry by Hackman (1958) and the fine structure as revealed by electron microscopy has been described and illustrated by Locke (1961). From the accounts given by these and other authors, the following composite and general picture emerges.

Cuticle is a secretion rich in proteins, some at least of which are conjugate. It is usually divided into two main regions: (a) a thick inner layer, or *procuticle,* which consists largely of glycoproteins and tanning agents, and (b) a thin outer region, or *epicuticle,* which is rich in lipoproteins and lipids (Fig. 3.1).

The procuticle, which may represent as much as 95% of the total thickness of the cuticle, is secreted in distinct layers and is rich in chitin. Although chitin may account for much of the total cuticular weight, it is probably not responsible for the rigidity of some types of cuticle and is certainly not responsible for the impermeability of cuticle to substances of many types. The rigidity is mainly due to a protein called *sclerotin* present in the outer region of the procuticle and the impermeability is largely or entirely due to the extremely thin outer layer of lipid-rich epicuticle.

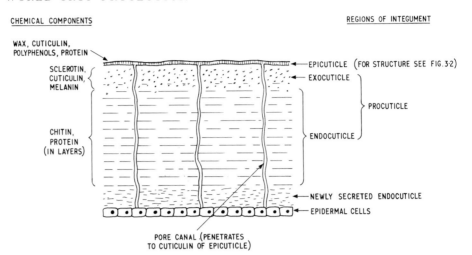

Fig. 3.1. Main features of insect integument

Despite its thinness, the epicuticle consists of three regions (Fig. 3.2). The inner layer contains much protein but is also rich in polyphenols and the lipoprotein-like substance, cuticulin. The central region is much richer in lipids and waxes. On the outside, there is usually a thin film termed the

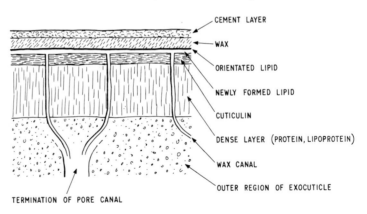

Fig. 3.2. Structure of the epicuticle

tectocuticle or cement layer. The lipophilic nature of these two outer regions of the epicuticle contrasts with the essentially hydrophilic characteristics of the remainder of the total cuticle, and is of great importance in relation to the uptake and selectivity of insecticides. The human skin, for example, does not possess any region corresponding to the outer layers of the epicuticle.

The epicuticle is not only an important barrier preventing polar substances from entering the insect, but is also a barrier preventing water from leaking out. If it is damaged as it sometimes is, for example, when soil organisms struggle through firm or dry soil, the insect risks desiccation. The simplest of all pesticides—and the only sort, perhaps, for which we can truly claim to know the mode of action—has, like the soil above, an abrasive effect. Abrasives, such as mineral dust have, in fact, been used to control insects in stored produce, especially in circumstances where the persistence of a poisonous insecticide would be hazardous.

Although it is valuable to divide the integument up into regions characterised by their chemical structure and physical properties, it must not be overlooked that it is, in fact, a single entity consisting of merging layers which show much diversity both in thickness and composition from one species of insect to another. Thus the cement layer may be absent altogether. Cases are also known where chitin, often regarded as the most characteristic component of insect cuticles, may be totally absent. Even in different parts of the same organism, the structure and thickness of the layers may vary considerably. In the intersegmental areas, the procuticle remains soft and is almost transparent. Elsewhere the layers of chitin are often less obvious and the outer part of the procuticle may darken and harden. This outer region, which contains chitin and the derived protein sclerotin, may then be distinguished as the exocuticle. Although hard, this exocuticular region is probably freely permeable to aqueous solutions and appears to be saturated with body fluids.

The thickness of the cuticle is extremely variable in different groups of arthropods. Richards estimated that a several thousand-fold difference in thickness exists between the thinnest and thickest insect cuticles so far investigated. The cuticle tends to be very thin in the regions of the nerve endings and in the lining of the tracheoles but nevertheless, even in these cases, electron micrographs reveal that the important lipophilic epicuticle remains intact. In insect larvae, the thickness of the cuticle also frequently varies with the stage in the life cycle; it often increases in thickness threefold or more between one moult and the next. At the time of moulting, the softer parts of the endodermis are dissolved by enzymes, and a new soft endocuticle is laid down over the epidermis. The new endocuticle acts as a protective layer when the old exo- and epi-cuticle shear off. The cuticle of the adult is not necessarily thicker than that of the final larval form but it may well be different in composition and tends, in particular, to contain more sclerotin and thus to be more rigid.

The cuticle is modified in the regions occupied by sensory cells, spines and microtrichia (which are cuticular projections around cellular filaments).

Richards disputes a widely-held view that the cuticle is perforated above the sensory cells; there is little evidence to suggest that the cuticle near such nerve endings differs in any respect other than thickness from the cuticle nearby. Nevertheless, in the region of the sense organs the nervous system is particularly vulnerable, for here it is very near the surface, the sensory nerves ending in receptor cells. These cells are enlarged epidermal cells which penetrate through most of the thickness of the cuticle (Fig. 3.3).

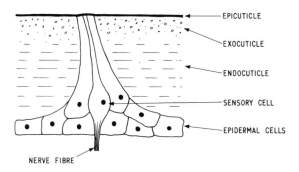

Fig. 3.3. The integument in the region of a sensory cell

Most insects, but not all of them, possess integuments perforated by pore canals leading from the epidermal layer up to the lower limit of the epicuticle. According to Locke (1961) they may play a part in the deposition of the waxy layers of the epicuticle.

SOME CHEMICAL CONSTITUENTS OF THE CUTICLE

Chitin is almost always present in insect endocuticles, and sometimes accounts for 60% of the cuticular weight. It is plentiful near the epidermis but the exocuticle may contain as little as 20%. It is of interest that a similar or identical substance is present in fungal spore walls. Chitin is a polymer of acetylated glucosamine, the molecular length probably being several hundred glucosamine units. Richards (1951) has pointed out that, despite the presence of the acetylated amino groups in chitin, a considerable similarity exists between the structure of cellulose (Fig. 3.4a) and the structure of chitin (Fig. 3.4b), and the average chain length may be approximately the same.

In pure chitin the individual molecules are arranged in an orderly manner in a space lattice. Rudall (1963) has described the chemistry of chitin in natural structures, and has provided X-ray evidence that three types of chitin occur in cuticle. These are believed to be associated with protein molecules to form protein-chitin complexes.

Pure chitin is a colourless substance which is extremely stable. It is insoluble in water, dilute acids and alkalies and is scarcely affected by organic solvents. Concentrated hydrochloric acid hydrolyses and dissolves

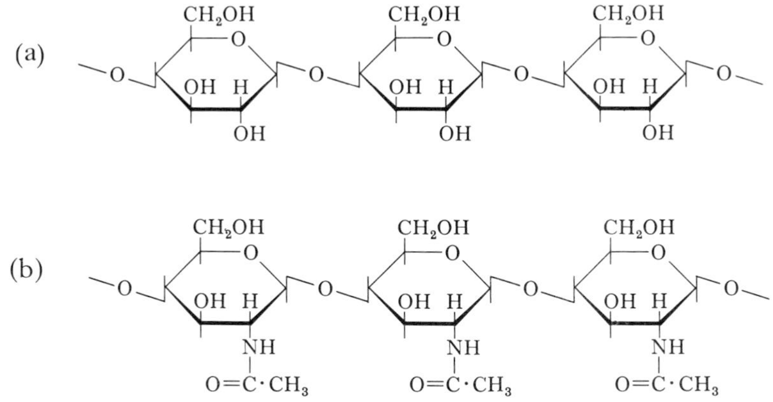

Fig. 3.4. (a) Cellulose; (b) Chitin

it, while concentrated potassium hydroxide removes some of the acetyl groups, to form a substance called chitosan which gives a violet colour with iodine.

Protein may account for more than half the weight of the cuticle, but information about it is scanty (Hackman, 1958). Different proteins have been isolated from the cuticles of different species of insect, and more than one protein can be extracted from the cuticle of any one insect. Most of this protein is probably bound more or less securely to chitin (though only a little over half may be attached by covalent bonding) but a residue of some 15% is probably not bound to any other component of the cuticle.

Polyphenolic substances are also present and are probably responsible for both the darkening of the exocuticle and for the hardening of the exocuticular region of the procuticle. Ortho- and possibly also para-dihydric phenols may participate in the tanning of the protein which leads to sclerotin formation. This is brought about by polyphenol oxidase, an enzyme widely distributed in insects. Mason (1955) has given an account of the biochemistry of this reaction. The brown or black pigment, melanin, is probably not a single chemical substance and it, too, may be formed by the activity of a polyphenol oxidase. Polyphenols are also present in the epicuticle, though it is doubtful whether they form a layer in any histological sense.

Cuticulin, according to Wigglesworth (1957), consists of lipoprotein subsequently tanned with quinones formed by oxidation of polyphenols. The lipid is believed by some observers to be of the sterol type. The cement layer, often to be found outside the layer of crystalline wax, is about 0.1μ in thickness. It is not continuous over the whole waxy surface and is sometimes absent. It is probably composed of lightly tanned lipoprotein.

The waxes of the outer epicuticle are of the paraffin type and are largely responsible for the water-impervious nature of the cuticle. The wax crystals appear to be arranged in a three-dimensional pattern and are orientated perpendicular to the cuticular surface. The nature of the wax varies considerably in different species of insects, a factor which may well determine how readily an insecticide is able to penetrate the cuticle of the insect in question. Thus the wax of the cockroach melts at $30°C$, whilst that of *Rhodnius* melts above $50°C$. The ability of a wax-soluble substance to penetrate into these two insects might be expected to be very different at, say, $37°C$. It has also been shown that a sudden rapid change in the permeability of the cuticle to water may occur above a certain temperature, an observation of importance in relation to water conservation by the insect.

The preceding account provides a very general model of the structure and composition of an 'average' and hence largely hypothetical insect cuticle. This must not disguise the very great variety of cuticular morphology which is actually to be observed; the skins of a hamster, a human and a hippopotamus could be described similarly in general terms, but everyone—scientist or layman—recognises that thickness, hairyness and penetrability nevertheless vary greatly for the three. Insect cuticles probably vary even more profoundly amongst themselves than do these mammalian skins. Indeed, we have seen that structure, thickness and hardness of the cuticle can vary in different parts of one insect, or in different stages of its life cycle, as well as between different insects. Similarly, the nature of the proteins present, and the extent to which they are bound to chitin or are tanned to sclerotin, differs in different cuticles. More important, perhaps, the wax in epicuticles is extremely variable in chemical composition and therefore in such properties as softness and melting point, while the cement layer, or tectocuticle, may sometimes be completely absent.

THE CUTICLE AS A TWO-PHASE SYSTEM

From the foregoing discussion it appears that the cement layer and wax of the epicuticle together form a thin but highly impermeable barrier to the outward passage of water or the inward diffusion of aqueous solutions of toxicants. Ionised materials would be expected to enter with difficulty unless their entry were facilitated in some way.

In practice, several means exist whereby the effectiveness of the epicuticle as a barrier may be overcome. Physical damage prior to, or simultaneously with, the arrival of solutes often increases the permeability of the cuticle to solutes. Thus, surfactants and carriers may bring about modification of the lipid (p. 33), while soil insects may so abrade their cuticle by movement that vulnerable areas are produced through which entry of aqueous solutes is less difficult. Again, weak electrolytes exist partly as ions and partly in the covalent form; since the equilibrium between the two forms is disturbed when undissociated molecules dissolve in lipid, many weak electrolytes actually gain access quite readily. It should also be remembered that insects, in common with other living organisms, have special mechanisms for the uptake of ions in the gut, and such mechanisms may well lead, as they do in higher organisms, to the incidental uptake of toxic ions.

A covalent, oil-soluble substance, on the other hand, might be expected to enter the epicuticle with reasonable ease, especially if its absorption affects the structural integrity of the cuticle. Once there, its fate is determined by characteristics of both a physico-chemical and a physiological nature. If it is a substance capable of attacking the sensory nerve endings (the toxic effect then being transmitted along the nerve fibre by a perversion of the usual biochemical mechanism), mere penetration of the epicuticle might result in contact between the toxicant and its site of action.

If, however, it does not attack sensory nerve cells, toxic action probably requires that it should leave the lipid layer and enter the body after penetrating the aqueous interstices of the endocuticular structure. This implies the need for a certain degree of solubility in water, and the existence of a suitable balance between solubility in water and solubility in oil. In other words, the oil-water partition coefficient of the substance must be favourable (Fig. 3.5). If the partition coefficient is too much in favour of oil, the substance may enter the cuticle with ease but will leave the cuticle only with difficulty.

When a substance possesses a very high oil-water partition coefficient, it could be anticipated that small quantities might be immobilised by physical solution in the bulk phase of the wax of the cuticle. Such physical solution may itself have deleterious effects on the organism, but, on the other hand, it sometimes provides time for the defence mechanisms of the insect to come into action with gradual destruction of the foreign molecules. The time factor involved here should be noted: an organism can often cope with even a very highly poisonous substance, so long as it is not all presented to the body in active form at the same time. If the absorbed substance enters a 'reservoir', out of which it leaks only gradually, it is sometimes inactivated as it escapes.

It must be admitted that problems concerning the permeability of the cuticle to any type of substance, let alone insecticides, are of extreme

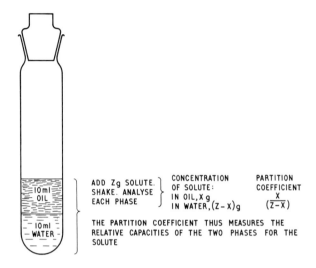

Fig. 3.5. The oil-water partition coefficient

complexity and that reliable experimental evidence is fragmentary. One author lists no less than twenty three independent variables capable of influencing the permeability of insect cuticle. Webb (1949) and Richards (1951), however, attempted to apply general physico-chemical principles to the problems of uptake and selective action of insecticides.

Webb (1949) described two ways in which penetration of the cuticle could be effected. The first of these is the method of three-dimensional diffusion which was discussed above. Even for this, the obvious method, there is some doubt as to whether diffusion occurs only so far as the tips of the pore canals or whether, at least for some substances, diffusion is the major factor determining entry through the whole depth of endocuticle.

When diffusion occurs, the driving force is the concentration gradient of the diffusing substance, and this is governed by the relative saturation of the poison in the wax near the outside of the cuticle, compared with the relative saturation near the epidermal cells. Should the substance remain in the cuticle, an equilibrium is achieved when the concentration of the toxicant is the same throughout the depth of the cuticle (Fig. 3.6). The same principle can be extended to cover phase distribution between the solute in a solution applied to the outside of an insect and the solute present

58

in each individual phase within the insect (Ferguson, 1939; Hassall, 1953), though a steady state, rather than a true equilibrium, normally exists. This concept has proved particularly rewarding for substances termed physical poisons, because, by knowing the relative saturation in the external phase

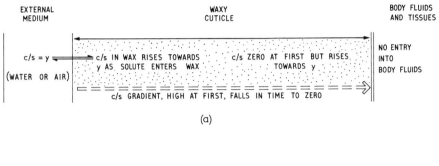

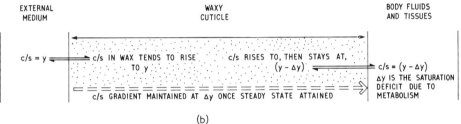

Fig. 3.6. *Diffusion and phase distribution as functions of relative saturation*
(a) Entry of a poison into, and its diffusion across, the epicuticle, when none of it leaves the inside. Relative saturation equals c/s, where c equals concentration of toxicant present and s its saturation concentration in that phase. When equilibrium is established, the relative saturation c/s is the same in all phases, though it will be less than y if depletion has occurred ;
(b) Steady state absorption and diffusion. The tissues, by destroying poison at a constant rate, reduce c/s in tissues and hence create a diffusion gradient. For clarity, it is assumed that the external concentration, c, is not allowed to fall

at equilibrium (a quantity which is readily measured), valuable conclusions can be reached regarding the internal distribution of the toxicant (pp. 182, 228).

If a solute is very sparingly soluble in a solvent, even a saturated solution may be very dilute, and hence little of the solute may be present in the phase even when the relative saturation is 1·0, its maximal value. This introduces the concept of a chemical capacity factor, the importance and implications of which have been discussed by Burtt (1945). The inability of substances with high oil–water distribution coefficients to leave the cuticle, once sorbed within it, is a capacity effect, for very little would need to leave the lipid to raise the internal aqueous concentration to saturation level. Extreme differences in the capacities of two adjacent phases to dissolve a poison may thus have the effect of hindering its inward movement.

The second possible mode of entry through the cuticle is by two-dimensional diffusion. It is hard to assess the importance of this method of entry in the complex situation presented by the cuticle. The cuticle has so far been regarded as a simple two phase system, rather like oil (outer exocuticle) resting on top of water (the remainder of the cuticle). But, as has been seen, the whole of the exo- and endo-cuticle is, in fact, a heterogeneous matrix of lipids and non-lipids, presenting a vast area of phase boundaries. On these boundaries, monomolecular layers of certain types of substances can be adsorbed. If the hydrophilic-lipophilic balance of an adsorbed substance is favourable, its molecules may slide along the surfaces and so reach the internal bulk aqueous phase by two-dimensional movement. No doubt surface active spray supplements influence diffusion by this method, but precise experimental information is lacking.

Whatever the method, or methods, whereby insecticides penetrate insect cuticles, there is no doubt about the ease with which certain covalent materials in suitable formulation can gain access to the bodies of many

Table 3.1 LD_{50}S FOR PESTICIDES APPLIED BY DIFFERENT ROUTES, INDICATING THE EXTENT TO WHICH CUTICLE AND SKIN CAN ACT AS BARRIERS TO PENETRATION

Substance	Insect	LD_{50}		Mammal	LD_{50}		
		Topical	Injected		Dermal	Oral	Injection
Rotenone	Cockroach	>2000	10	Rat	—	60-150	6
	Japanese beetle	40	25	Rabbit	>940	600	—
Pyrethrins	Cockroach	6·5	6	Rat	>1880	570	200[a]
	Japanese beetle	40	40	Rabbit	400	240[b]	—
				Dog	—	—	7
DDT	Cockroach	10	5-8	Rat	2500+	400	10-15
	Japanese beetle	93	162	Rabbit	300 to 2800	400	45
	Bee	114	0·2				
Lindane	Cockroach	5	4	Rat	500+	200	35+[c]
				Rabbit	180 to 4000	60+	<6
Parathion	Cockroach	1·2	0·95	Rat	—	6	3
	Japanese beetle	3·3	0·45	Rabbit	50	—	—
Malathion	Cockroach	—	8·4	Rat	>4000	1400 to 1900	50
DNOC	Cockroach	20	14	Rat	200+	25+	10[d]

Most of the figures for mammals from Edson, Sanderson and Noakes (1966).
(a) Intraperitoneal LD_{90} (Negherbon, 1959, p. 637).
(b) Sub-acute dose leading to spastic inco-ordination.
(c) Intraperitoneal LD_{50} (Negherbon, 1959, p. 438).
(d) Subcutaneous LD_{50} (Negherbon, 1959, p. 292).

insects. The LD_{50}s in Table 3.1 for various insecticides applied topically or injected into insects show that, with a few notable exceptions, the cuticle gives little protection against oil-soluble materials. The values should be contrasted with the overall picture presented by mammalian toxicity tests in which mammals have been treated dermally, by oral administration and by intravenous injection. In all cases the figures are expressed as mg per kg body weight.

Generalisations relating to the penetration of insecticides through cuticles also apply in a qualitative manner to entry into eggs of insects, for eggs are covered with a waxy layer which is disrupted by organic solvents and penetrated by lipophilic substances. Nevertheless, there is some doubt about whether an insecticide always has to enter an egg in order that it should be ovicidal. It has, for example, been reported that oil can be lethal without penetration. Nicotine appears to enter through the micropyles rather than through the waxy surface, so other water-soluble materials might be able to do the same.

NERVE IMPULSES

TRANSMISSION ALONG THE AXON

Many insecticides attack some part of the nervous system. A frequently observed symptom of their toxic action is that an instability develops in the delicately maintained difference in voltage on the two sides of certain membranes. The physiological effects of neurotoxic poisons will be described later, but it is first necessary to provide a brief account of the way in which a typical nerve of any animal—vertebrate or invertebrate—is believed to function in the absence of poison. For further details, the account by Katz (1952) or the more advanced monograph by Hodgkin (1964) should be consulted.

A nerve axon can be regarded as a cable of aqueous fluid insulated from the circumambient fluid by a lipid or lipoprotein membrane. The total osmotic concentration operating inside and outside the membrane is the same, but the compositions of the two solutions differ. The inside fluid is richer in potassium ions than is the fluid outside, a situation which indicates that the membrane is relatively impermeable to ions when the nerve is resting. The inside of the membrane is some 70 millivolts (mV) negative relative to the outside, a figure which can be predicted from the Nernst Equation if it is assumed that this 'resting' or 'membrane' potential is due to the potassium ion gradient (Hodgkin, 1964).

$$\mathscr{E} = \frac{1000 \text{ RT}}{\text{F}} \times 2 \cdot 3 \log_{10} \frac{[\text{K}^+]_{\text{outside}}}{[\text{K}^+]_{\text{inside}}}$$

where $\mathscr{E}$ is the equilibrium potential in millivolts, F is the Faraday in coulombs per g equivalent, T is the absolute temperature ($290°$) and R is the gas constant ($8 \cdot 3$ joules per degree per mole).

Substituting the observed equilibrium concentration of potassium ions, $[\text{K}^+]$, outside (400 mE) and inside (20 mE) the membrane,

$$\mathscr{E} = \frac{1000 \times 8 \cdot 3 \times 290}{96,500} \times 2 \cdot 3 \log_{10} \frac{400}{20}$$

$$\approx 57 \times \log_{10} 20 = 57 \times 1 \cdot 3, \text{ or } 74 \text{ mV}$$

A stimulus causes an electrical impulse to pass along a nerve at a speed of up to 100 feet per second. The transmission is occasioned by a local and rapidly self-adjusting reversal of the potential; momentarily, the outside of the membrane becomes negative and the inside positive (Fig. 3.7). The

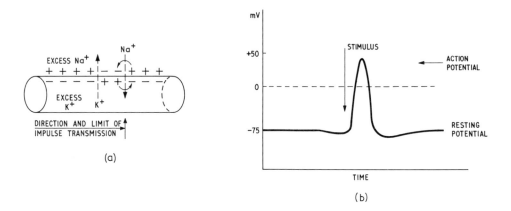

Fig. 3.7. (a) Wave of action potential moving along an axon. The inrush of sodium ions precedes the efflux of potassium ions by a few microseconds;
(b) Resting and action potential. Note the abscissa here is time, not distance, for the graph represents the changes occurring at any one place along the axon

reversal is caused by a temporary alteration in the permeability of the membrane in one area so that sodium ions rush into the nerve from outside. Hodgkin has described how the magnitude of the reversed charge, some 50 mV positive, can be predicted from the same equation by assuming that the potential is developed by the membrane becoming permeable to sodium ions. The impulse is carried along the axon by the movement of the area of depolarisation.

The general effect of this transient reversal of charge—the *status quo* is rapidly restored by efflux of potassium ions—is that a signal passes through a set of 'booster stations' in an electrochemical relay system. The nerve message generates a current which excites the next portion of the nerve; this alters the permeability of the nearby membrane, again generating a current. It has been estimated that the boosting is so efficient that only 10% of the current generated by annulment of the sodium ion gradient is necessary to transmit the message. It will be apparent from what has just been said that the functioning of the transmission system depends upon the remarkable property of selective permeability possessed by the membrane of the nerve. If this membrane were to be damaged in any way— and its thickness is only 7·5 mμ—interference with the transmission of impulses would be expected.

The precise mechanism whereby the permeability of the membrane is altered by the nerve impulse remains obscure, as does the nature of the 'ion-pump' needed to drive the sodium ions out again to restore the resting state. Some authors believe that acetylcholine (Fig. 3.8) may be implicated

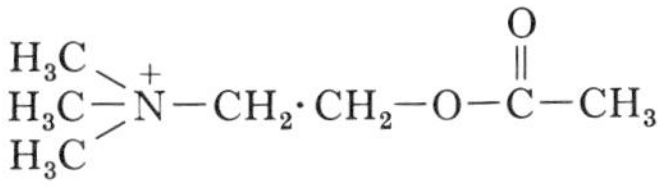

$$\begin{array}{l} H_3C \\ H_3C \overset{+}{-} N - CH_2 \cdot CH_2 - O - \overset{\overset{\displaystyle O}{\displaystyle \|}}{C} - CH_3 \\ H_3C \end{array}$$

Fig. 3.8. Acetylcholine

in the permeability sequence. Depolarisation by the impulse could, for example, release acetylcholine from one protein and enable it to join with another protein, differently positioned with regard to the membrane. The enzyme cholinesterase might then be responsible for destroying the acetylcholine on its second protein site, as a step towards the restoration of the *status quo*. This interesting speculation has, however, not yet been verified experimentally (Hodgkin, 1964).

While the general picture is probably similar for nerves of insects and vertebrates, relatively little is known about the significance of the differences which appear to exist. Some of these differences will be described later; for the present, the outline given above may be regarded as being applicable to nerves of all types of organisms.

TRANSMISSION AT NERVE-MUSCLE JUNCTIONS

It was seen above that changes in the permeability of the nerve membrane to ions are responsible for the transmission of the impulse along the fibre, and that acetylcholine could possibly play some part in this process. However, at the neuromuscular junctions, where nerve fibres meet the muscles they innervate, and also at nerve-to-nerve junctions which occur in certain nerves, there are gaps which interrupt the electrical conduction. In these regions, the arrival of a nerve impulse occasions the release of a chemical substance, or mediator. The task of this mediator is to diffuse across the gap, which is extremely small, and to induce a muscular response (or to generate another electrical impulse, as the case may be) on the far side. Having fulfilled its task, the mediator is then rapidly destroyed by a specific enzyme. The importance of the lability of the mediator is illustrated by an analogy drawn by O'Brien (1962), in which the nervous system was compared to a signalling device operated by the make-and-break of a morse key. The mediator and the operator's finger both serve as contact makers; if the key is not released, in both cases a protracted 'noise' rather than an intelligible message is transmitted.

In different parts of the nervous system of higher animals, different mediators operate. The neuromuscular junctions of voluntary muscles, and of those involuntary muscles innervated by the parasympathetic nervous system, are bridged by acetylcholine. So are the synapses (nerve-to-nerve junctions) of the sympathetic nervous system, and, in all probability, at least some of the synapses of the central nervous system. On the other hand, *nor*-adrenaline is the mediator at the neuromuscular junctions of the sympathetic nervous system.

Where acetylcholine is the mediator, the destruction is achieved by the activity of acetylcholinesterase, which is present at these junctions in very considerable excess. In mammals, and probably also in insects, this or a very similar enzyme is the target of the organophosphorus compounds; its inactivation leads to the organism being poisoned by the effects of an excess of its own acetylcholine. Returning to the analogy, the 'noise' replacing the message causes a response to the nonsense signal which leads to death. In mammals, death is a consequence of respiratory failure, caused by the paralysis of the muscles of the diaphragm or of the respiratory centre of the brain. If acetylcholine is also concerned in the production of the nerve action potential, cholinesterase inhibitors could well interfere with the transmission of impulses in a second and quite distinct way.

In insects the picture is somewhat different, for the respiratory system of insects is simpler than that of higher animals and is no more vulnerable than several other physiological processes. Instead, the blockage of nerve conduction resulting from the inhibition of acetylcholinesterase or some similar enzyme leads to more diffuse effects, characterised frequently, prior to death, by a loss of the ability to feed and move.

REFERENCES

BURTT, E. T. (1945), *Ann. appl. Biol.,* **32,** 247

EDSON, E. F., SANDERSON, D. M. and NOAKES, D. N. (1966), *Wld Rev. Pest Control,* **5,** 143

FAST, P. G. (1964), *Insect lipids ; a Review.* Mem. Ent. Soc. Canada, No. 37

FERGUSON, J. (1939), *Proc. R. Soc.,* **127(B),** 387

HACKMAN, R. H. (1958), *Proc. 4th Internatn. Congr. Biochem.,* **12,** 48

HASSALL, K. A. (1953), *Ann. appl. Biol.,* **40,** 688

HODGKIN, A. L. (1964), The Sherrington Lectures, VII. *The Conduction of the Nervous Impulse,* Liverpool
    University Press

KATZ, B. (1952), *Scient. Am.* November issue

LOCKE, M. J. (1961), *J. biophys. biochem. Cytol.,* **10,** 589

MASON, H. S. (1955), *Adv. Enzymol.,* **16,** 105

O'BRIEN, R. D. (1962), *Wld Rev. Pest Control,* **1,** (1), 29

RICHARDS, A. G. (1951), *Integument of Arthropods,* Univ. Minnesota Press

RUDALL, K. M. (1963), *Adv. Insect Physiol.,* **1,** 257

WEBB, J. E. (1949), *Symp. Soc. exp. Biol.,* **3,** 143

WIGGLESWORTH, V. B. (1947), *Proc. R. Soc.,* **134(B),** 163

WIGGLESWORTH, V. B. (1957), *A. Rev. Ent.,* **2,** 37

4

ORGANOCHLORINE INSECTICIDES

The ill-fated organochlorine compounds, discovered during the second world war, were at first heralded as almost ideal insecticides. They have since become notorious because of their toxicity to wild life especially when used as seed dressings, their high persistance, their potential chronic toxic hazard to man, and their tendency to induce resistance in the insects against which they are used (Carson, 1963). To appreciate the reasons for this change in outlook it is necessary to describe the structure, physical properties and physiological effects of certain members of the group.

The organochlorine compounds, $C_xH_yCl_z$, may be divided into several sub-groups or families. Some members of these groups contain oxygen or sulphur as well as carbon, hydrogen and chlorine. Structurally, almost the only feature common to all the members of different families is the presence of an alicyclic ring. Three typical organochlorine insecticides, belonging to the three principal families, are DDT, BHC and aldrin (Fig. 4.1, a, b and c).

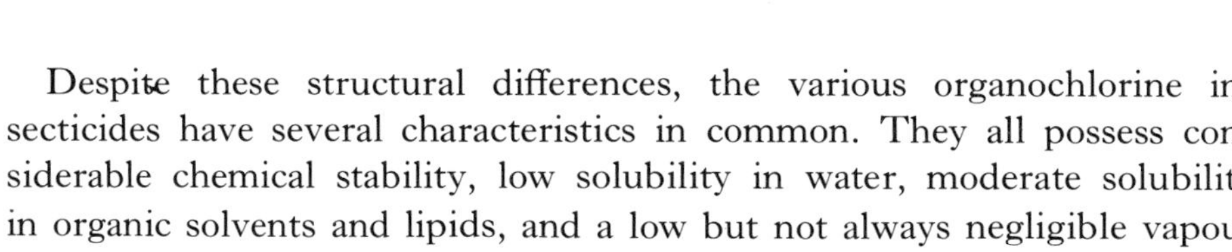

Fig. 4.1. (a) p,p'-DDT: dichlorodiphenyl trichloroethane; (b) γ-BHC: benzene hexachloride; (c) Aldrin: a cyclodiene derivative

Despite these structural differences, the various organochlorine insecticides have several characteristics in common. They all possess considerable chemical stability, low solubility in water, moderate solubility in organic solvents and lipids, and a low but not always negligible vapour pressure. When pure, they are white or yellow waxy solids. Excepting members of the aldrin sub-group, they lose one or more molecules of hydrogen chloride per molecule in the presence of alcoholic (and sometimes aqueous) alkali. These attributes of stability and solubility render most of the group very persistent, and organochlorine compounds therefore tend to accumulate in soil, in fatty parts of animals and in the cuticle of leaves of plants. Also, despite their different constitutions, they produce physiological responses of similar types when applied to insects.

Their acute toxic doses to rats on intravenous injection have been reported by Barnes (1957), and Edson, Sanderson and Noakes (1966) have collected data on the toxicity of these and other pesticides when applied to skin or given by mouth. Some selected examples appear in Table 4.1.

Table 4.1 TOXICITIES OF SOME ORGANOCHLORINE COMPOUNDS TO RATS
(AFTER BARNES, 1957, AND EDSON, SANDERSON AND NOAKES, 1966)

Substance	LD_{50} as mg/kg body weight		
	Intravenous	Oral dose	Dermal application
Endrin	1·5	3*	60*
Endosulfan	—	35	75*
Dieldrin	8	40	> 100
Heptachlor	—	40	200
Aldrin	18	40*	> 200
Lindane (BHC)	5	200	500*
DDT	75	300*	2500
DDD (or TDE)	250	3400	—
Methoxychlor	75	5000*	6000

*signifies that, of a range of reported values, the lowest is recorded here.
>signifies that the highest dose tested failed to kill 50% of the organisms.
The acute oral LD_{50} is dependent on the strain of rat used; this may account for the poor agreement between some of the figures collected by Edson *et al* and those given in the *Insecticide and Fungicide Handbook* (1963).

These data show that the toxicities of organochlorine insecticides are of intermediate magnitude, and few cases of accidental acute poisoning have been reported (but see Carson, 1963, pp. 22, 23, 157). Of those commonly employed, gamma (γ)–BHC is amongst the most toxic, the LD_{50} by intravenous injection being 5 mg/kg body weight, the toxic dose of aldrin being three and of p,p′–DDT fifteen times this value.† However, when

†Hereafter, p,p′-DDT will be called DDT and γ-BHC will be called BHC, unless the context requires otherwise.

administered by mouth or applied to the skin, the magnitudes of the LD_{50}s are several times as great, the acute oral LD_{50} of DDT, for example, being 300 mg/kg body weight (Table 4.1).

METHODS OF APPLICATION

Since the behaviour of compounds belonging to the three main families is very similar, much of the following account will centre upon DDT (Fig. 4.1(a)), one of the most important organochlorine compounds. When physical characteristics such as lipid solubility (Table 4.2) are considered

Table 4.2 PHYSICAL PROPERTIES OF p,p′ -DDT

Property	
Melting point	109°C
Boiling point/1 mm Hg	185°C
Relative density	1·6
Vapour pressure	$1\cdot5 \times 10^{-7}$ mm at 20°C
Solubility in benzene	780 g/l
Solubility in alcohol	20 g/l
Solubility in kerosene	40–80 g/l
Dipole moment	0·9–1·12
Heat of vaporisation	20 Kcal/mole
Solubility in water	1–3 parts per thousand million at 25°C. Values from 0·2 to 1000 p.p.th.m. have been recorded. The most recent work shows apparent solubility decreases with increasing speed of centrifugation from 3·4 p.p.th.m. at zero centrifugation to 1·7 p.p.th.m. at 18,000 r.p.m. (Biggar, Dutt and Riggs, 1967)

in conjunction with chemical stability and the nature of the insect cuticle, it is clear that several methods of formulation and application are possible.

DDT may be applied in the vapour phase as a fog of colloidal particles in which the toxicant is almost as well dispersed as it would be in a true vapour; before the persistence hazard was appreciated, this was a common practice in premises where food was processed or sold (Dyte, 1962). This can be done by volatilising the solid by heating, though the temperature must be controlled since volatilisation is accompanied by partial decomposition. Another method, the aerosol technique, has already been described (p. 46). In solution, it may be applied to some target surface as a suspension in water; the water eventually evaporates, leaving the DDT and the dispersing agent on the surface. Or it may be dissolved in an organic solvent which is then either emulsified in water or employed in the absence of water. DDT may also be used in the dry state, the active ingredient being incorporated into a powder containing 90% or more of inert diluent.

ROUTES OF ENTRY INTO THE INSECT

The solubility of DDT in waxy materials enables the poison to enter the insect integument readily. In contrast, it usually penetrates rather slowly into animal skin. This difference in penetrative ability may explain its selective toxicity to insects, for when the barrier presented by the skin is by-passed by injecting DDT intravenously into mammals, its LD_{50}, on a mg/kg body weight basis, is of the same order as that observed for most insects.

The toxicity of DDT to insects also varies somewhat with the method of application, but seldom by so much as when mammals are the test organisms. Metcalf (1955, p. 158) has, however, quoted a few apparent exceptions. For example, the LD_{50} for *Melanoplus* species is over 9,000 mg/kg by dermal application, 2,500 mg/kg when administered orally, but only 2 mg/kg when the DDT is injected.

Cuticle thickness, as such, does not seem greatly to influence the susceptibility of insects to DDT, although the DDT may penetrate more readily through flexible regions such as intersegmental membranes. Solution in epicuticular waxes appears to be an essential prerequisite to effective toxic action. The rate of penetration increases with temperature, often approximately doubling for a 20°C rise in temperature. There is evidence that solid particles do not normally penetrate directly into the spiracles or other body openings.

The precise location of the site of action of DDT and of other organochlorine insecticides is uncertain, though the nervous system undoubtedly is attacked. The extremely low aqueous solubility of DDT suggests that it may be able to induce a lethal effect by a direct action either on the sensory nerve cells or on the nerve fibres which lead to them. DDT may, therefore, be an example of a substance capable of initiating a toxic response before any large quantity of it has entered the haemolymph (Fig. 3.6). On the other hand, a rapid initial attack upon these vulnerable parts of the nervous system does not preclude the possibility of a further action on the central nervous system if and when the insecticide succeeds in reaching it through the intervening aqueous phases.

A curious characteristic of DDT is that its toxic action sometimes has a negative temperature coefficient (McIntosh, 1957; Das and McIntosh, 1961). That is to say, it is more toxic to insects maintained at a lower temperature *after* treatment than insects treated in exactly the same way and then kept at a higher temperature. DDT is not unique in this respect, the pyrethrins (Potter and Gillham, 1946), BHC and certain DDT analogues sometimes showing a similar effect against certain organisms. Small negative temperature coefficients have also been observed with a few fungicides. Nevertheless, DDT does differ qualitatively from most, if not all, common poisons in two respects: (1) its effect is reversible to an extent not observed with other materials—as the temperature is lowered after suitable dosing, the paralysis increases, while larvae paralysed at a low temperature recover when the after-treatment temperature is raised; (2) the negative influence of temperature on the action of DDT is very large; using *Tenebrio molitor* as test species, Das and McIntosh observed that at 28°C the LD_{50} was more than ten times the LD_{50} at 10°C.

Whatever the biochemical significance (if any) of the positive or negative sign of temperature coefficients, the observed size and direction of this quantity depends on numerous experimental factors. As well as being a function of the poison and dependent on the insect species under test, the size and direction of the coefficient has been found to vary with the formulation and dose, with the method of application, with the range of temperatures being considered and with the length of time passing after treatment and before measurements of response are recorded (McIntosh, 1957).

Some authors have attempted to explain negative temperature coefficients in terms of some property of the cuticle. Munson, Padilla and Weissmann (1954), for example, suggested that the solubility of DDT in the general cuticular lipids might increase more rapidly with temperature than does its solubility in some important lipid at the site of action. In view of the likelihood that lipids or lipoproteins in the nervous system are the ultimate target, this theory cannot be lightly dismissed, but the difficulty of this and similar physical theories is that it fails to explain why some lipid-soluble materials have negative coefficients while others have positive coefficients; nor does it indicate which particular physical characteristic of DDT leads to the accentuation of the negative temperature effect in the case of this compound. Another possibility is that the coefficient depends on the relative effect of temperature on the activity of DDT, on the one hand, and on detoxication mechanisms on the other. The weaknesses of both explanations have been described in a review by Yamasaki and Ishii (1954).

Das and McIntosh (1961) and, more recently, Eaton and Sternburg (1964), have concluded that the negative temperature coefficient is an immediate function of a physiological change induced in nervous tissue, and assign the response specifically to events occurring in the central nervous system rather than in the peripheral nerves. Until more is known, however, about the physiological change which DDT induces, and how it differs from physiological changes induced by other neurotoxicants, the problem of the negative temperature coefficient cannot be regarded as having been satisfactorily resolved.

THE MODE OF ACTION

If the members of the three main families of organochlorine compounds differ at all in their effect on organisms, the difference probably relates to the precise site, rather than to the mode, of their action. Thus, whereas the initial action of DDT may be upon the peripheral nervous system, there is some evidence that BHC and aldrin attack the central nervous system (Winteringham and Lewis, 1959). The picture is not, however, entirely clear, for synapses as well as sensory receptors are believed by some authors to be readily affected by DDT. Again, Eaton and Sternburg (1964) provided evidence that the negative temperature coefficient associated with the action of DDT arises as a result of its effect on the central nervous system—it is not evident when the insecticide acts upon peripheral nerves. Conversely, BHC, which is supposed to affect the central nervous system, does not have a negative temperature coefficient.

At the physiological level, the effect of DDT on nerve-muscle systems has been investigated extensively. The action of other organochlorine insecticides has been studied to a lesser extent, but despite some differences, the general effect seems to be rather similar for them all. DDT has an unstabilising action on the nervous system, an effect manifested by a hyper-excitability of nerves and muscles. Whereas in the normal nerve one stimulus leads to one muscular response, poisoned insects undergo multiple uncontrolled muscular spasms. This is shown diagrammatically in Fig. 4.2.

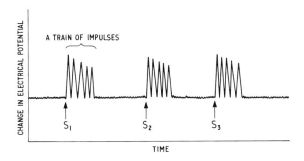

Fig. 4.2. Trains of impulses following stimulation of DDT-poisoned nerve. S_1, S_2, S_3 are points of electrical stimulation. At high levels of DDT, S_2 and S_3 are unnecessary

The trains of impulses which replace the normal response to an applied electrical impulse last longer as the concentration of DDT increases. At high concentrations the trains arise spontaneously—i.e. electrical stimulation of the nerve is no longer necessary to induce them. They continue at intervals of a few seconds until eventually the muscle innervated by the poisoned nerve assumes a state of permanent contraction. However, the primary effect of DDT, except at very high concentrations, is not upon the motor nerve but upon a more distant sensory nerve; hence the whole

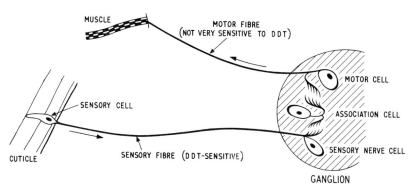

Fig. 4.3. Diagram of a reflex arc

reflex arc (Fig. 4.3) appears to be concerned in the transmission of the multiple impulses induced by the insecticide. Isotope work has recently confirmed that DDT increases the permeability of nerve tissue to potassium ions (Matsumura and O'Brien, 1966).

Unfortunately, it is still uncertain what these physiological changes represent at the biochemical level. The possible effects of organochlorine insecticides fall under at least two headings. Firstly, they might inhibit some enzyme or compete with some metabolite essential to the proper functioning of the nervous system. Secondly, they might cause an accumulation of substances normally destroyed during nerve transmission. A third possibility, not necessarily distinct from the others, is that they might induce a physical change in the delicate machinery of the nerve fibre or of nerve endings.

Substances within the three main families of organochlorine insecticides possess toxicities which are intimately dependent on constitution. If, for example, the two phenyl rings of DDT are substituted with chlorine in the *meta* position instead of the *para,* the toxicity is greatly reduced. The same thing happens when one of the phenyl rings is substituted *ortho* instead of *para.* Similarly, only one stereo-isomer of BHC, namely the gamma isomer, is highly toxic to insects. This close relation between structure and toxicity appears at first to favour the classical concept of fitment to an enzyme surface or competition with an essential metabolite. At this point, however, an apparent biochemical dilemma is encountered. Not only has no enzyme been isolated which could be regarded as the principal actor in the drama, but the three families of organochlorine compounds, despite the divergence of molecular architecture, evoke similar physiological responses. Thus the specificity which clearly exists *within* a family is not apparent *between* different families. One solution would be to postulate the existence of several enzymes, the inhibition of each of which produces similar physiological responses. In view of the failure to isolate any such enzymes, such a theory seems only to multiply the difficulties.

There is no shortage of evidence showing that organochlorine insecticides cause abnormal biochemical effects. When an insect is poisoned with DDT its respiration increases greatly, but, unlike the action of dinitrophenol and its derivatives (p.225), it does not uncouple oxidation from phosphorylation. The increase may be a secondary effect, a consequence of intensified neuromuscular activity. Some of its effects on oxidative metabolism cannot, however, be explained so simply. Work on sub-cellular particles, for example, has indicated that Krebs cycle intermediates are oxidised less rapidly in the presence of DDT—although *non*-insecticidal analogues of DDT are also able to inhibit the oxidation of α-keto-glutarate (Winteringham and Lewis, 1959). Similarly, preparations of brain mitochondria liberate esters of betaine coenzyme-A when treated with dieldrin (Hosein and Proulx, 1960). These esters have physiological properties similar to those of acetylcholine. It is possibly significant that the concentration of acetylcholine itself often appears to increase in insects poisoned with DDT.

The failure to discover any important enzyme which could be regarded as the specific target of organochlorine compounds has led many researchers to consider the possibility that, in fact, no such specific attachment occurs. The apparent paradox is explicable if numerous enzymes, participating in quite different biochemical processes, operate not as individual substances in solution, but take part in *integrated* reactions on an organising surface. Should a material, by its mere presence in the vicinity, distort, alter or disrupt such a surface, enzymes carrying out quite unrelated transformations would appear to be adversely affected by the foreign substance. Such a view was put forward by Albert (1960) as a development of the concept of the 'physical poison' first proposed by Ferguson (1939). Mullins (1954) applied the same idea to the organochlorine insecticides. Another group of pesticides, the aliphatic hydrocarbon oils, could also be physical poisons, for their chemical inertness would appear to preclude specific action. It is of interest that Ferguson and Hawkins (1949) demonstrated that even the inert gases possessed toxic properties under appropriate conditions.

It is therefore possible, but by no means certain, that organochlorine insecticides affect nervous tissue by altering the structure, and hence the permeability to ions, of the delicate lipid or lipoprotein membrane which forms the wall of the nerve axon. An objection to such a theory is that not all oil-soluble substances are neurotoxic, but since molecular architecture and physical properties other than lipid solubility will determine approach to, and fitment on, a lipoprotein surface, it is doubtful whether physical toxicity implies that the target-toxicant relationship must necessarily be one of low specificity. A more serious criticism is that little work has been done to determine the effect of DDT on the gradient of sodium and potassium ions on each side of the membrane of the axon, and such as has been done has been inconclusive (Winteringham and Lewis, 1959). It has, however, been shown very recently that HEOD, the active principle of dieldrin, is strongly bound to the lipoprotein membranes of the endoplasmic reticulum and DDT complexes with cockroach nerve components have also been reported.

It is possible, however, that the site of action of organochlorine insecticides is not the nerve axon itself, but the nerve endings or 'end-plates'. It has long been known that the liberation and rapid destruction of acetylcholine at certain end-plates plays an important part in the transmission of nerve impulses from one nerve fibre to the next or from nerve fibre to muscle fibre. Although organochlorine insecticides cause acetylcholine to accumulate, there is no evidence that this is a consequence of inactivation of acetylcholinesterase (p. 64).

Vesicles are present near the presynaptic membrane at the end-plate. They normally store acetylcholine until it is released by the arrival of a nerve impulse. Winteringham (1962) has suggested that organochlorine insecticides might damage these vesicles, allowing acetylcholine to seep out. Should such leakage occur, not only would normal transmission of nerve impulses be impeded, but excessive production of acetylcholine within the leaking vesicles might occur in an attempt to maintain saturation of the storage sites. However, Lewis, Waller and Fowler (1960) have demonstrated that physical prostration of an insect also causes the accumulation of excessive quantities of acetylcholine. Although this observation is not necessarily at variance with the suggestion of Winteringham, the precise manner in which the insect nervous system is disturbed by organochlorine compounds cannot yet be regarded as settled. In view of their side effects, the possibility also exists that membranes other than nerve membranes may be affected, in such a way that permeability to ions is altered.

74

SIDE EFFECTS OF ORGANOCHLORINE INSECTICIDES

1. SIDE EFFECTS ON SOIL ORGANISMS AND IN PLANTS

The high chemical stability and low aqueous solubility of most organo-chlorine compounds favour their persistence in soil for months or even years (Table 4.3). This is especially so when they are applied at high dosage to clay soils and to soils rich in organic matter (Wheatley, Hardman and Strickland, 1962). Davis (1964) quoted the case of a field, treated with 6 lb BHC per acre, which still contained about 1 lb per acre 14 years later. In Britain, DDT and its degradation products are the main organochlorine contaminants in soil. Such persistence may be an advantage, in that it ensures protection of the crop for a period of time—so long as the organisms against which it is used do not become resistant—but it also introduces a risk of undesirable side effects.

Table 4.3 HALF-LIVES OF SOME ORGANOCHLORINE INSECTICIDES IN ANIMALS AND SOIL

Substance	Environment or organism	Half-life
Dieldrin (active principle, HEOD)	soil	0·5 to 4 years
	rat	12–15 days
	pigeon	47 days
	human	90 days
DDT (p,p'-)	soil	2·5 to 5 years
BHC (γ-)	soil	1·5 years

One such side effect is that beneficial soil organisms or micro-organisms might be seriously affected by the continued presence of DDT, with consequent reduction in the fertility of the soil. Martin and his co-workers (1958, 1959) have described the effect of pesticides on the soil population. They concluded that none of the eight organochlorine compounds investigated had a significant effect on bacteria or fungi when applied at normal concentrations.

Little appears to be known about the long term effects of most organo-chlorine insecticides on soil fauna, although a disturbance of the equilibrium existing between the populations of the various species of soil micro-arthropods has been demonstrated using DDT at the rate of 1 lb per acre. The number of *Collembola* (a genus feeding on vegetable matter) suffers a sharp initial decline but then increases again, eventually exceeding the original level. The higher steady state level is due to the effective absence of predators, and especially of soil mites, the mites having been decimated by the action of DDT. Earthworms which, according to Davis (1964), account for a biomass of some 526 g/m^2 of soil surface in pastures, do not seem to be seriously affected except, perhaps, by chlordane. Jönsson and Fåhraeus (1960) obtained direct experimental evidence that aldrin could act as a source of carbon for certain soil organisms. Other aspects of the effect of organochlorine compounds on aquatic and soil-inhabiting invertebrates have been described by Rudd (1964).

A second difficulty is that soil water may become contaminated with minute but not negligible amounts of these sparingly soluble substances and so become a potential hazard to fish, fish-eating birds and even to the domestic water supply. Important sources of pollution of ponds, rivers and lakes are discharges from sheep dips and from industrial effluent (Holden, 1966). Water running off the surface of soil after heavy rain or flooding is another cause of contamination; drainage water, as such, is usually almost free from organochlorine insecticides because of the high adsorption on to soil particles or organic matter, to which reference was made earlier (p. 75). In a similar way, predators may be threatened indirectly if they eat earthworms which have been in contact with soil or soil water containing the pesticides. These and related hazards arising from the use of highly persistent poisons have been emphasised—perhaps a little too strongly—by Carson (1963).

Finally, over a period of time, substantial amounts of even a very sparingly soluble substance may be able to enter through the roots of a rapidly transpiring plant. Such material often moves up the plant and, if it is not metabolised, may accumulate in the edible parts of food crops, to become a potential threat to animals or man.

Organochlorine compounds are absorbed locally by foliage, but mobility within the plant has only been observed when certain of them enter through the roots. BHC is probably translocated more readily than most other members of the group, although even for this substance uptake from the soil may be limited except at high rates of soil application (Lichtenstein and Schulz, 1960). Bradbury (1963) showed that wheat plants placed in saturated BHC solution sorbed the material readily, although only 10% of a BHC seed dressing entered wheat plants when seeds were sown in compost. On the other hand, the amounts of aldrin and heptachlor (including their oxidation products) stored by plants is negligible when soil is treated with these substances at normal levels of application (Lichtenstein, 1960), and Lichtenstein and Schulz (1960) could obtain no evidence for the translocation of DDT to the aerial parts of pea plants.

When organochlorine compounds do gain access to plant tissues they can have a variety of effects, some of which appear to be advantageous. Foliage, for example, may become insecticidal to sucking or biting insects, while MacLagan (1957) observed that suitable concentrations of BHC and dieldrin in soil or compost were able both to stimulate the growth of roots of certain plants and to increase the rate of germination. Lichtenstein, Millington and Cowley (1962) found that organochlorine compounds inhibited plant growth and respiration of root tips less than did most organophosphorus compounds. More usually, however, the main problem is to adjust the dose and method of application so that the pesticide does not have harmful effects. For example, most of the early attempts to use BHC as a seed treatment resulted in reduced germination of seed, inhibition of sprouting of potatoes, suppression of growth, or the induction of atypical growth such as a thickening of root or stem (Reynolds, 1958). As foliage sprays, organochlorine compounds are usually of low phytotoxicity except to the Cucurbitaceae.

There is evidence that tainting of root crops by BHC and certain other insecticides is in part due to impurities in the technical material, and the marketing of lindane (as the purified gamma isomer is called), has reduced this problem in recent years. However, San Antonio (1959) referred to several instances where off-odours and off-flavours of edible crops have followed the use of lindane and he concluded that metabolic products of pure lindane could be responsible for them.

A more disturbing effect which has occasionally been observed is that organochlorine compounds, when applied to meristematic tissue, may be able to induce abnormal nuclear divisions. Some, at least, of the macroscopic abnormalities referred to above can be attributed to this cause. Poussel (1948) noted abnormal mitosis in the presence of BHC; her work has been confirmed and extended by Hyypio, Tsou and Wilson (1955).

2. SIDE EFFECTS IN HIGHER ANIMALS, BIRDS AND FISH

The 'dilution' of a contaminated foodstuff with wholesome food from other sources reduces the risk to omnivores arising from the use of most types of persistent insecticides. But when organochlorine compounds are used, the dilution effect may be less marked than it is for other substances, because DDT and BHC are used for pest control on a wide range of crops both before harvesting and during storage. Much work has been undertaken to discover whether repetitive intake of small quantities of these highly stable substances over a long period of time can lead to continuing accumulation within the body, or whether, for a specified low daily intake, the body concentration rises to a constant level. This research, undertaken by numerous workers on a range of different species of mammals, has demonstrated that without exception, at all doses *of a magnitude at all relevant to the residue problem,* a constant internal level is achieved for a constant small daily intake. The explanation is both simple and important: at low levels of daily intake, the various mechanisms within the body which lead to detoxication and elimination result in the eventual establishment of a steady state between uptake and disposal of the pesticide (Fig. 4.4). Sometimes, in fact, eventual increased effectiveness of defence mechanisms can cause the internal level to *fall,* even though the daily dosage remains unchanged.

A Report of President Kennedy's Science Advisory Committee (Anon, 1963) stated that the level of DDT in American human body fat was about 12 ppm in 1951. Despite the continued ingestion of about 0·2 mg DDT per day per person, the amount stored has apparently not increased significantly in the intervening years although the amount of the DDT metabolite, DDE may possibly have risen (Table 4.4, based on Hoffman, Fishbein and Andelman, 1964). Other evidence suggests that the steady state concentration in body lipids is reached within a few months of initial contact with food contaminated with DDT. As the magnitude of the dose of ingested DDT rises, so does the level of the steady state concentration in the body fats (Hayes, 1963), but for all realistic doses of DDT a steady internal con-

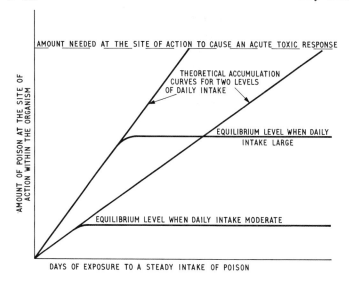

Fig. 4.4. Levels of intake of poison and the equilibrium concentrations which may induce chronic responses

centration is eventually reached. In relation to the restriction placed on the magnitude of the applied dose both here and in the previous paragraph, the reader should guard himself against a common scientific non-sequitur— to argue from the effects of a high dose of a poison in animals by extrapolation to the danger inherent in man's exposure to low doses. This is

Table 4.4 DISTRIBUTION OF DDT RESIDUES IN HUMAN FAT

Range ppm in body fat	Percentage of cases				
	Laug, 1951	Hayes, 1956	Hayes, 1958	DDT only	DDT+DDE
				Hoffman, 1964	Hoffman, 1964
0·0	20	0	3	1	0
0·1 — 1·0	9	0	0	20	1
1·0 — 5·0	28	25	69	65	19
5·1 —10·0	28	61	25	13	39
10·1 —20·0	12	14	3	1	34
over 20	3	0	0	0	7

Mean American human pesticide residue in fat (1964):

$$\begin{array}{ll} \text{DDT}+\text{DDE} & \text{10·3 ppm in fat} \\ \text{BHC} & \text{0·56 ppm in fat} \end{array}$$

American human daily intake   0·184 mg per day
(Figures from Hoffman, Fishbein & Andelman (1964).

particularly misleading when it is done without regard to possible qualitative differences at different dilutions or to the sometimes dramatic changes in the statistical probability of an event occurring, even when quantitative effects persist as the dose becomes extremely small.

The amount of DDT now present in the body fat of an American appears to be innocuous, for the Presidential Report quoted an investigation in which volunteers received 35 mg DDT per day for some months without any short term ill effect, yet the concentration of DDT and its metabolites in their body fats, at 270 ppm, was some 20 times the average level for the population. Hayes (1962) reported that a level of 648 ppm had been observed in the fat of certain workers occupationally exposed to DDT and concluded that man can probably tolerate a dose at least two hundred times that to which the population of America is now exposed—although the statistical distribution of susceptibility of different individuals within a population may not have been fully taken into account. As Frazer (1963) has pointed out, such a safety margin compares favourably with that existing between the dose of acetylsalicylic acid in a single aspirin tablet, and the lethal dose of this 'poison'.

Experiments with animals have indicated that these conclusions, based largely upon the level of DDT in human beings, can be extended both to other organochlorine compounds and to other animals. Reference has been made elsewhere to certain of these investigations (Hassall, 1965a, b; 1966). In addition, Robinson (1967) has quoted figures showing that residues of the active principle of dieldrin in British human adipose tissue have not risen since 1961. He has also shown that for dieldrin, as for DDT, when a small dose (211μg) is fed daily for 18 months, the relationship between internal concentration and time is asymptotic, not additive, and so rises to a finite upper limit as in the hypothetical case of Fig. 4.4.

Since man depends on the meat, milk and eggs of his domestic animals for a major part of his diet, the knowledge that steady state concentrations are established in animals is of great importance. The reliance of the young upon cow's milk places this food in a very special position. It is of interest that Zweig *et al* (1961) observed that when DDT was fed to dairy cows, the concentration of DDT in the milk came, within a fortnight, into steady state with the amount in the diet. When the cows were taken off the contaminated diet the concentration in the milk fell rapidly.

Since it has been proved conclusively that a constant level of organochlorine insecticide is attained in the tissues when *small* amounts are fed directly to any animal, the main problem requiring further investigation concerns the possible harmful effects of each steady state level. Carson (1963) considered that the only concentration which could be regarded as safe was a zero concentration. By the same type of reasoning, the only completely safe number of cars, oil-stoves or swimming pools is zero. In any case, for some types of poisons, many specialists believe a threshold limit exists below which no harm whatsoever is caused. Whether or not this is so for organochlorine insecticides, an Advisory Committee of the Ministry of Agriculture, Fisheries and Food under the Chairmanship of Sir James Cook (1964) concluded that there is no evidence for Carson's contention that organochlorine compounds (other than carbon tetrachloride) are powerful liver poisons and only meagre evidence for suspecting them of being weakly carcinogenic. In a recent book, based on an American Congressional report, Whitten (1966) is often critical of some of Carson's conclusions concerning the magnitude of the hazards from residues, although in no way denying that such hazards exist.

If the acute and chronic toxic effects considered so far were the only threat to man, to livestock and to wild life arising from the use of organochlorine compounds, the problem would probably be a small one when viewed in the light of world requirements for food. But there are other problems, especially so far as wild life is concerned, and Carson (1963) has done well to draw attention to them.

When organisms are dependent on each other in a biological sequence, many members of a species forming an earlier link in the chain may be eaten by one forming the next link. If, then, a small quantity of a *highly stable* pesticide should be present in each of the lowliest organisms, the possibility exists that the lipid concentration of the material may rise with the trophic level of the organisms (Fig. 4.5). The most notorious example

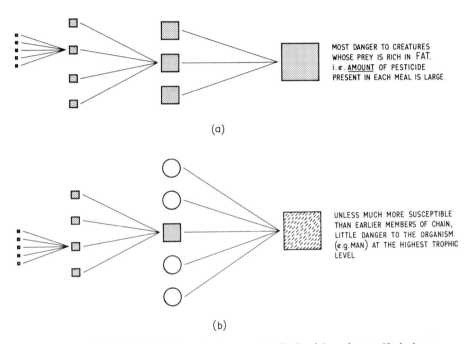

MOST DANGER TO CREATURES WHOSE PREY IS RICH IN FAT. i.e. AMOUNT OF PESTICIDE PRESENT IN EACH MEAL IS LARGE

(a)

UNLESS MUCH MORE SUSCEPTIBLE THAN EARLIER MEMBERS OF CHAIN, LITTLE DANGER TO THE ORGANISM (e.g. MAN) AT THE HIGHEST TROPHIC LEVEL

(b)

Fig. 4.5. The food chain (a) in a closed community (b) involving a less specific feeder

of a chain operating in this way is one terminating in fish-eating birds such as certain marine species (Robinson *et al.*, 1967), herons and grebes (Mellanby, 1967, pp. 127, 156) and ducks (Walker and Mills, 1965). However, as Mellanby has pointed out, the overall importance of the food chain effect has probably been over-estimated.

The analysis of tissues of birds and their eggs carried out by Walker, Hamilton and Harrison (1967) showed a striking difference in the quantity of organochlorine insecticides present in birds whose food stemmed mainly from plants and those whose diet was mainly flesh. They found that particularly high levels were present in birds feeding upon fish or upon other birds. A brochure issued by the Royal Society for the Protection of Birds (1964) lists the results of numerous analyses and concludes that organochlorine compounds are a threat to the existence of certain species of fish-eating birds in some areas. On the other hand, despite the high level of residues often found in the tissues of herons and shags, there is no evidence that their populations have as yet seriously declined. The plight of birds of prey is much more serious in some localities, probably because they attack preferentially birds which have acquired far higher than average levels of the poison and which have thereby been incapacitated (Mellanby, 1967, p. 1567).

Birds are frequently more susceptible to certain organochlorine compounds, and especially to the cyclodienes (p. 92), than are most mammals and are, furthermore, exposed to a danger which arises from the fact that certain species select one type of seed as their main diet. Should that seed be the farmer's newly sown cereal, treated with insecticidal or fungicidal seed dressings, the birds may well pay heavily for their 'predations'. Moreover, seed dressings are efficient, economical and amongst the safest of all methods of application so far as man and his livestock are concerned. For these reasons, it is a method which should, and probably will, be used increasingly; it is therefore to be hoped that selection of suitable toxicants will minimise the hazard to birds. Even without abandoning the organochlorine insecticides, this can be achieved in fair measure by replacement of dieldrin and aldrin by BHC. Other materials, such as chlorfenvinphos, which possess relatively low avian toxicity, can also be used.

Owing to the existence of alternative food supplies at the end of summer, seed dressing of autumn-sown cereal does not present the same hazard as its use on spring-sown cereal. In Britain, an agreement not to employ aldrin, dieldrin and heptachlor, after January, 1962, on spring-sown cereal, greatly reduced wood-pigeon mortality—in the spring of 1961 Murton and Vizoso (1963) estimated that at least 8% of the birds in one area were killed. In order, however, that this mortality should be kept in perspective, it should be added that a much larger proportion than this perishes each winter through natural causes. Murton (1965) estimated that, to achieve a reduction in population the next season, no less than 90% of the population would need to be destroyed, whether the instrument of killing were chemical or climatic.

Not surprisingly, birds which have eaten sub-lethal doses of organochlorine compounds contain variable amounts of these compounds in their eggs. Rightly or wrongly, decreased egg production, lower fertility and lower hatchability have all been ascribed, from time to time, to the presence of organochlorine compounds in adults or in eggs. The researches of De Witt (1956) and of Ware and Naber (1961) have demonstrated that aldrin, dieldrin and endrin are more likely to affect hatching than a similar dose of

DDT or BHC, but it must be emphasised that the presence of an organo-chlorine compound in unhatched eggs does not, in itself, constitute proof that it has acted as a toxicant. The more recent investigations of Brown *et al* (1965) have led to the tentative conclusion that the biochemical effect of small amounts of dieldrin residues in eggs may not be as great as was originally feared; in particular, the hatchability of eggs containing up to 25 ppm dieldrin in the yolk was no less than that of the controls. A delay in ovulation caused by DDT and noticed by Jefferies (1967) is possibly more significant in relation to population numbers of certain species. Jefferies considered that the delay was caused by some effect of the poison on the pituitary or hypothalamus, and pointed out that large sub-lethal doses might so delay egg laying that double-brooded birds might produce a late brood at a time when the food supply was failing. Less well grounded is the fear of Carson (1963) that fertility not only of birds but of animals and man might have been affected by these materials. Although trite, it must be pointed out that the large scale use of pesticides has been precipitated by the fact that the world population will double in the next forty years; fertility is the main *threat* to the survival of the human race at the present time.

It was mentioned above that, due to run-off and to pollution by waste from sheep dips or by industrial effluent, organochlorine insecticides occasionally enter rivers in considerable amounts; they may then be carried many miles from their place of application. They have been detected, according to the Presidential Report (Anon, 1963), in the fats of fish living far out at sea; as much as 300 ppm has been found in certain fish oils. Occasionally, valuable fish have been killed off in streams and rivers (Carson, 1963). Holden (1962) studied the absorption and internal distribution of C^{14}-labelled DDT in trout and was able to demonstrate that minute amounts were rapidly removed from water and accumulated in the lipids of all the main body organs. In the light of such accumulation, Holden and Marsden (1966) conclude that dieldrin or DDT concentrations above about 10^{-5} mg/l are undesirable from the long term aspect of wild life protection; they demonstrated that this figure was often detectable in 'clean' streams in Scotland. It is exceeded at least ten times when sheep dips are sited near streams, and also when sewage effluents enter waterways.

The contamination of fish with organochlorine insecticides represents a possible threat to man himself, for whereas his food chain is normally only two or three links long when land plants and animals participate, the chain is of indeterminate length once it includes aquatic organisms. Shellfish and crustacea could present a certain hazard for similar reasons.

THE DEVELOPMENT OF RESISTANCE TO ORGANOCHLORINE COMPOUNDS

Resistant strains of insects tend to develop whenever a species survives in a locality in spite of the use of an insecticide. As a general rule, the more rapid the life cycle of the organism and the more persistent the poison, the greater is the risk that the development of resistance will be rapid.

By 1950, instances of insects becoming resistant to insecticides were sufficiently numerous to occasion concern (see, for example, Brown, 1950). During the next decade the problem became increasingly serious, especially in relation to the use of organochlorine compounds (Hoskins and Gordon, 1956, Brown, 1958 and Gordon, 1961). A report of a Committee (Cook, 1964) emphasised the importance of this problem to public health. The report also mentioned a few cases where pests of agricultural importance had become difficult to control by organochlorine and certain other insecticides, a particularly important case being the resistance to dieldrin recently developed by the cabbage root fly. The severity of the problem varies greatly with the insect species and with the insecticide. In the laboratory, selective breeding under 'pressure' of an organochlorine compound sometimes only alters the tolerance a few-fold after several years, but instances are known where a hundredfold, or even a thousandfold, increase in tolerance has occurred. Experimental techniques have been worked out for the detection and measurement of resistance; some of these are compared and criticised by Busvine (1968).

It must be stressed that an individual insect exposed to a toxicant does not become resistant. Brown (1958) mentioned several instances where pre-exposure of insects to sub-lethal doses of organochlorine compounds rendered them more, rather than less, susceptible to later administration of the same poison. Hadaway and Barlow (1962) confirmed these observations using DDT, dieldrin and BHC. The effect of these materials is, in fact, to kill off the more susceptible organisms in a population, leaving a few naturally resistant individuals to re-colonise the area. Breeding rapidly in the absence of competitors of their own and of predatory species, these resistant organisms produce offspring which have a greater mean tolerance to the poison than had the earlier population (Fig. 4.6). Also, since it is usually the *logarithm* of tolerance which is the normally distributed characteristic, selective breeding over only a few generations may raise the dose needed to control the pest to a level which is uneconomic or hazardous.

In theory, the problem of resistance could be avoided by destroying every individual of the species in the sprayed area, but, in practice, this is seldom possible. The next best thing is not, as the unwary might imagine, to attempt to kill off as many organisms as possible, but rather to apply that concentration of poison which gives the *mimimal control of the pest consistent with economic considerations*. This approach does not prevent the development of resistance, but it reduces its rate of increase.

When the treatment leading to selection ends, the resistance it has

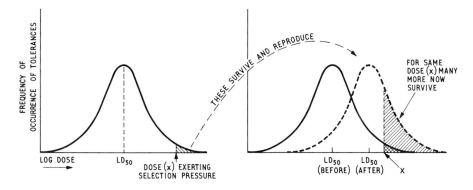

Fig. 4.6. Normal distribution of logarithms of tolerances before and after exerting selection pressure

induced continues for many generations, though some reversion towards the susceptible state normally takes place in the end. Precisely why reversion occurs is not clear, but is probably related to the fact that some degree of heterogeneity still exists in a phenotypically resistant population. The resistant genes are, according to Keiding (1967) 'better integrated into the genome' after each period of selection pressure. In the field, the apparent 'reversion' is largely due to untreated insects moving into the sprayed area from nearby districts once the insecticide concentration has diminished to a sub-lethal level.

Winteringham (1962) and Georghiou (1965), distinguished two types of factors, behaviouristic and physiological, which could control the development of resistance. Some authors (e.g. Hoskins and Gordon, 1956) consider that morphological characteristics such as a particularly impermeable cuticle, or simply the possession of physical robustness, may also contribute to a form of tolerance termed 'vigour tolerance'. Behaviouristic factors are those which enable the insect to avoid the poison more successfully than susceptible insects are able to. Some mosquitoes and flies, for example, tend to avoid landing on surfaces treated with DDT. But the majority of cases involving insect resistance can probably be attributed, in part, to the development of a more effective physiological or biochemical defence mechanism than is present in susceptible organisms (Potter, 1965).

When insects are exposed to any one organochlorine compound, there is a tendency for resistance to develop not only to that one compound but also to certain others to which the insect has never been exposed. According to the extent to which *cross-resistance* occurs, it is possible to divide organo-chlorine compounds into two groups. The first group contains DDT and its analogues. Development of resistance to any substance in this group usually involves simultaneous development of resistance to all the others, but compounds such as BHC and dieldrin usually remain effective against DDT-resistant strains. All the organochlorine compounds not related to DDT are therefore placed in a second group. For compounds within this second group, a more or less marked correlation usually exists between the resistance developed by an insect to one member and that developed to another. Conversely, selection pressure from BHC, chlordane or dieldrin does not generally induce resistance to DDT and its analogues, at least in the case of the housefly, the organism most studied (Brown, 1958, p. 383). Within the second group there may be a low correlation between resistance to BHC and resistance to the remaining members. It should be pointed out, however, that insects already resistant to DDT may develop resistance to compounds such as BHC or dieldrin much more rapidly *on exposure* to these materials than insects not initially resistant to DDT.

The mechanisms whereby DDT and its analogues are detoxified are better understood than are those which lead to the destruction of other organochlorine compounds. As was mentioned above, it is possible that intensification of such mechanisms by 'un-natural selection' could be a primary cause of the development of insect resistance. Rarely, however, has such a primary causal relationship been demonstrated unambiguously. To do this, it would be necessary to demonstrate that greater quantities of a detoxifying enzyme can be isolated from a resistant strain than from a sus-ceptible one—and also to show that the specific inhibition of such an enzyme in resistant organisms leads to a reduction in their resistance to DDT.

Two biochemical mechanisms which lead to the destruction of DDT have been observed. In the housefly, an enzyme has been isolated from resistant organisms capable of removing the elements of hydrogen chloride from the molecule of DDT with the formation of DDE, the dichloroethylene derivative. The latter is a persistent compound but it is far less toxic than DDT to insects. It is formed in a degradation process which usually terminates in the production of the much more water soluble DDA (Fig. 4.7). The dehydrochlorination is accomplished by the intervention of an enzyme which only occurs in very small quantities in strains susceptible to DDT (Lipke and Kearns, 1960). Such evidence as this favours the view that resistance to DDT is causally related to the action of the dehydro-chlorinase. It is consequently interesting to find that in *Drosophila,* and

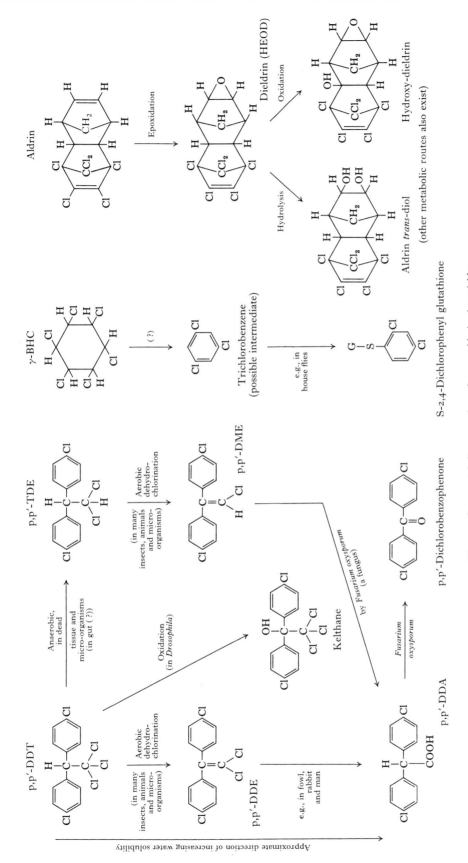

Fig. 4.7. Some metabolic conversions of organochlorine insecticides

perhaps in the cockroach, a quite different type of detoxication system operates in resistant strains (Gordon, 1961; Agosin *et al*, 1961). An oxidase replaces the central aliphatic hydrogen atom of DDT by a hydroxyl group with the formation of p,p'-dichloro (trichloromethyl) benzhydrol (Fig. 4.7).

Unfortunately, it is not possible to invoke either of these mechanisms to account for the increased resistance which some insects have developed to substances in the other two families of organochlorine compounds. Thus, although some strains of insects may be up to a thousand times more tolerant of dieldrin than are their susceptible counterparts, attempts to detect a difference in the pattern of uptake, metabolism and excretion between susceptible and resistant strains have been unsuccessful (Winteringham, 1962). Bridges and Cox (1959) were similarly unable to detect a difference in the rate of metabolism of BHC in resistant and susceptible strains of house fly.

Evidence such as that provided by Brooks (1960) and Ray (1963) points to the possibility that approximately equal amounts of dieldrin reach the site of action in resistant and susceptible strains. The difference in response may therefore reflect some physiological or structural modification of the

STRUCTURAL VARIABILITY AMONGST ORGANOCHLORINE COMPOUNDS

THE DDT FAMILY

The success of DDT led to an extensive study into the biological properties of related compounds, partly in the hope that some insight might thereby be obtained into the relationship between structure and toxicity, and partly in an attempt to find materials of the same order of toxicity as DDT but without some of its disadvantages.

Two of the derivatives which were eventually marketed with some success match DDT in toxicity for specialist purposes, though neither has its all-round effectiveness. The first is methoxychlor, in which each of the two aromatic chlorine atoms of DDT is replaced by the isosteric (equal sized) methoxy group. The other is TDE (also called DDD), in which one of the chlorine atoms of the trichloromethyl part of the molecule is replaced by a hydrogen atom. Methoxychlor, Fig. 4.8a, shows a lower tendency than DDT to dissolve in animal fats and also possesses a much lower acute oral toxicity to higher animals. It is therefore used on and near livestock for purposes of veterinary hygiene. Dichlorodiphenyl dichloroethane, or TDE,

(Fig. 4.8b) is somewhat less toxic than DDT to mammals and also to most insects, but it is sometimes used for the control of mosquito larvae, against some strains of which it is superior to DDT.

The extensive literature on the relation of structure to toxicity amongst DDT analogues has been reviewed by several authors and only a brief summary will be given here. For further information, reference should be made to the general review of Sexton (1950), to the very detailed account of Metcalf (1955), or, for photographs of models showing the structural topography of DDT analogues, to the article by Riemschneider (1958).

All potent analogues are, like DDT itself, substituted in at least one, and nearly always in both, of the *para* positions (Fig. 4.8c). If other halogens

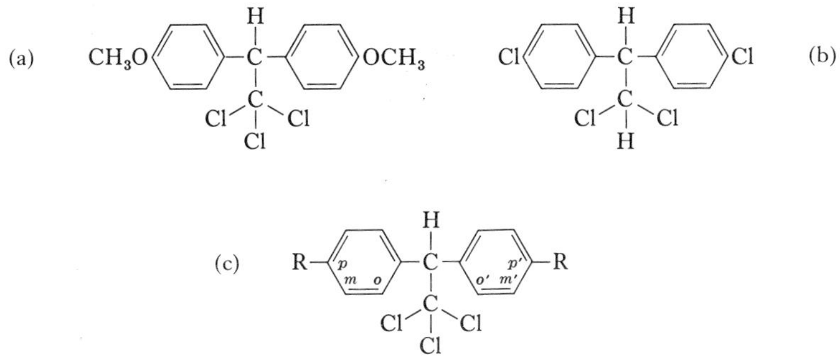

Fig. 4.8. (a) Methoxychlor; (b) TDE; (c) General formula for most DDT analogues

are substituted for chlorine in these two positions it is found that, relative to DDT, the fluoride is sometimes rather more toxic, the bromide usually considerably less so, while the iodide is almost inactive. In view of the possible future emphasis upon deterrence rather than lethal action, it is of interest that Ascher (1964) has reported that several fluoride derivatives of DDT tend to deter oviposition by insects.

The introduction into the parent hydrocarbon of groups isosteric with chlorine often results in derivatives of comparable toxicity to DDT. In addition to methoxychlor (Fig. 4.8a), the methyl analogue is moderately insecticidal (Fig. 4.8c, R = CH_3). As the alkyl or alkoxy group in each of the two *para* positions is increased in size, toxicity rapidly declines, the four-carbon homologue being almost non-toxic both in the alkyl and in the alkoxy series. Thus, toxicity is dependent upon the molecule possessing a particular shape and size, but it must be remembered that on ascending an homologous series, many physical and chemical properties other than molecular volume alter automatically. All these factors are interdependent, and probably the alteration of no one of them can be singled out as the specific cause of loss of toxicity. It is of interest that the remarkably low *mammalian* toxicity of methoxychlor vis-à-vis DDT (Table 4.1) declines rapidly as the series ethoxy, propoxy, butoxy is ascended; thus the propoxy derivative (Fig. 4.8c, $R = C_3H_7$) is no less toxic to mammals than DDT and at the same time is only one-fifth as effective against insects.

Replacement of one chlorine atom in the trichloromethyl group with a hydrogen atom gives TDE (Fig. 4.8b), a useful insecticide; but if a second chlorine is similarly replaced, the compound so formed possesses only about one-fiftieth the toxicity of DDT. Replacement of all three chlorine atoms causes almost complete loss of toxicity to insects, though the compound so formed has been employed as an acaricide (mite-killer). If the trichloromethyl group is replaced by a tribromomethyl group the resulting compound has about one-tenth the toxicity of DDT.

BENZENE HEXACHLORIDE, BHC

The ring which forms the framework of the benzene hexachloride molecule is chair-shaped, not planar, and it is possible by constructing models to demonstrate that eight distinct stereo-isomeric forms of BHC exist, and that one of these has optical enantiomorphs. Of these eight isomers, only the gamma (γ) isomer shows consistently high toxicity to insects, being from ten to several thousand times as toxic as the α or δ isomers, the relative

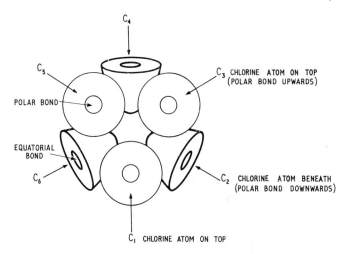

Fig. 4.9. Model of the cyclohexane ring, showing configuration of lindane

toxicity varying from one insect species to the next. The β and ε isomers are usually inert. There is no obvious correlation of toxicity with either physical properties or chemical reactivity, for the vapour pressure, the solubility in oil, and the chemical reactivity of the gamma isomer all lie between those of various inactive isomers.

The structure of the gamma isomer can best be appreciated by constructing a model (Fig. 4.9). It will be observed that three carbon atoms have valency bonds directed up out of the plane of the ring and that the three carbon atoms alternating with them have valency bonds directed downwards. Such valency bonds, whether directed upwards or downwards, are termed polar bonds (p), whilst the remaining bonds, which project almost but not quite sideways out of the ring, are termed equatorial (e) bonds. To construct a model of the gamma isomer, attach one chlorine atom to each of the six carbon atoms; dealing with the carbon atoms in strict rotation, put chlorine atoms in the following positions: p,p,p,e,e,e. Note that if the first p-chlorine is 'up' the second must be 'down' and the third 'up' once more. Six hydrogen atoms are then attached to the remaining valency bonds.

Before purification, the technical material only contains about 13% of the gamma isomer. From this mixture, the pure gamma isomer, lindane, is obtained by exploiting differences in the solubilities of the isomers in various solvents. As has been mentioned earlier (p. 77), the tendency of impure BHC to taint foodstuffs can often be reduced or avoided by using the purified gamma isomer. Lindane is an almost odourless white solid sparingly soluble in water (0·001%), slightly soluble in kerosene (2%) and very soluble in acetone (43%). It has a vapour pressure of about 10^{-5} mm Hg at 20°C and it does not decompose on heating.

There is some difference of opinion as to whether the toxicity of the gamma isomer is reduced in the presence of other isomers. Such competitive action, should it occur, does not appear to be of practical importance, for toxicity is not impaired unless the molecules of lindane are outnumbered hundreds to one by molecules of the other isomers. It is not known why only one of the eight isomers is extremely toxic. Furthermore, this high correlation of toxicity with structure within the cyclohexane group makes it even harder to explain why flies, when treated with lindane, exhibit a response which Busvine (1954) termed 'wing-fanning'. The same response occurs when cyclodiene compounds, but not DDT, are used. This similarity of response seems hardly coincidental when it is recalled (p. 86) that cross-resistance frequently occurs between BHC and the cyclodiene group of insecticides but rarely occurs to any marked extent between BHC and compounds belonging to the DDT family.

It has long been known that, under mildly alkaline conditions, a molecule of γ-BHC loses three molecules of hydrogen chloride to yield symmetrical trichlorobenzene. The metabolism of γ-BHC in living organisms probably follows a similar pathway in the presence of a dehydrochlorinase. More recently, Clark, Hitchcock and Smith (1966) have shown that, in flies, further changes occur, and lead to the formation of the S-2,4-dichlorophenyl derivative of glutathione.

THE CYCLODIENE (ALDRIN) FAMILY

All the members of this group are derivatives of hexachloro-cyclopentadiene (Fig. 4.10). Numerous organochlorine compounds can be made by con-

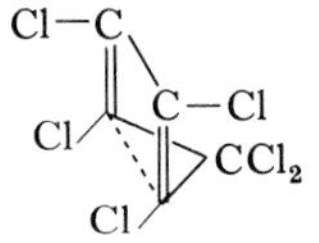

Fig. 4.10. Hexachloro-cyclopentadiene

densing this substance with suitable cyclic hydrocarbons containing five or seven carbon atoms per molecule. The reaction which leads to the condensation is termed the Diels-Alder reaction, the chemistry of which has been described by Fieser and Fieser (1961). Two of the best known insecticidal members of the group, dieldrin and aldrin, are named after two chemists who won the Nobel Prize in 1950 for discovering the diene synthesis. Dieldrin (Fig. 4.11) is an oxidised form (an epoxide) of aldrin (Fig. 4.1c). Other members of the group are endrin (Fig. 4.12), heptachlor

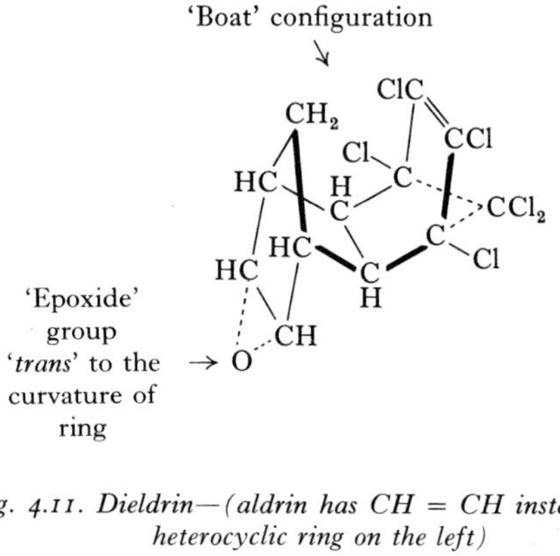

Fig. 4.11. Dieldrin—(aldrin has CH = CH instead of the heterocyclic ring on the left)

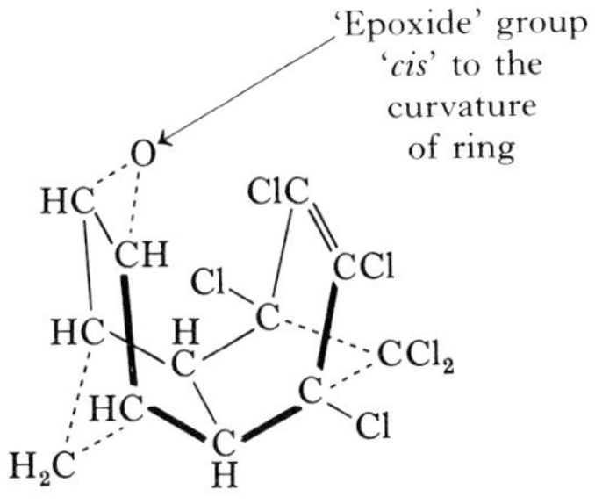

Fig. 4.12. Endrin

(Fig. 4.13) and chlordane (Fig. 4.14). Heptachlor and chlordane are shown as projection formulae.

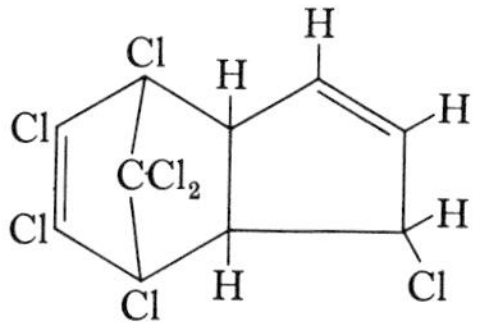

Fig. 4.13. Heptachlor

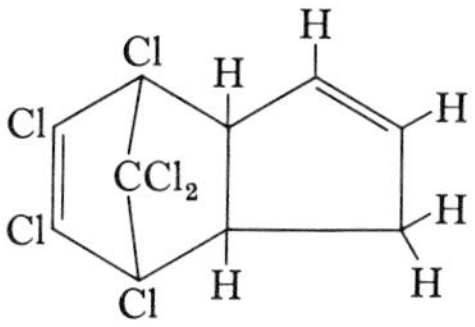

Fig. 4.14. Chlordene—(chlordane is a mixture of compounds, corresponding roughly to a dichlorinated chlordene)

The structural chemistry of the cyclopentadienes is complex, for numerous stereo-isomers exist. This is because the molecule is not planar—in fact, the molecular geometry recalls the 'chair' configuration of BHC, although the alternative 'boat' form provides the framework of the cyclodienes. When such a 'boat' structure exists it is possible for a type of isomerism akin to geometrical isomerism to occur, as an example will illustrate. Formulae (Fig. 4.11) and (Fig. 4.12) show the probable configuration of the isomers dieldrin and endrin. In dieldrin, the epoxide grouping, C_2H_2O, is directed towards the convex surface of the 'boat', whereas in endrin it is directed towards the concave side. The stereo-chemistry of the compounds mentioned above, and also of some newer materials such as alodan, bromodan, telodrin and endosulfan, has been reviewed by Riemschneider (1963).

Some of the unoxidised chlorinated cyclopentadienes have been used for soil and seed treatment. Thus aldrin, possibly because it has a somewhat higher vapour pressure than lindane at normal soil temperatures in Britain (Fig. 4.15), is often a more efficient soil insecticide than BHC, and is applied

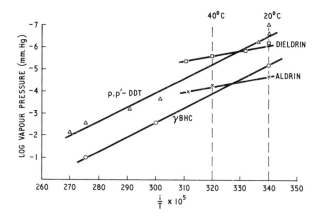

Fig. 4.15. Relationship between vapour pressure and temperature for some organochlorine insecticides. T is the temperature on the absolute scale

to soil to control wireworms and the larvae of various root flies. The epoxides, on the other hand, are more frequently used as seed dressings and for the treatment of the roots of seedlings by dipping prior to planting.

In Britain, the use of cyclodienes has been subjected to legal restrictions following investigations into the hazards inherent in the use of organo-chlorine compounds carried out by a Ministry Advisory Committee. While the Report (Cook, 1964) should be consulted for details, the Committee was much more critical of the cyclodiene compounds than it was of other organochlorine insecticides. It was recommended that, whenever possible, DDT, BHC or organophosphorus compounds should be employed instead of the cyclodienes. The Committee accepted that in Britain the use of aldrin and dieldrin saved the equivalent of about 4,000 acres of winter-sown wheat and about the same acreage-equivalent of cabbage and sugar beet, but considered their use should cease in fertiliser mixtures and in sheep dips. In view of the high toxicity of cyclodienes to birds, the use of aldrin, dieldrin and heptachlor in most seed dressings was also considered undesirable, though exceptions were made, in certain stated circumstances,

94

for the treatment of autumn-sown wheat and of sugar beet. It was agreed that aldrin and dieldrin should continue to be used for the time being against wireworm in potatoes and to control cabbage root fly, though a hope was expressed that less persistent materials might soon replace all groups of organochlorine hydrocarbons.

In addition to the usual neurotoxic action, several cyclodienes appear to affect the activity of the Malpighian (excretory) tubules in insects. Roan and Hopkins (1961) reviewed work which indicated that excretory activity almost ceased in insects poisoned with endrin. DDT derivatives do not have this effect. Zavon (1961) prepared, on behalf of the Shell Petroleum Company, a Bulletin which describes the toxicology of endrin to higher animals. One or two parts per thousand million in water will cause the death of fish and it is also highly toxic to mammals. Prolonged absorption of large doses has been known to cause diffuse degenerative lesions of the brain, kidney and adrenal tissues. The toxicology of aldrin and dieldrin was described in a similar Bulletin (Zavon, 1963). Birds were found to be approximately five times as susceptible to these compounds as were mammals, but microscopic examination revealed changes in certain viscera of animals fed aldrin at concentrations which had no visible external effect.

METABOLISM OF ORGANOCHLORINE INSECTICIDES

When a suitable tissue, such as bird liver, is homogenised and then subjected to differential centrifugation, it is possible to separate sub-cellular components into fractions. If, after centrifugation at 9000 G to separate heavier particles, the supernatant liquid is subjected to ultracentrifugation for about 40 minutes at 100,000 G, a particulate solid separates which is termed the microsomal fraction. It consists of fragments of the endoplasmic reticulum, comprising lipoprotein membranes and the ribosomes which, in life, are associated with it.

Within the last few years it has become apparent that certain enzymes responsible for the ultimate breakdown of complex and potentially harmful molecules are located in the microsomal fraction and, for this reason, microsomes are now being studied intensively by research workers interested in many aspects of toxicology. Work is still in its infancy, but we know already that some of the enzymes participating in the breakdown of pesticides occur in this fraction—although, of course, this does not mean that all breakdown processes occur in the microsomes. The 'processing enzymes' in the microsomes fall, for the present purposes, into at least three groups, comprising respectively systems which formally (though not necessarily mechanistically) involve hydroxylation (a), oxidation (b) and the addition of water (c) (Fig. 4.16).

It was pointed out earlier (p. 47) that the route of oxidative degradation of some pesticides may involve the production of an intermediate substance

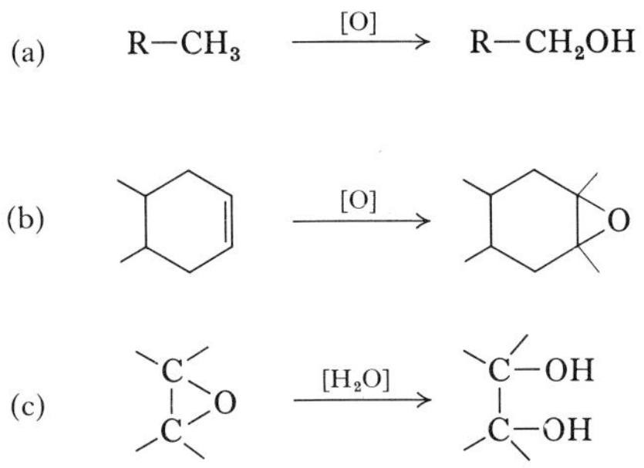

(a) $\qquad$ $R-CH_3 \xrightarrow{[O]} R-CH_2OH$

(b)

(c) $\xrightarrow{[H_2O]}$

Fig. 4.16. *Some microsomal reactions (a) Hydroxylation: replacement of the linkage C-H by C-OH; (b) Oxidation: epoxide formation; (c) Addition of water: formation of diols*

which, fortuitously, happens to be more toxic to the organism than was the original foreign molecule. *In such cases,* we are faced with the paradoxical situation that the protective enzymes in the microsomes may, at least temporarily, actually enhance the toxicity of the original poison. This is shown diagrammatically in the following scheme:

Pesticide $\xrightarrow{\ \ 1\ \ }$ Oxidised form with $\xrightarrow{\ \ 2\ \ }$ Further oxidised or
(toxic)   'activating'   higher toxicity than   Detoxifying   hydroxylated inactive
  step   the pesticide   step or steps   form

Here, a toxic molecule is first converted to a more active molecule and this in turn to one or more inactive forms. If an inhibitor applied with the toxic molecule *preferentially* retards the activation process (it may have some effect on both step (1) and step (2) above), it functions as an antagonist, because it causes the concentration of the activated intermediate to be lower than it would be in the absence of the inhibitor. Conversely, if it retards the detoxifying process(es) more strongly than the activating step, the concentration of the active intermediate will be higher than it would be if the inhibitor were not present, and the microsomal oxidase inhibitor thus functions as a synergist (p. 47).

The three main types of microsomal processing systems mentioned above are probably of low specificity, as indeed is to be expected in view

96

of the miscellaneous and ever-changing substrates that they need to act upon. On the other hand, like better known oxido-reductases elsewhere in the cell, they almost certainly depend upon various co-factors—there is evidence that most of them show high specificity in this respect. So far as is known, many systems reponsible for the metabolism of organochlorine insecticides require NADPH rather than NADH but, as will be seen later (p. 121), microsomal systems dependent upon NADH appear to participate in the breakdown of certain organophosphates. The diol-forming system (Fig. 4.16c) needs neither NADH nor NADPH. It should be added that two cytochromes (b_5 and P450) present in microsomes are different from the cytochromes in the mitochondria; such evidence as exists strongly suggests that these special cytochromes take part in some of the redox systems concerned with the processing of toxicants. The role of the pyridine nucleotides must be indirect, for it is the reduced forms in each case which are found experimentally to be necessary additives to microsomal preparations.

All three types of microsomal processing enzymes play a part in the metabolism of cyclodiene insecticides, though the relative importance of the role to be ascribed to each probably varies in different species of organisms, or indeed, in different strains or varieties of one species in certain circumstances. The initial step in the sequence of changes leading to breakdown frequently results in the production of an epoxide of high toxicity (e.g., aldrin is oxidised to dieldrin; heptochlor to heptachlor epoxide). In due course—and if the organisms or at least their enzymes survive—the epoxide may be hydroxylated or suffer cleavage of the three-membered epoxide ring; in either case, toxicity decreases and, so far as is known, the inactivation process is thereafter straightforward.

In the few examples investigated so far using the housefly as test organism, it appears that the NADPH-dependent oxidases which catalyse first the formation and then the destruction of epoxides are inhibited by sesamex

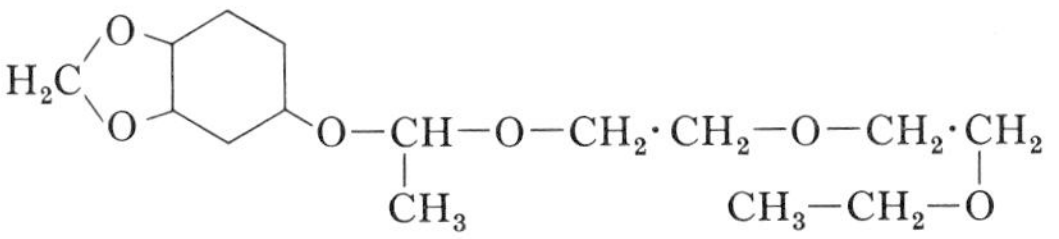

Fig. 4.17. Sesamex

(Fig. 4.17), though the two steps in the oxidative sequence are not always inhibited to an equal extent (compare, steps 1 and 2 of the sequence on p. 96). Work on commercial organochlorine insecticides has so far been rather limited, but using chlordene (Fig. 4.14), a compound closely related to the insecticide chlordane, Brooks (1966) has shown that both steps of the

97

oxidative sequence were slowed down by simultaneous use of sesamex. In consequence, sesamex causes chlordene toxic symptoms in flies to appear later than when chlordene is used by itself. On the other hand, the stabilisation of the epoxide, once it has been formed, leads to an overall increase in toxicity in the presence of sesamex.

There is some evidence that the (hydrolytic?) ring cleavage is brought about by enzymes which add or subtract water, which are not dependent upon NADH or NADPH and are not inhibited by sesamex. Furthermore, there is evidence, so far fragmentary, that some higher animals may possess these hydratases to a quantitatively greater extent than do most insects. This difference in microsomal processing capability is of interest for, should it prove to be fairly general, it clearly raises the possibility of using mixtures of two or more substances which act synergistically when they come into contact with one sort of organism but lack synergistic action in another (due to the rapid destruction of epoxide by a pathway not sensitive to the synergist). Microsomal enzymes thus offer a further mechanism which may be exploited to achieve selective toxic action.

It is of interest that under anaerobic conditions, the microsomal oxidoreductases act in reverse—i.e., as reductases. Walker (1966) has demonstrated that bird liver preparations can, under anaerobic conditions, transform p,p′–DDT into TDE (DDD) by a process which has been termed reductive dechlorination (Fig. 4.18).

This reaction is of practical as well as theoretical importance, for, upon death, anaerobic conditions develop in many tissues and so may switch the route of degradation of any DDT present in the body. Consequently, an

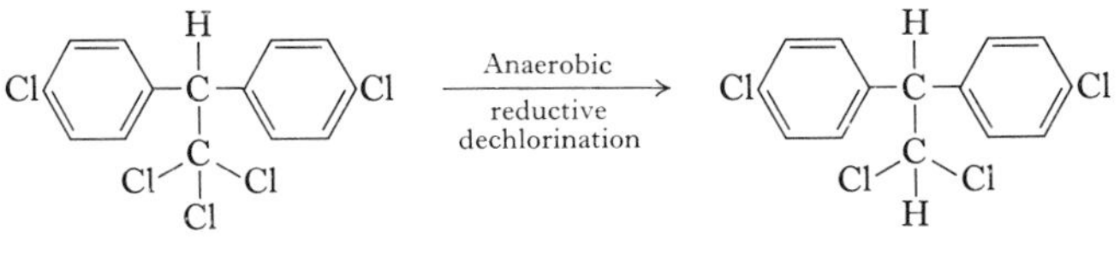

Fig. 4.18. Anaerobic reductive dechlorination of p, p′–DDT to give p, p′–TDE

analyst investigating corpses of wild life killed by pesticide needs to recognise that any TDE present may be of post mortem origin as well as possibly originating from the (minor) pesticide rhothane, which is a formulation of TDE.

The routes whereby p,p′–DDT is degraded under normal aerobic conditions have been left till last because the cellular location of the several types of enzymes involved remains uncertain. The same is true of the enzymes concerned with the degradation of γ-BHC. So far as is known,

the breakdown of DDT does not result in the production of any intermediate compound more toxic than DDT itself. On the other hand,
as was seen earlier in a different connection, the principal pathway by
which degradation occurs is different in different types of organisms (Fig.
4.7). Sometimes the overall breakdown can be formally, though not
necessarily mechanistically, represented as oxidation, sometimes as hydrolytic (compare the hydrolysis of benzo-trichloride) and sometimes as a
dehydrochlorination process. The route by which BHC is metabolised in
flies has been mentioned already (p. 92).

It will be noted that, whatever the route whereby compounds highly
soluble in lipid are degraded, the final product is much more soluble in
water than was the original material. For example, the cyclodienes are
converted to more soluble hydroxylated derivatives, DDT to hydroxylated
or carboxylic acid derivatives and γ-BHC is changed to water-soluble
S-(2,4-dichlorophenyl) glutathione. All such changes, no matter how their
detailed chemistry may differ, can be regarded as metabolic devices for
ensuring that a lipid-soluble substance can eventually be eliminated from
the body in the form of an aqueous solution of a suitable derivative.

REFERENCES

AGOSIN, M., MICHAELI, D., MISKUS, R., NAGASAWA, S. and HOSKINS, W. M. (1961), *J. econ. Ent.*, **54**, 340
ALBERT, A. (1960), *Selective Toxicity*, Methuen, London
Anon (1963), Report of the President's Science Advisory Committee, *Use of Pesticides*, The White
    House, Washington, D.C.
ASCHER, K. R. S. (1964), *Wld Rev. Pest Control.* **3**, (1), 7
BARNES, J. M. (1957), *Adv. Pest Control Res.*, **1**, 1
BIGGAR, J. W., DUTT, G. R. and RIGGS, R. L. (1967), *Bull. Environ. Contam. Toxicol.*, **2**, 90
BRADBURY, F. R. (1963), *Ann. appl. Biol.*, **52**, 361
BRIDGES, R. G. and COX, J. T. (1959), *Nature, Lond.*, **184**, 1740
BROOKS, G. T. (1960), *Nature, Lond.*, **186**, 96
BROOKS, G. T. (1966), *Wld Rev. Pest Control*, **5**, 62
BROWN, A. W. A. (1950), Symposium on the development of resistance of insects to insecticides, *81st
    Rept. Ent. Soc. Ontario*, p. 33
BROWN, A. W. A. (1958), *Adv. Pest Control Res.*, **2**, 351
BROWN, V. K., RICHARDSON, A., ROBINSON, J. and STEVENSON, D. E. (1965), *Fd Cosmet. Toxicol.*, **3**, 675
BUSVINE, J. R. (1954), *Nature, Lond.*, **174**, 783
BUSVINE, J. R. (1968), *Wld Rev. Pest Control*, **7**, (1) 27
CARSON, R. (1963), *Silent Spring*, Hamish Hamilton and Co. London
CLARK, A. G., HITCHCOCK, M. and SMITH, J. N. (1966), *Nature, Lond.*, **209**, 103
COOK, J. (1964), *Review of the Persistent Organochlorine Pesticides*, Ministry of Agriculture, Fisheries
    and Food, H.M.S.O.
DAS, M. and MCINTOSH, A. H. (1961), *Ann. appl. Biol.*, **49**, 267
DAVIS, B. N. K. (1964), *Food supply and Nature conservation—A Symposium.* Held at the Cambridgeshire
    College of Arts and Technology.
DE WITT, J. B. (1956), *J. agric. Fd Chem.*, **4**, 863
DYTE, C. E. (1962), *Fd Trade Rev.*, **33**, (3), 35
EATON, J. L. and STERNBURG, J. (1964), *J. insect Physiol.*, **10**, 471
EDSON, E. F., SANDERSON, D. M. and NOAKES, D. N. (1966), *Wld Rev. Pest Control*, **5**, 143
FERGUSON, J. (1939), *Proc. R. Soc.*, **127(B)**, 387

FERGUSON, J. and HAWKINS, S. W. (1949), *Nature, Lond.,* **164,** 9

FIESER, L. F. and FIESER, M. (1961), *Advanced Organic Chemistry.* Reinhold Publ. Corpn., New York (see pp. 206–211)

FRAZER, A. C. (1963), British Food Manufacturing Industries Research Assoc., Presidential Address

GEORGHIOU, G. P. (1965), *Adv. Pest Control Res.,* **6,** 171

GORDON, H. T. (1961), *A Rev. Ent.,* **6,** 27

HADAWAY, A. B. and BARLOW, F. (1962), *Ann. appl. Biol.,* **50,** 633

HASSALL, K. A. (1965a), *Brit. vet. J.,* **121,** 105

HASSALL, K. A. (1965b), *Brit. vet. J.,* **121,** 199

HASSALL, K. A. (1966), *Scient. Hort.,* **18,** 103

HAYES, W. J. (1962), *Chemical and Biological Hazards in Food,* Iowa State University Press

HAYES, W. J. (1963), *Natn. agric. Chem. Ass. News,* **22,** (1), 3

HOFFMAN, W. S., FISHBEIN, W. I. and ANDELMAN, M. I. (1964), *Natn. agric. Chem. Ass. News,* **22,** (6), 3

HOLDEN, A. V. (1962), *Ann. appl. Biol.,* **50,** 467

HOLDEN, A. V. (1966), *J. appl. Ecol.,* **3,** (suppl.), 45

HOLDEN, A. V. and MARSDEN, K. (1966), *J. and Proc. Inst. Sewage Purification,* Part 3, 3

HOSEIN, E. A. and PROULX, P. (1960), *J. agric. Fd Chem.,* **8,** 428

HOSKINS, W. M. and GORDON, H. T. (1956), *A rev. Ent.,* **1,** 89

HYYPIO, P. A., TSOU, T. M. and WILSON, G. B. (1955), *Cytologia,* **20,** 166

Insecticide and Fungicide Handbook (1963), (Ed. Martin, H.) Blackwell Publications, Oxford

JEFFERIES, D. J. (1967), *Ibis,* **109,** 266

JÖNSSON, A. and FÅHRAEUS, G. (1960), *Kungl. Lanthr. hogsk. Ann.,* **26,** 323

KEIDING, J. (1967), *Wld Rev. Pest Control,* **6,** (4), 115

LEWIS, S. E., WALLER, J. B. and FOWLER, K. S. (1960), *J. insect Physiol.,* **4,** 128

LICHTENSTEIN, E. P. (1960), *J. agric. Fd Chem.,* **8,** 448

LICHTENSTEIN, E. P., MILLINGTON, W. F. and COWLEY, G. T. (1962), *J. agric. Fd Chem.,* **10,** 251

LICHTENSTEIN, E. P. and SCHULZ, K. R. (1960), *J. agric. Fd Chem.,* **8,** 452

LIPKE, H. and KEARNS, C. W. (1960), *Adv. Pest Control Res.,* **3,** 253

MCINTOSH, A. H. (1957), *Chemy. Ind.,* January, p. 2

MACLAGAN, D. S. (1957), *Nature, Lond.,* **179,** 1197

MARTIN, J. P., HARDING, R. B., CANNELL, G. H. and ANDERSON, L. D. (1959), *Soil Sci.,* **87,** 334

MARTIN, J. P. and PRATT, P. F. (1958), *J. agric. Fd Chem.,* **6,** 345

MATSUMARA, F. and O'BRIEN, R. D. (1966), *J. agric. Fd Chem.,* **14,** 39

MELLANBY, K. (1967), *Pesticides and Pollution.* Collins, London

METCALF, R. L. (1955), *Organic insecticides.* Interscience Publishers Ltd., London

MULLINS, L. J. (1954), *Chem. Rev.,* **54,** 289

MUNSON, S. C., PADILLA, G. M. and WEISSMANN, M. L. (1954), *J. econ. Ent.,* **47,** 578

MURTON, R. K. (1965), *The Wood Pigeon,* New Naturalist Special Vol. No. 20. Collins, London

MURTON, R. K. and VIZOSO, M. (1963), *Ann. appl. Biol.,* **52,** 503

POTTER, C. (1965), *Sci. Progr.,* **53,** 393

POTTER, C. and GILLHAM, E. M. (1946), *Ann. appl. Biol.,* **33,** 142

POUSSEL, H. (1948), *Gallica biol. Acta,* **1,** 114

RAY, J. W. (1963), *Nature, Lond.,* **197,** 1226

REYNOLDS, H. T. (1958), *Adv. Pest Control Res.,* **2,** 144

RIEMSCHNEIDER, R. (1958), *Adv. Pest Control Res.,* **2,** 307

RIEMSCHNEIDER, R. (1963), *Wld Rev. Pest Control,* **2,** (4), 29

ROAN, C. C. and HOPKINS, T. L. (1961), *A. Rev. Ent.,* **6,** 333

ROBINSON, J. (1967), Paper read to the VIth Int. Congress Plant Protection, Vienna

ROBINSON, J., RICHARDSON, A., CRABTREE, A. N., COULSON, J. C. and POTTS, G. R. (1967), *Nature, Lond.,* **214,** 1307

Royal Society for the Protection of Birds (1964); 4th Rept. on toxic chemicals, 1962–1963 *The risk to bird life from chlorinated hydrocarbon pesticides*

RUDD, R. L. (1964), *Pesticides and the Living Landscape.* Faber and Faber, London

SAN ANTONIO, J. P. (1959), *J. agric. Fd Chem.,* **7,** 322

SEXTON, W. A. (1950), *Quart. Rev. Chem. Soc.,* **4,** 272

WALKER, C. H. (1966), *J. appl. Ecol.,* **3,** (suppl), 213

WALKER, C. H., HAMILTON, G. A. and HARRISON, R. B. (1967), *J. Sci. Fd Agric.,* **18,** 123

WALKER, C. H. and MILLS, D. A. (1965), *16th Rep. Wildfowl Trust,* p. 56

WARE, G. W. and NABER, E. C. (1961), *J. econ. Ent.,* **54,** 675

WHEATLEY, G. A., HARDMAN, J. A. and STRICKLAND, A. H. (1962), *Plant Path.,* **11,** 81

WHITTEN, J. L. (1966), *That We May Live,* D. van Nostrand Co. Ltd., London

WINTERINGHAM, F. P. W. (1962), *J. R. Soc. Arts,* **110,** 719

WINTERINGHAM, F. P. W. and LEWIS, S. E. (1959), *A. Rev. Ent.,* **4,** 303

YAMASAKI, T. and ISHII, T. (1954), *Sci. Insect Control, Kyoto,* **19,** 39

ZAVON, M. R. (1961), *Agricultural chemical bulletin: the toxicology and pharmacology of endrin.* Shell Petroleum Company, Bulletin ADB:882/Da, 31

ZAVON, M. R. (1963), *Agricultural chemical bulletin: the toxicology and pharmacology of aldrin and dieldrin.* Shell Petroleum Company, Bulletin ADB:881/Da, 30

ZWEIG, G., SMITH, L. M., PEOPLES, S. A. and COX, R. (1961), *J. agric. Fd Chem.,* **9,** 481

5

ORGANOPHOSPHORUS INSECTICIDES

It is of interest to contrast the history of the organophosphorus insecticides with that of the organochlorine compounds (p 66), for both groups were developed during the second world war and together they now account for a very large percentage of the total tonnage of marketed insecticides.

The organophosphorus compounds were discovered by a German team concerned primarily with the investigation and development of nerve gases, which are amongst the most toxic materials known to man. This association of insecticides with war gases was hardly auspicious; it aroused fears which at first seemed only too justified, for the earliest insecticidal members of the group, TEPP and parathion, were of high mammalian toxicity. Many years elapsed before it became apparent that it was possible to prepare organophosphorus compounds which were very poisonous to insects yet were less toxic to mammals than were many of the organochlorine insecticides. Furthermore, since some of them undergo degradative changes with moderate ease and others are soluble in water, inconveniently high persistence (a property which has proved so damaging to the reputation of the organochlorine compounds) can be avoided by synthesising organophosphorus insecticides of suitable molecular structure. Consequently, whilst problems have occasionally arisen in relation to the acute toxicity of concentrates or of spray mixtures, the more troublesome problem of accumulation in animal tissues has seldom, if ever, been encountered. Another advantage of organophosphorus compounds is that their primary, and perhaps only, mode of action is largely understood, whereas only a hazy understanding exists as to why organochlorine compounds are poisonous. Thus, while organochlorine compounds have fallen under an ever-increasing cloud of disapproval, the reputation of the organophosphorus insecticides has risen as their variety and their uses have multiplied.

In terms of tonnage they are now in some countries the most commonly used insecticides.

Most organophosphorus insecticides are based upon one particular molecular pattern (Fig. 5.1), where X and Y are alkoxy or substituted

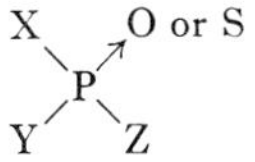

Fig. 5.1. General molecular pattern of organophosphorus insecticides

amino groups, and Z is often, but not always, a group derived from an acid HZ. Table 5.1 indicates in more detail the range of structure encountered in the group, together with the nomenclature employed.

Table 5.1 MAIN CHEMICAL GROUPS TO WHICH
ORGANOPHOSPHORUS INSECTICIDES BELONG

1. Amidohalogen phosphates	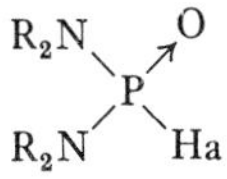	e.g. Dimefox (Fig. 5.16)
2. Orthophosphates	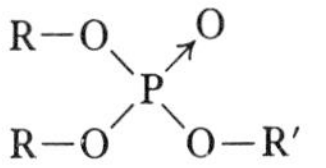	e.g. Dichlorvos (Fig. 5.14) Chlorfenvinphos (Fig. 5.30)
3. Ortho*thion*phosphates	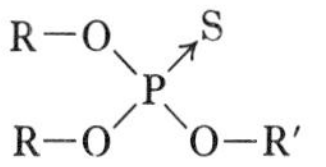	e.g. Parathion (Fig. 5.10) Diazinon (Fig. 5.15)
4. *Dithio*phosphates *or* phosphorodithioates	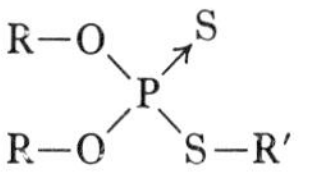	e.g. Malathion (Fig. 5.7) Azinphos-methyl (Fig. 5.8)
5. Thionphos*phon*ates	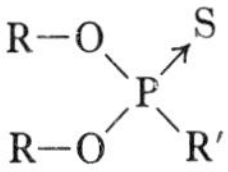	e.g. 'EPN' (Fig. 5.2)
6. *Pyro*phosphates	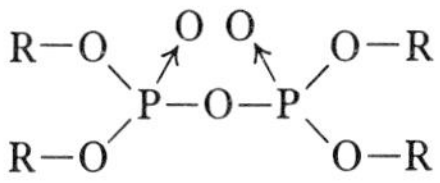	e.g. TEPP (Fig. 5.9)
7. *Pyro*phosphoramides	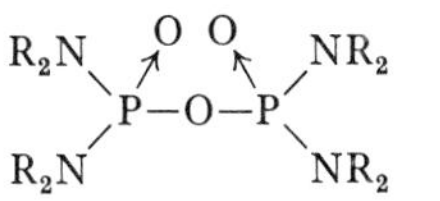	e.g. Schradan (Fig. 5.11)

Price Jones and Edgar (1961) have given the common names and formulae for fifteen organophosphorus compounds which are, or have been, used as aphicides; for further information about the naming of organophosphorus compounds, the monograph by O'Brien (1960) should be consulted. However, it will not be necessary to discuss the rather complex nomenclature of phosphorus derivatives more fully here, for they can be conveniently classified by reference to their field uses as contact and systemic poisons, and these field uses are not closely correlated with chemical classification.

Symptoms of sub-lethal poisoning of mammals by organophosphorus compounds include a development of a tightness of the chest, vomiting, muscular twitching, contraction of the pupil of the eye, and in severe cases, convulsions. References to work describing the detailed symptomology of poisoning by insecticides of this group have been given by O'Brien (1960 p. 175) and by Heath (1961, Chapter 14).

MODE OF ACTION

In all probability, the mode of action of organophosphorus compounds in insects is the same as it is in mammals (p. 64). In both cases, acetylcholinesterase, or some very similar enzyme, appears to be the primary site of action, although minor differences may well exist in the nature (or perhaps the location) of the enzyme in vertebrates and insects. Nevertheless, while cholinesterase is probably the *primary* site of action of organophosphorus compounds *in vivo,* there is considerable evidence that other esterases are also inhibited to a greater or lesser degree. Indeed, Frawley (1965) has pointed out that a few members of the group appear preferentially to

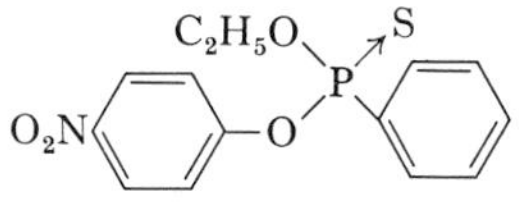

Fig. 5.2. Ethyl p–nitrophenyl benzene thionphosphonate (trade name 'EPN')

inhibit esterases capable of hydrolysing aliphatic esters and amides—i.e., while they inhibit carboxyesterases *and* cholinesterase, the former are inhibited at lower concentrations. Ethyl p-nitrophenyl benzene thionphosphonate, 'EPN' (Fig. 5.2), is a particularly well documented example of a compound acting selectively on carboxylic acid esterases. The action on the carboxyesterases (aliesterases) of 'EPN' and of some other compounds will be referred to later in the chapter, for it is of importance in relation to the synergism sometimes apparent when two organophosphorus compounds are applied simultaneously.

Some of the observations which suggest that small differences may exist between the cholinesterase(s) in vertebrates and insects deserve brief comment, for differences in the nature or location of the enzyme might affect its vulnerability to inhibitors and hence be contributory factors in determining the selective toxicity to insects or to mammals shown by some members of the group.

In mature insects, there is evidence that acetylcholine is not the mediator at neuromuscular junctions. Exogenous acetylcholine, which is extremely toxic to mammals, is without effect when injected into insects, yet there is evidence that endogenous acetylcholine, readily detectable in the nervous system of insects, is probably pharmacologically active there (Chang and Kearns, 1955). Another problem arose when Hopf and Taylor (1958) noted that a quaternary ammonium organophosphate had no effect on locusts at concentrations which totally inhibited locust nerve cholinesterase *in vitro*. Conversely, it has been shown that insects killed by organophosphorus compounds do not always have their (acetyl)cholinesterase substantially inhibited at the time of death. Again, even if it were established that the inhibition of cholinesterase was the principal or only effect of these compounds on insects, asphyxiation is not the actual cause of death, as it is in mammals, for in insects there is no elaborate respiratory system. Finally, insect eggs can be killed by organophosphates before the nervous system has been differentiated.

More or less adequate explanations have been advanced for most of these apparent anomalies. They have been summarised by O'Brien (1960, pp. 171, 248, 263) and only one aspect of the problem needs emphasis here. It appears that the nervous system of insects, but not of mammals, is surrounded by a connective tissue sheath which is of low permeability to many types of ions. If the sheath is peeled off, the exposed nerve fibre becomes much more susceptible to ionic poisons. It has therefore been suggested that in insects, but not in higher animals, a barrier exists between the nerve cord and exogenous ions. This barrier must not, of course, be confused with the membrane, impermeable to sodium and potassium ions (except when an impulse is being transmitted) which is essential to the functioning of all nerves (p. 61).

If such a barrier does indeed exist in insects, it could be anticipated that ions of certain weakly basic or acidic organophosphates may have more difficulty in penetrating to their site of action in insects than have unionised molecules. It should be added, however, that so far as is known, selective *insecticidal* action depends primarily upon various metabolic changes to be described later, rather than upon structural differences between the nervous systems of insects and mammals.

THE INHIBITION OF CHOLINESTERASE

Acetylcholine, Fig. 5.3, is the natural substrate of acetylcholinesterase, although it can also be split by a number of related cholinesterases. Since

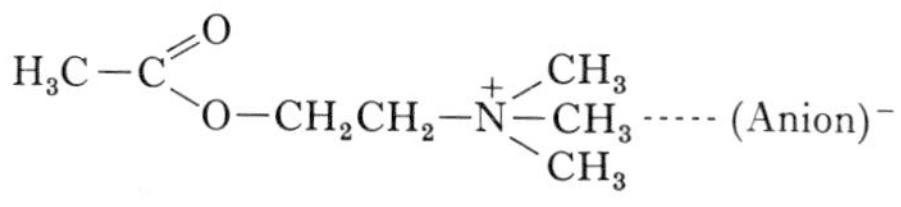

$$H_3C-C\underset{O-CH_2CH_2-\overset{+}{N}-CH_3}{\overset{O}{\diagup}}\cdots (Anion)^-$$

Fig. 5.3. Acetylcholine

the different roles of these closely related esterases has not been defined, what is said below probably applies to all the cholinesterases, though the kinetics will, of course, vary with the specificity of each enzyme for the substrate.

Acetylcholine is believed to become bound to (acetyl)cholinesterase at two, or possibly three, attachment sites. The following account, which is a simplified version of those provided by Casida (1956) and O'Brien (1960), assumes the existence of one anionic and one ester-forming site on the surface of the enzyme. According to O'Brien (1962), the hydroxyl group shown in Fig. 5.4(a) belongs to a vital serine molecule.

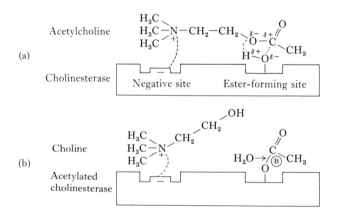

Fig. 5.4. Diagram illustrating the reaction of acetylcholinesterase with acetyl-choline: (a) Orientation of substrate on enzyme surface; (b) Splitting gives rise to free choline (which rapidly breaks off) and an acetylated enzyme. The latter is quickly hydrolysed at bond Ⓑ

The bond ⓑ is weak and is rapidly hydrolysed once the choline fraction of the molecule has split off, so that choline molecules and acetate ions diffuse away, leaving the cholinesterase surface unoccupied.

Organophosphates of suitable constitution, by masquerading as the natural substrate, orientate themselves at the surface of the enzyme and undergo, up to the moment of fission, changes analogous to those undergone by the natural substrate. The esteratic site is now, however, associated with phosphate rather than with acetate and the bond ⓑ is relatively stable to hydrolysis (Fig. 5.5). The phosphorylated esteratic site is consequently

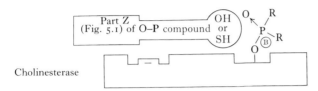

Fig. 5.5. Diagram illustrating the reaction between cholinesterase and an organophosphate inhibitor. Bond ⓑ is not readily hydrolysed, so only one cleavage fraction vacates surface

unable to accept any of the natural substrate and the enzyme ceases to function.

It was soon apparent to those responsible for the synthesis of new compounds that, if the mode of action of these insecticides was along the lines suggested above, phosphorylative ability was one of several molecular properties likely to be important in potential new poisons. A systematic search eventually led to the discovery of many useful materials, although it also brought to light other molecular factors of importance (Sherlock, 1962).

Casida (1956) pointed out that an organophosphorus compound of sufficient persistence to be of practical value must, paradoxically so it appears, combine stability to oxidation and hydrolysis *away* from the site of action with phosphorylative ability (i.e., instability) *once it reaches* that site. One way in which the difficulty could be resolved would be to effect a compromise between stability and instability, so sacrificing inherent toxicity for the sake of persistence. Alternatively, a stable substance could be chosen which undergoes a chemical change (activation) to a more reactive phosphorylating agent within a living organism. In practice, both mechanisms influence the reactivity and selectivity of most organophosphorus insecticides.

The earlier insecticides of the group contain anion-producing (electron-attracting) groups Z, linked to phosphorus through an oxygen atom. They react readily in the presence of cholinesterase, as shown in Fig. 5.6.

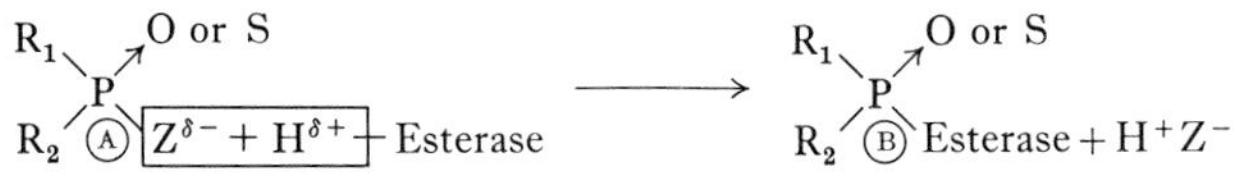

Fig. 5.6. Reaction of an anion-producing (electron-attracting) group Z, linked to phosphorus through an oxygen atom, in the presence of cholinesterase

The bond Ⓐ is weakened by the electron pull of Z, whereas the bond Ⓑ, as has been seen above, is relatively stable to hydrolysis. The somewhat complex theory underlying these changes has been outlined by Heath (1961, Chapter 1).

In compounds of more recent discovery, the atom connecting the (often rather large) group Z to the phosphorus atom is one of sulphur instead of oxygen (contrast Figs. 5.7 and 5.8, for example, with Figs. 5.9, 5.10 and 5.11). The use of sulphur, which is below oxygen in Group 6 of the

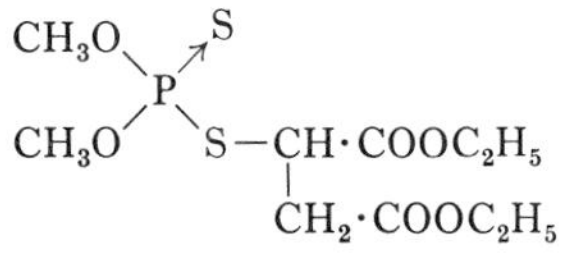

Fig. 5.7. Malathion: dimethyl (diethylsuccinic) phosphoro-dithiolate. ('Thiol' indicates that at least one S atom is in a covalent linkage)

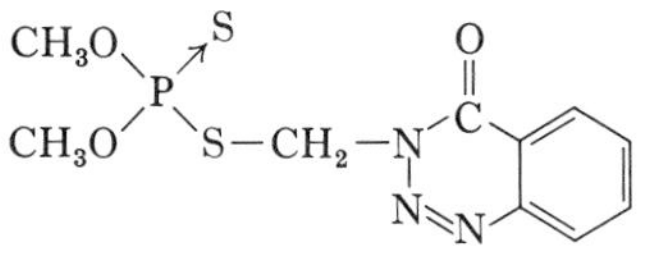

Fig. 5.8. Azinphos-methyl: (dihydro-oxobenzotriazin–3–yl methyl phosphorodithioate

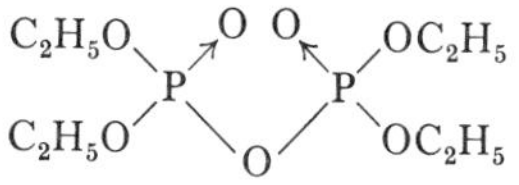

Fig. 5.9. TEPP: tetraethyl pyrophosphate

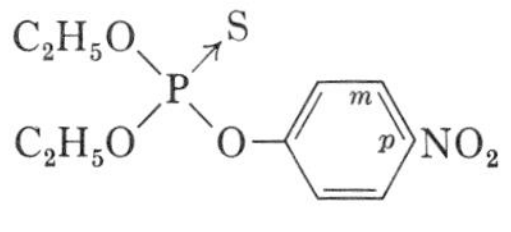

Fig. 5.10. Parathion: diethyl p–nitrophenyl phosphorothionate. ('Thion' indicates that the S atom is in the dative linkage)

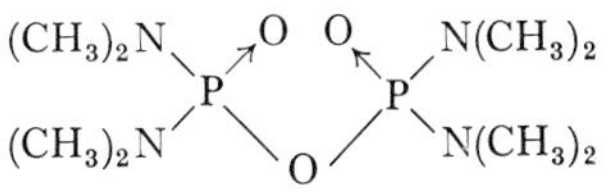

Fig. 5.11. Schradan: tetramethyl phosphorodiamidic anhydride

Periodic Table, renders the thiols somewhat more electropositive than their oxygen counterparts, and hence less readily attacked by hydrogen ions. It simultaneously makes them more readily attacked by *negative* groups. According to Sherlock (1962) this may explain why thiols are often quite stable in a neutral solution but are nevertheless readily attacked by a negative site on the cholinesterase surface. The negative group induces a positive charge upon the sulphur atom which lays the molecule open to disruption, the phosphorus part of the molecule then phosphorylating the hydroxyl group of the serine.

Phosphorylative ability is not, however, the only factor determining toxic effectiveness. As would be expected, the total molecular similarity in shape, size and ionising potential are of importance, and these are all influenced by the nature of the remainder of group Z. If all other factors could be kept constant, it would be anticipated that those organophosphorus compounds most like acetylcholine would attach themselves best to the surface by association with the enzyme's anionic site. It is of interest in this respect that the distance between anionic and cationic sites differs some-what in the acetylcholinesterase of insects and the acetylcholinesterase of mammals; consequently, it does not follow that a compound which binds strongly to the enzyme surface in the one case would also attach itself firmly to the surface of the other.

The part of acetylcholine which corresponds to group Z has the structure:

$$-O-CH_2-CH_2-N^+(CH_3)_3$$

It would therefore be expected that suitable compounds with the following structures could be cholinesterase inactivators:

$$-S-CH_2-CH_2-N^+(alkyl)_3 \text{ (Quaternary ammonium compounds)}$$

$$-S-CH_2-CH_2-N^+H(alkyl)_2 \text{ (Tertiary amine salts)}$$

and it is found that many are, in fact, potent esterase inhibitors *in vitro*. But not all are potently insecticidal. Their ionic nature appears to restrict their entry through the ion barrier sheathing the insect nervous system to which reference was made above. A compromise in structure is necessary; some degree of similarity with the ionic state of *endogenous* acetylcholine must be sacrificed to allow these *exogenous* materials to penetrate through the barrier to their site of action. On the other hand, the specific *mammalian* toxicity of such materials as amiton (Fig. 5.12) could be anticipated, for an ion-impermeable barrier is absent in higher animals.

Recent work has suggested that for some organophosphates, the nature

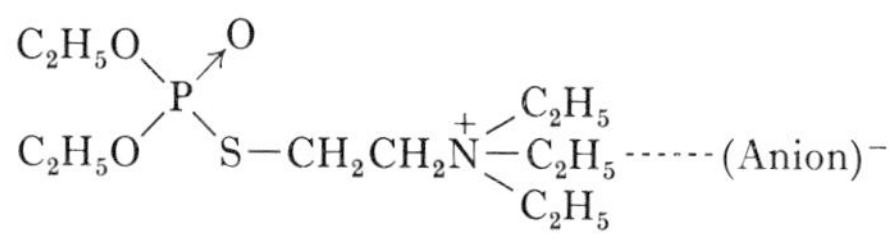

$$C_2H_5O \diagdown \diagup O$$
$$P \diagup \diagdown \diagup C_2H_5$$
$$C_2H_5O \diagup \diagdown S-CH_2CH_2\overset{+}{N}-C_2H_5 \cdots (Anion)^-$$
$$\diagdown C_2H_5$$

Fig. 5.12. Amiton: 2–(diethoxyphosphinyl–thio)–ethyl triethylammonium ion

of the side groups attached to the phosphate may play a definite role in determining the overall toxicity (O'Brien, 1963). For the reason given above, these side groups must not be ionised; consequently, non-coulombic forces must be implicated in any binding for which they are responsible. Such forces appear to be important in relation to the toxic action of the oxygen analogue of azinphos-methyl (Fig. 5.8) but not in the cases of dichlorvos or paraoxon.

CLASSIFICATION OF ORGANOPHOSPHORUS COMPOUNDS

Organophosphorus compounds may be classified according to their field use on crops, since, although their primary mode of action is probably the same, their field uses differ widely. Some, for example, can be applied to crops to give long term protection from insects, while others are used specifically to eliminate a sudden late infestation just prior to harvesting the crop. Hartley (1951) attributed such differences to the physical characteristics and chemical stability of the compounds concerned. Later investigations covering a wider range of materials demonstrated that this view is an over-simplification, but it will be adopted here, since it provides a simple explanation of the uses and limitations of many organophosphorus compounds. The chief characteristics of compounds in each of the three sub-groups are:

Sub-group 1. Compounds of low chemical stability. Soluble in water and usually somewhat soluble in oil. The sprayed substance is usually also the effective substance at the site of action in insects.

Sub-group 2. Compounds of moderate or high chemical stability. They are of low solubility in water but usually soluble in oil. The sprayed substance is activated before it reaches its site of action in insects.

Sub-group 3. Compounds of moderate or high chemical stability. Usually of moderate to high solubility in both water and oil and translocated within plants. The sprayed substance is activated before it reaches its site of action in insects.

Classification and properties of some organophosphorus compounds in these sub-groups are given in Table 5.2.

SUB-GROUP I

The low hydrolytic stability of compounds in the first group precludes the possibility of their persisting for more than a few hours after spraying. Their field use must therefore be almost immediate, and this, in turn, requires that they act by direct contact with the pest. Where solubility in covalent solvents is sufficiently high, penetration through the cuticle of leaves and translocation within the plant may occur, but low chemical stability ensures that their presence there is transient. Tetraethyl pyrophosphate, TEPP (Fig. 5.9), one of the first organophosphates to be employed as an insecticide, belongs to this group. Under optimal conditions *in vitro* it has a half-life of about eight hours (under field conditions the half-life of organophosphorus compounds is found to be much less than *in vitro* studies suggest). This instability, and its high acute toxicity to higher animals (Table 5.2) has rendered it obsolete in Britain.

Mevinphos (Fig. 5.13), which superseded TEPP, has an acute toxic dose about four times as great as that of TEPP. It is somewhat more stable

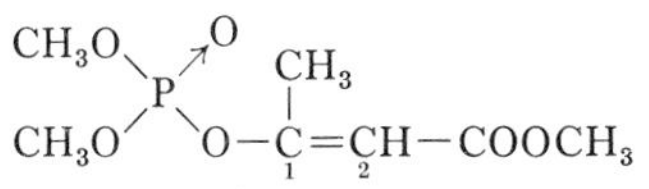

$$CH_3O \diagdown \nearrow O \qquad CH_3$$
$$\qquad P \qquad \qquad |$$
$$CH_3O \diagup \diagdown O - C = CH - COOCH_3$$

Fig. 5.13. Mevinphos: 2–methoxycarbonyl–1–methyl-vinyl dimethyl phosphate (trade name 'Phosdrin')

than TEPP. This stability, together with its solubility in oils and miscibility with water, provide it with a definite but very temporary systemic action. The effective duration within the plant has been variously estimated as from one to eight days; the Ministry of Agriculture (loose leaf dossier *User and Consumer Safety—Advice of Government Departments)* advises that a minimum of three clear days should elapse between the last application of mevinphos and the harvesting of edible crops. It has been

Table 5.2 CLASSIFICATION AND PROPERTIES OF SOME ORGANOPHOSPHORUS COMPOUNDS

Substance	Formula see Fig No.	Aqueous solubility in ppm; (ref 2)	Acute oral toxicity to higher animals LD_{50} mg/kg	Other properties
Sub-group 1				Low contact selectivity between pests and predators. Negligible persistence
TEPP	5·9	Miscible	0·5 (rat; ref. 8) / 2 (rat; ref. 1)	
Mevinphos	5·13	Miscible	7 (rat; ref. 1)	
Dichlorvos	5·14	10,000	25 (rat; ref. 8)	
Sub-group 2				Contact selectivity slight. Usually not very persistent. Quasi-systemic
Parathion	5·10	24	3–6 (rat; ref. 8) / 10 (rat; ref. 1)	
Chlorfenvinphos	5·30	—	10–39 (rat; ref. 8)	
Azinphos-methyl	5·8	33	16 (rat; ref. 1)	Somewhat phytotoxic
Phenkapton	—	—	50 (rat; ref. 8)	
Diazinon	5·15	40	120 (mouse; ref. 3) / 235 (rat; ref. 5)	
Trichlorfon	—	—	650 (rat; ref. 8)	
Malathion	5·7	145	1400 (rat; ref. 1) / 200 (hen; ref. 4) / 20 (calf; ref. 4)	Low phytotoxicity
Paraoxon	5·24	2400	More toxic than is parathion	Some systemic action; see text
Menazon	5·18	250	1980 (rat; ref. 1)	Some systemic action; see below
Sub-group 3				Most have strong systemic properties. Highly persistent
Dimefox	5·16	Miscible	3 (rat; ref. 1)	
Phorate	5·27	—	3 (rat; ref. 8)	
Schradan	5·11	Miscible	5 (rat; ref. 8) / 10 (rat; ref. 1)	Moderately persistent
Demeton (thiol)	—	100	10 (rat; ref. 9)	
Amiton oxalate	5·12	5000	6 (rat; ref. 8)	
Demeton-methyl (thiol)	—	3300	40 (rat; ref. 6)	Moderately persistent
Demeton-methyl (thion)	5·19	330	180 (rat; ref. 6)	
Morphothion	—	—	200 (rat; ref. 8)	
Dimethoate	5·17	25,000	200 (rat; ref. 8) / 500 (rat; ref. 7)	
Menazon	5·18	250	1200 (rat; ref. 8) / 1980 (rat; ref. 1) / More toxic to ruminants	Fairly persistent Selective when applied *via* roots. Only enters slowly through leaves

References: 1. Price Jones and Edgar (1961)
2. Mitchell, Smale and Metcalf (1960)
3. Margot and Gysin (1957)
4. Spiller (1961)
5. Gasser (1953)
6. *Insecticide and Fungicide Handbook* (1963)
7. Pietri-Tonelli (1965)
8. Edson, Sanderson and Noakes (1966)
9. Negherbon (1959).
   See also p. 22 of this book.

recommended for use particularly on fruit and vegetables just before harvesting (Ministry of Agriculture, Fisheries and Food, 1968).

Unlike many or all of the substances in the remaining two groups, compounds such as TEPP and mevinphos appear to be the actual toxicants at the site of action—they do not seem to be altered or 'activated' to more potent cholinesterase inhibitors. They therefore show little selectivity between pests (usually sap-sucking insects such as aphids) and beneficial insects which happen to be in the neighbourhood at the time of spraying.

Dichlorvos (Fig. 5.14) is a substance which lies intermediate between

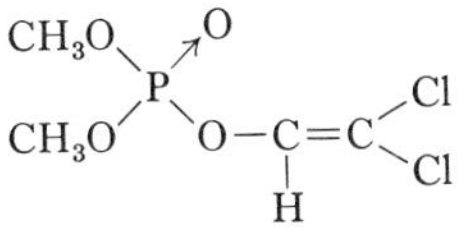

$$CH_3O \diagdown P \diagup O$$
$$CH_3O \diagup \diagdown O-C=C \diagdown Cl \atop Cl$$
$$\underset{H}{|}$$

Fig. 5.14. Dichlorvos: 2,2–dichlorovinyl dimethyl phosphate

groups 1 and 2, for while its solubility in water (1%) is much lower than is that of members of group 1, it is rapidly hydrolysed and is therefore non-persistent. It is applied as a mist or in the form of resin strips in glasshouses and mushroom houses, but it can also be applied as a water emulsion by means of a watering can. With a vapour pressure of 0·032 mm Hg at 32°C it is about a thousand times more volatile than most other organophosphorus insecticides (e.g., malathion, parathion and diazinon); hence it possesses an appreciable fumigant action not possessed by these other materials (Attfield and Webster, 1966). It is decomposed rapidly by mammals, half of it being excreted as dichlorovinyl phosphate within 12 hours, and within 24 hours no unchanged dichlorvos can be detected in the mammalian body. The complex it forms with cholinesterase in erythrocytes and plasma is not very stable and consequently the cholinesterase activity, especially of the plasma, tends to return to normal levels more quickly than it does after the enzyme has been attacked by most other organophosphorus compounds. This is of importance in relation to the problem of possible harmful effects arising from exposure to successive small doses of the poison.

SUB-GROUP 2

The substances in the second group are soluble in oil but of very limited solubility in water. Parathion (Fig. 5.10), malathion (Fig. 5.7), azinphosmethyl (Fig. 5.8), diazinon (Fig. 5.15), also ethion and mecarbam, are representative of the group. When sprayed on to foliage they penetrate into the wax, and, if applied in sufficient amounts, may diffuse to the lower surfaces of the leaves. This property has practical value for the control of insects on low-growing plants, where direct spraying would be difficult. Low aqueous solubility precludes the possibility of gross translocation,

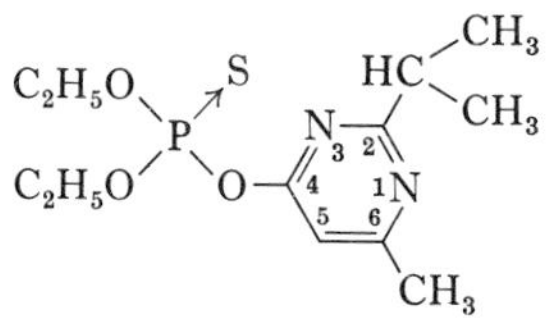

Fig. 5.15. Diazinon: diethyl 2–isopropyl 6–methyl 4-pyrimidinyl phosphorothionate

although radioactive labelling techniques have shown that minute amounts are transported, especially after application through the roots. With this exception, and so long as the compound is not metabolised to more soluble toxic derivatives, movement of the material from the point of application is dependent solely on physical diffusion. Such local penetration has been termed quasi-systemic action, to distinguish it from the truly systemic action characteristic of substances in the third group. In contrast to substances such as TEPP, most, and perhaps all, substances in this second group undergo activation before they reach their site of action in the insect.

Parathion and certain other quasi-systemic compounds are of high toxicity to animals, of limited selectivity to insects and of moderate persistence. Some of the more recently discovered compounds have, however, a remarkably low mammalian toxicity (Table 5.2). Again, some of the first discovered members of this group were sufficiently persistent to occasion a serious residue problem, especially when applied to edible crops too close to the time of harvesting; the more recent introduction of such materials as malathion has dramatically altered this situation. Thus, in view of the relative instability and low mammalian toxicity of malathion, the Ministry of Agriculture, Fisheries and Food (1968) allows its use on edible crops up to one day before harvesting. The corresponding requirement for parathion is four weeks, while azinphos-methyl and diazinon have the intermediate requirements of three weeks and (usually) two weeks, respectively.

The preparation, properties and toxicology of diazinon have been described by Gasser (1953) and by Gysin and Margot (1958). Spiller (1961) has provided an excellent digest of the literature on malathion. The selective toxicities to insects and higher animals of parathion, malathion and their oxygen analogues have been discussed by Metcalf (1964).

SUB-GROUP 3

The third group of organophosphorus compounds comprises the systemic poisons. Many hundreds have been investigated, and about a dozen of them are included in the Ministry of Agriculture, Fisheries and Food (1968) *List of Approved Products*. They are materials which are able to enter the plant through its leaves, though they may sometimes be applied through the roots. By their persistence *within* the plant, they give a degree of protection against a variety of insects for a shorter or longer time after application. They are usually of moderate solubility in oil and of moderate to high solubility in water; the former allows them to penetrate the lipophilic cuticle of plant leaves, while the latter enables them to move about in the aqueous fluid of xylem or phloem once they have gained access to it.

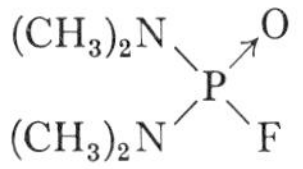

$$
\begin{array}{c}
(CH_3)_2N \\
\qquad\qquad\diagdown \\
\qquad\qquad\qquad P \nearrow^{O} \\
\qquad\qquad\diagup \quad \diagdown F \\
(CH_3)_2N
\end{array}
$$

Fig. 5.16. Dimefox: tetramethylphosphorodiamidic fluoride

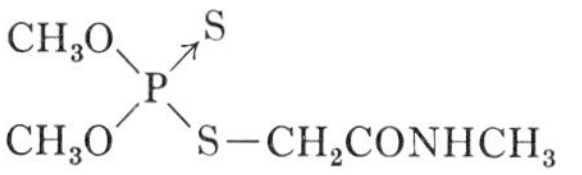

$$
\begin{array}{c}
CH_3O \\
\qquad\diagdown \\
\qquad\qquad P \nearrow^{S} \\
\qquad\diagup \quad \diagdown S-CH_2CONHCH_3 \\
CH_3O
\end{array}
$$

Fig. 5.17. Dimethoate: dimethyl (N–methylcarbamoyl-methyl) phosphorodithioate

$$
\begin{array}{c}
CH_3O \\
\qquad\diagdown \\
\qquad\qquad P \nearrow^{S} \\
\qquad\diagup \quad \diagdown S-CH_2- \\
CH_3O
\end{array}
$$

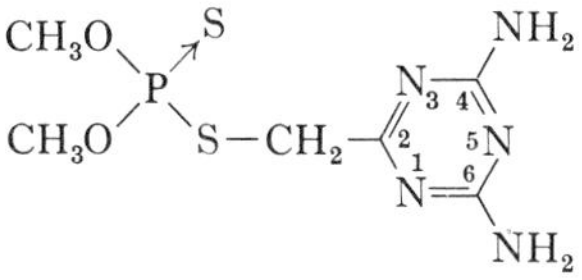

Fig. 5.18. Menazon: dimethyl (diaminotriazin–2–yl methyl) phosphorodithioate

Schradan (Fig. 5.11), dimefox (Fig. 5.16), dimethoate (Fig. 5.17), menazon (Fig. 5.18), demeton ('Systox',* Fig. 5.19), demeton-methyl ('Metasystox'*, Fig. 5.19), phorate (Fig. 5.20) and morphothion are representative members of the group; they clearly show a wide range of both structure and complexity, cutting right across the chemical classification of Table 5.1.

*Trade name.

$$RO \diagdown P \diagup S \qquad RO \diagdown P \diagup S \qquad O$$

Oxidation

Fig. 5.19. Demeton–O and its oxidation product. In demeton (trade name 'Systox') R = ethyl. In demeton–methyl (trade name 'Metasystox') R = methyl

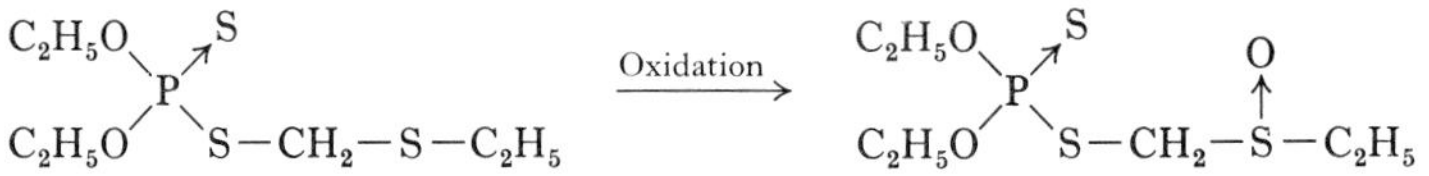

Oxidation

Fig. 5.20. Phorate and its oxidation product

Schradan (Fig. 5.11) and dimefox (Fig. 5.16) were amongst the earliest systemic compounds to be investigated, though, for reasons of safety dimefox is now normally applied so that it enters plants through their roots rather than their leaves. Both compounds are miscible with water, but unlike the water-miscible compounds of the TEPP group, they possess marked chemical stability to hydrolysis. Ripper (1952) reported the half-life at pH 6 of schradan to be about thirty years and of dimefox to be two years, although it must be repeated that such figures do not provide a measure of the time of persistence within a metabolising plant. A practical indication of level of persistence is the time which must elapse, between application and harvesting, to ensure that there should be negligible residue hazard to the consumer. This time is, of course, discovered experimentally during the testing phase of the pesticide, and is provided for each compound in the Ministry publication mentioned above.

Systemic compounds have several important advantages over other types of persistent insecticides. First, they enable substances to persist inside the plant, where they are not susceptible to wash-off by rain. Secondly, translocation away from the point of application increases the availability of the toxicant by distributing it more evenly than would be possible by direct spraying. Moreover, since they often tend to move in the xylem towards the regions of growth, they protect the more vital and more vulnerable tissue near the meristems—tissue which may have been undifferentiated at the actual time of application. Thirdly, some systemic compounds have only a weak contact toxicity, with the result that beneficial organisms in the vicinity at the time of application may not be seriously affected by the poison. This last possibility opens up a new dimension in pest control, for as Carson (1963) so ably illustrated, one of the principal objections to chemical pest control is that indescriminate destruction of the pest and its predators can occasionally result in a worse situation than that existing before spraying. Their limited contact toxicity is due to the fact that the sprayed substance itself is usually only a weak cholinesterase inhibitor, the actual toxicant at the site of action being a more potent inhibitor formed from it by one of the metabolic processes described in a later section.

Schradan and dimefox, in common with other early organophosphorus insecticides, are of high toxicity to vertebrates (Table 5.2), but some of the materials which have been introduced more recently are much less toxic—dimethoate (Fig. 5.17) and menazon (Fig. 5.18) are two examples. Indeed, not only are organophosphorus compounds employed extensively as systemic compounds in plants, but in recent years certain of them have been found suitable for both systemic and superficial application to animals for the control of endo- and ecto-parasites. They have, for example, been employed in veterinary hygiene for the control of grubs of blowfly and warble fly. Hassall (1965) has referred to some of the literature on this subject. Clearly, the mammalian toxicity of organophosphorus compounds of suitable structure can be very low in comparison with the toxicity they show towards insects and to some other invertebrates.

Compounds which are systemic in plants have a wide range of uses against phytophagous insects, but they excel as aphicides and as killers of red spider mites (i.e. as acaricides). Their limited contact action when applied at appropriate concentrations minimises the risk of explosive reproduction of surviving pests in the absence of the predators (the pheno-menon termed 'flare-up'). It also ensures maximal safety to pollinating insects. Menazon (Fig. 5.18) is reported by Price Jones and Edgar (1961) to possess low contact toxicity to predatory and competitive insects but to have the disadvantage of a relatively local systemic action against aphids. It can, however, enter crop plants through their roots, and, by movement in the transpiration stream, render foliage aphicidal. According to Pietri-Tonelli (1965), who has reviewed the chemistry and uses of dimethoate, the systemic effect is most marked when a relatively concentrated solution is applied to a small area of the plant, rather than a dilute solution to a larger surface.

The minimal interval of time to be observed between the last application and harvesting an edible crop is one week for dimethoate and three weeks for menazon. In the case of schradan, the time varies with the season—that is, with the level of metabolic activity of the plants. Dimefox, which is a highly dangerous substance and the only substance which carries a Part 1 schedule in the Regulations of the Ministry of Agriculture, Fisheries and Food (1968), is applied to the soil and in Britain is employed principally for the control of aphids and red spider mites on hops.

It should be observed that while the classification of organophosphorus compounds into three sub-groups is convenient, no perfectly clear cut distinction exists. It has already been seen that mevinphos (group 1) has a transient systemic activity, while menazon (group 3) is of limited systemic action. In addition, many of the substances in group 2 undergo metabolic changes to provide more water-soluble, and therefore somewhat systemic, derivatives. For example, although parathion is of very limited solubility in water, and hence quasi-systemic, its metabolic product, paraoxon, is much more soluble and possesses a far more general systemic activity. Finally, certain organophosphorus compounds are now finding increasing use as granular formulations which are applied to the soil. These formulations naturally present new problems and are considered separately (p. 125).

SELECTIVITY, ACTIVATION AND DEGRADATION

Selectivity of action, whether it is between insects and higher animals or between one insect and another, is dependent upon one or more of three possible selective processes which O'Brien (1962) termed target selectivity, penetration selectivity and metabolic selectivity.

In all probability cholinesterase is the target for the organophosphorus compounds in all insects and higher animals, hence target selectivity is only to be expected where the enzyme surfaces are spatially different (p. 109). Nevertheless, there has been considerable debate as to whether acetylcholinesterase plays exactly the same role in insects as it does in higher animals; in particular, it is possible that, in insects, its function may be usurped by closely related enzymes. Such enzymic differences, should they exist, might again permit some target selectivity. In general, however, it seems that for this group of compounds, a search for this type of selectivity is unlikely to be very profitable. O'Brien (1962) mentions two cases where selectivity could possibly be attributed to some difference at the target level.

It has already been observed that barriers to penetration and movement of poisons differ in different organisms and that this variability may be responsible for selective action. Thus the lipophilic insect cuticle contrasts sharply with the mammalian skin and the difference is an obvious factor influencing the rate of entry of a substance into the two types of organisms (Chapter 3). In addition, the sheath of tissue around the insect nervous system forms a barrier which is relatively impermeable to the entry of ionised or highly polar substances (p. 105).

Metabolic activity can lead to selectivity as a result of one or both of two opposing modifications which can occur after a substance is sprayed. If one type of organism is able to *destroy* a substance more rapidly than is a second type, the first type might well be unaffected by doses of that substance which are lethal to the second. Alternatively, one type of organism may possess an enzyme system capable of changing the sprayed substance into a more toxic derivative (as we have already seen can occur in the case of certain chlorinated cyclodienes) while a second type of organism lacks such an activating system. If so, the organism capable of *activating* the sprayed material would inadvertently bring about its own destruction. It is probable that both activation by the enzyme systems of insects and decomposition accelerated by enzymes in higher animals contribute to the selective action of insecticidal organophosphorus compounds.

TEPP is a strong cholinesterase inhibitor *in vitro* and probably undergoes no (activating) change either in insects or in higher animals prior to reaction with cholinesterase. Spontaneous and also enzymic hydrolysis destroy it rapidly in all organisms. Thus, although hydrolysis accounts for its low persistence, neither selective destruction nor selective activation appears to occur. It is hydrolysed by a group of enzymes capable of attacking the anhydride linkage, as shown in Fig. 5.21.

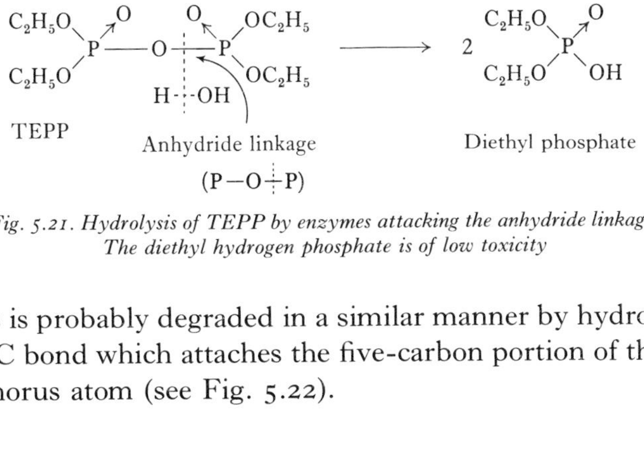

Fig. 5.21. Hydrolysis of TEPP by enzymes attacking the anhydride linkage. The diethyl hydrogen phosphate is of low toxicity

Mevinphos is probably degraded in a similar manner by hydrolytic cleavage of the O-C bond which attaches the five-carbon portion of the molecule to the phosphorus atom (see Fig. 5.22).

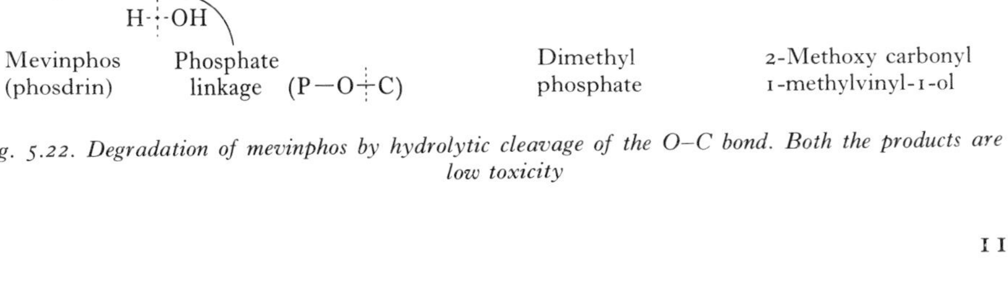

Fig. 5.22. Degradation of mevinphos by hydrolytic cleavage of the O–C bond. Both the products are of low toxicity

Malathion differs from parathion and many other members of the second sub-group in being readily hydrolysed. The enzyme concerned is apparently not an anhydride esterase or a phosphate esterase, for it does not attack phosphorus compounds from which the carboxylic ester linkage is absent. The disruption leads to the formation of a non-toxic and more water-soluble mono-ethyl succinate ester (see Fig. 5.23).

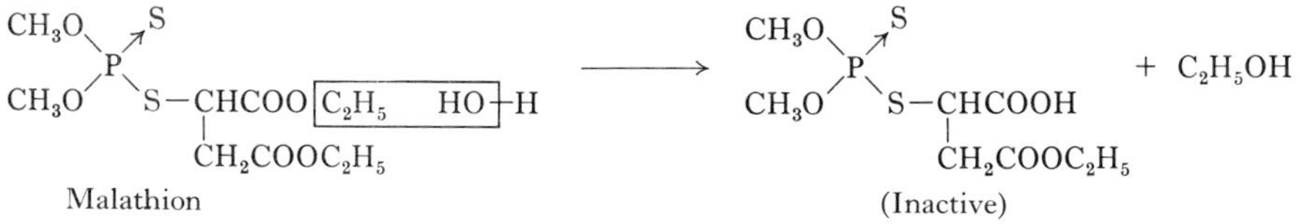

Fig. 5.23. Hydrolysis of malathion

This reaction, together with an oxidative change to be described below (Fig. 5.25) appears to account for the selectivity of malathion, for while the carboxyesterase responsible for the change is distributed widely in mammals, Weidhaus (1959) reported that it is absent from the heads and bodies of house flies. Since it is now known that a few organophosphorus compounds attack carboxyesterases more powerfully than they attack cholinesterase, it was to be anticipated that mixtures of malathion (or any similar cholinesterase inhibitor possessing a labile carboxylic ester linkage) with a carboxyesterase-inhibiting substance, should exhibit a synergistic action. Such an effect has indeed been observed *in vitro,* the synergism between EPN and malathion having been particularly closely studied (Frawley, 1965). This sort of interaction may well explain why malathion, normally so safe to higher animals, may be unsafe to workers previously exposed to such substances as mevinphos, parathion or schradan. Synergism has also been observed between dichlorvos (Fig. 5.14) and mevinphos (Fig. 5.13), though here it would be dangerous to assume that carboxyesterases were involved. It looks rather as though a phosphate-esterase capable of attacking the P-O-C linkage is also sensitive to certain organophosphorus compounds (in this case, dichlorvos), for mevinphos is attacked at the phosphate linkage; and the work of Dauterman and Matsumara (1962), described below, throws doubt upon the ability of carboxyesterases to attack rapidly the carboxymethyl linkage.

Many phosphorothionates, including parathion and malathion (sub-group 2, Table 5.2) undergo enzymic oxidation in insects and mammals. When this occurs, their cholinesterase activity, at first weak, is sometimes greatly enhanced. The reaction involves the substitution of oxygen for sulphur on the dative bond of the molecule. Thus, parathion is oxidised to the more potent and more water-soluble paraoxon, as shown in Fig. 5.24. Reference has already been made to the fact that the phosphate is a more efficient phosphorylator of the enzyme than its thion counterpart. The oxidation responsible for the activation has been studied by the preparation of a system containing liver microsomes and reduced nicotine adenine dinucleotide (NADH), together with several other co-factors

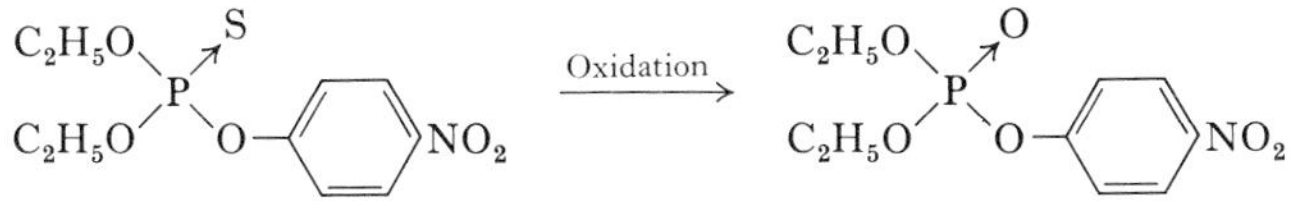

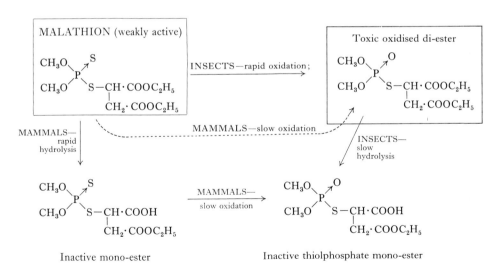

Fig. 5.24. Oxidation of parathion to paraoxon

(O'Brien, 1960, page 134; Heath, 1961, page 170). It is known that insect fat bodies and preparations from insect gut also activate thionates.

Similar activation has been noted for malathion, diazinon (Fig. 5.15) and some half dozen other common insecticidal phosphorothionates; it is apparent that for some of these, such as malathion, both hydrolytic and oxidative systems may play a part in their metabolism. Such metabolism may result in activation or in destruction. It seems likely that the point of balance between the hydrolytic and oxidative actions varies in different organisms and this variability is said to account for the remarkable selectivity of malathion (Fig. 5.25). In mammals, the hydrolytic process which

Fig. 5.25. Malathion: activation and inactivation

leads to inactivation normally occurs quite rapidly, whereas oxidation leading to activation is slow; in insects the opposite is usually the case.

When insects develop resistance to malathion, this is often due to an increase in the quantity or activity of a carboxyesterase operating in the same way as the carboxyesterase present in mammals. It is therefore of considerable interest that Dauterman and Matsumara (1962) observed that, while the higher homologues of malathion had higher LD_{50}s when applied to a malathion-resistant strain of *Culex tarsalis* than when applied to a malathion-sensitive strain, this was not the case when the methyl ester was employed (Table 5.3).

Table 5.3 TOXICITIES OF MALATHION HOMOLOGUES APPLIED TO MALATHION-SENSITIVE AND MALATHION-RESISTANT STRAINS OF *Culex tarsalis*.
FIGURES ARE LD_{50}s IN PARTS PER MILLION

Alkyl group of the carboxyalkyl groups	Susceptible strain	Resistant strain	Ratio
Methyl	0·12	0·13	1·1
Ethyl (malathion)	0·025	1·5	60·0
n-Propyl	0·09	3·1	34·4
iso-Propyl	0·19	0·86	4·5

A probable interpretation of these data is that the carboxyesterase capable of inactivating malathion and its two propyl homologues is unable to attack the carboxymethyl linkage. If this is so, it could be important both in relation to the problem of insect resistance and to the mammalian toxicity of new insecticides containing the carboxymethyl linkage.

Many organophosphorus compounds, both of the phosphate and of the thionate type (which have a P→O and a P→S group respectively) possess a sulphide linkage in the side chain. This sulphide linkage can undergo oxidation to the sulphoxide and sulphone both chemically and by enzymic action. In the latter case, the system effecting the oxidation is similar to, or identical with, that which oxidises thionates to phosphates. Moreover, oxidation of sulphide to sulphoxide, which occurs, for example, in demeton-O and phorate, often takes place more rapidly than the oxidation of thionate to phosphate. For this reason, many workers consider that the activation of demeton and phorate occurs in the manner illustrated in Figs. 5.26 and 5.27.

When oxidation occurs, however, it does not necessarily lead to activation. A minor difference in stability may determine whether an oxidation product is a potent phosphorylator of the enzyme or whether it is largely destroyed

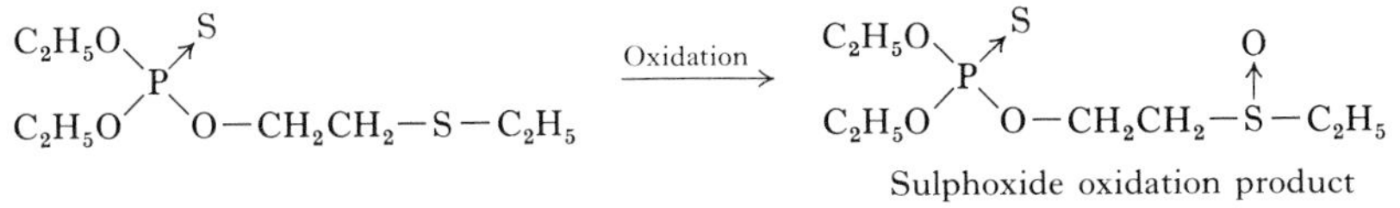

C₂H₅O   S   C₂H₅O   S   O
    ＼   ↗   ＼   ↗   ↑
     P   ──Oxidation──→   P   S
    ╱   ＼   ╱   ＼
C₂H₅O   O—CH₂CH₂—S—C₂H₅   C₂H₅O   O—CH₂CH₂—S—C₂H₅

Sulphoxide oxidation product

Fig. 5.26. Activation of demeton-O (the thion isomer)

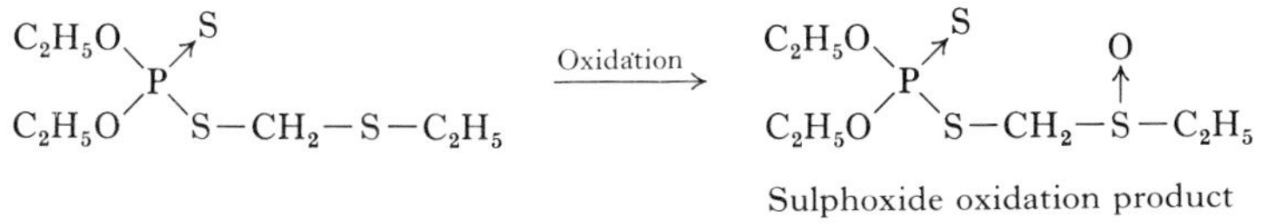

C₂H₅O   S   C₂H₅O   S   O
    ＼   ↗   ＼   ↗   ↑
     P   ──Oxidation──→   P   S
    ╱   ＼   ╱   ＼
C₂H₅O   S—CH₂—S—C₂H₅   C₂H₅O   S—CH₂—S—C₂H₅

Sulphoxide oxidation product

Fig. 5.27. Activation of phorate

before it reaches the surface of the enzyme. In the first case, the oxidation could lead to the sprayed substance becoming activated in the manner described above, whereas in the second case, the same type of biological oxidation would result in loss of toxic action completely. The thiol sulphur of amiton (Fig. 5.12), for example, is rapidly oxidised, but the sulphoxide-like compound so formed is almost immediately hydrolysed (Scaife and Campbell, 1959). Again, a supplemented microsomal preparation from mammalian liver can effect the oxidation.

A second example illustrating how the bounds of instability can be overstepped is provided by the three compounds depicted in Fig. 5.28.

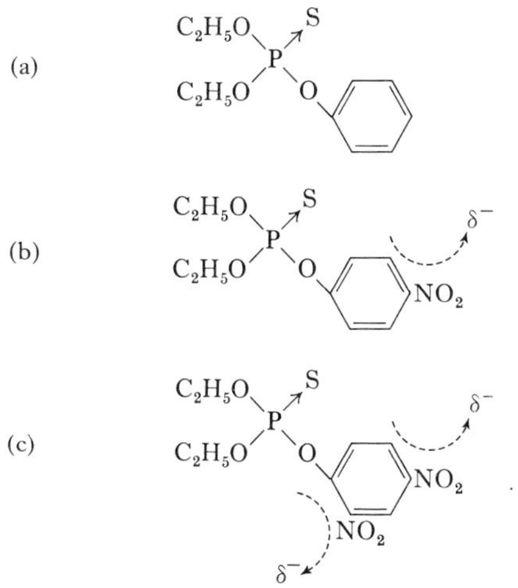

(a)

(b)

(c)

Fig. 5.28. Diagram to show that ease of oxidation, and possibility of activation or destruction, varies with molecular structure:
(a) Un-nitrated derivative of parathion: not easily hydrolysed, not easily oxidised;
(b) Parathion: not easily hydrolysed, easily oxidised, then hydrolyses near enzyme surface;
(c) Dinitro derivative of parathion: the electron-attracting substituents so weaken the molecule that oxidation and/or hydrolysis occurs before the enzyme is reached

(The author is indebted to Dr. R. Galley of Shell Chemicals Ltd. for bringing it to his attention). The un-nitrated substance (a) is moderately stable to oxidation. The introduction of one electron-attracting nitro-group into the phenyl ring of phenyl diethyl thionphosphate increases instability both by weakening the attachment of the sulphur atom and by weakening the ester linkage between the phosphorus atom and the phenyl ring. In consequence, oxidation to paraoxon proceeds readily, but hydrolysis of the paraoxon so formed still occurs sufficiently slowly to enable the majority of the molecules to reach the surface of cholinesterase. On introduction of a second nitro-group, however, the fact that oxidation may occur even more readily is immaterial, for the ester linkage is now so weak that hydrolysis inactivates the molecule before it reaches the vicinity of the enzyme.

The dimethyl phosphoramides are oxidised by enzyme systems similar to those which oxidise thionates to phosphates and sulphides to sulphoxides. A reduced nucleotide, probably NADPH, and other co-factors must be added to microsomal preparations to produce a system similar to that needed to bring about the *in vitro* oxidation of certain organochlorine compounds. Dimefox and schradan are the best known insecticidal phosphoramides; both are systemic (sub-group 3, Table 5.2) and both are oxidised to materials possessing high anti-cholinesterase activity. In higher animals, the oxidation of schradan may only take place in the liver, but in insects it can occur in many tissues (Casida, 1956). Oxidation products of tetramethyl phosphoramidic compounds of many sorts, including schradan, have been found to be very unstable, having at most half-lives of a few hours. Comparative studies have shown that ethyl analogues of the commercial phosphoramides are oxidised far less rapidly, if they are oxidised at all.

The precise nature of the activated oxidation product of schradan *in vivo* is uncertain, but it is the same compound that is formed by chemical oxidation (for references, see O'Brien, 1960, page 136). The activated form of schradan is likely to be either the amine oxide or the hydroxymethyl derivative (Fig. 5.29). Experimental evidence now seems to favour the second of

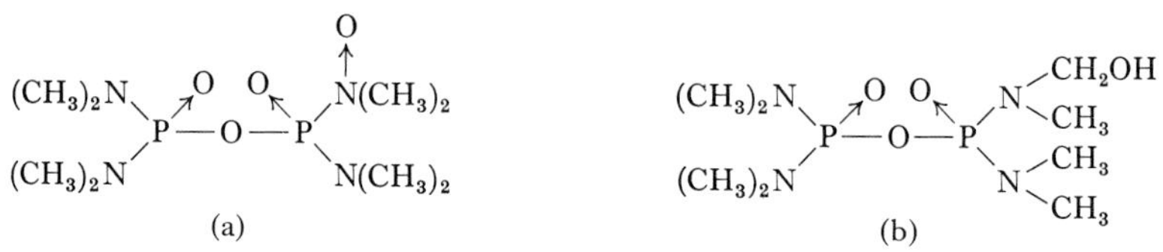

Fig. 5.29. Possible oxidation products of schradan:
(a) The amine oxide; (b) The hydroxymethyl derivative

these, although the latter may rapidly isomerise *in vivo* to a less active N-methoxide ($-N-O-CH_3$). The corresponding metabolite of dimefox (Fig. 5.16) does not appear to have been isolated, and may be very unstable. Arthur and Casida (1958) consider that, as in the case of schradan, the oxidation product is the active cholinesterase inhibitor, and is probably either the hydroxymethyl derivative or the amine oxide.

GRANULATED FORMULATIONS OF PESTICIDES

A relatively new method of formulation of pesticides—the use of granules —is becoming increasingly important for the application of certain organophosphorus insecticides to the soil. The method is applicable to many types of pesticides, but since most of the granular formulations mentioned in the 1968 brochure of the Ministry of Agriculture, Fisheries and Food, *Agricultural Chemicals Approval Scheme—List of Approved Products* are, in fact, organophosphorus compounds, a brief discussion of the factors governing the use of granules is appropriate at this point.

A major advantage of granular products, as was seen earlier (p. 30) is that the pesticide can be placed in such a manner that it gives maximal protection to crop plants with minimal danger of large scale soil pollution. This is of particular importance when the chemical is highly toxic, for while beneficial insects and earthworms in the neighbourhood of the granules may be killed, the soil population is not decimated in the way it would be if powders or suspensions were distributed uniformly. Other advantages are that the rate of release of the pesticide can be controlled; pesticides somewhat unstable in soil can sometimes be 'protected' within the granule; and particles can by-pass foliage and so reach the soil under conditions which would result in wastage if dusts or suspensions were used.

Since many pesticides are strongly adsorbed in soil, it is not always essential to control the release of pesticide from granules. The degree of control which is required will depend upon such factors as the extent of adsorption on soil particles, the rate at which the poison decomposes once it reaches the soil, and the rate of leaching from the soil. The rate at which the pesticide escapes from granular formulations is largely determined by the extent of leaching by rainwater, and leaching is in turn influenced not only by the duration and intensity of rain, but by temperature, by dosage, and by the size, composition and formulation of the granules. It should be added that organophosphorus compounds used in granules are usually of low aqueous solubility.

The theory of granule leaching has been discussed by Furmidge *et al*

(1966, 1967), who consider that the amount of pesticide leached per unit area of land is expressed approximately by the equation:

$$\text{Amount leached per unit area} \propto R\alpha/Dp\rho$$

where R is the volume of rain per unit area, α is the amount of toxicant applied per unit area, D is the diameter of the granules, p is the percentage of toxicant in the formulation and ρ is the density of the granules.

By reference to the equation above, Furmidge, Hill and Osgerby conclude that the quantity of toxicant released from a granular formulation by the action of a given volume of rain water should be proportional to the weight of toxicant per unit area of land, all other factors being kept constant. On the other hand, if dose per acre is kept constant, the release will vary inversely with the percentage of toxicant in the formulation. Similarly, the equation predicts that the rate of release of poison will fall as the size of the granules increases. Experimental evidence to justify the use of the equation is presented by the same authors.

At least four organophosphorus compounds are currently formulated as granules for use in soil treatment. Chlorfenvinphos (Fig. 5.30) is used

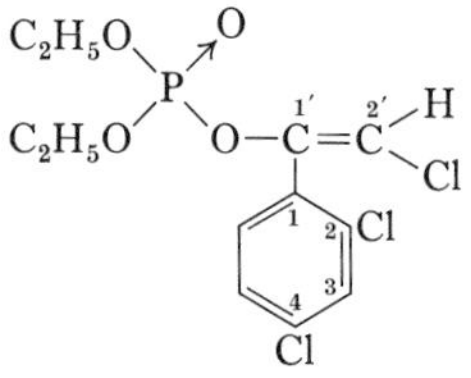

Fig. 5.30. Chlorfenvinphos : 2'–chloro 1–(2,4–dichloro–phenyl) vinyl diethyl phosphate

on brassicas, carrots and sweet corn for the control of cabbage root fly, carrot fly and frit fly respectively, the formulation being called Birlane Granules. Diazinon (Fig. 5.15), in addition to being used in sprays and drenches, is marketed as granules for the control of cabbage root fly and carrot fly. Phorate (Fig. 5.20) and disulfoton are often employed for similar purposes, but are also used to control aphids and, indirectly, aphid-borne virus diseases. They are also sometimes of value to potato growers to diminish damage caused by wireworms.

REFERENCES

ARTHUR, B. W. and CASIDA, J. E. (1958), *J. econ. Ent.*, **51**, 49
ATTFIELD, J. G. and WEBSTER, D. A. (1966), *Chemy. Ind.*, February 12, p. 272
CARSON, R. (1963), *Silent Spring*, Hamish Hamilton and Co., London

CASIDA, J. E. (1956), *J. agric. Fd Chem.,* **4,** 772

CHANG, S. C. and KEARNS, C. W. (1955), *3rd A. Meeting Ent. Soc. Am.* (Cincinnati, Ohio, Nov., 1955)

DAUTERMAN, W. C. and MATSUMARA, F. (1962), *Science,* **138,** 694

EDSON, E. F., SANDERSON, D. M. and NOAKES, D. N. (1966), *Wld Rev. Pest Control,* **5,** 143

FRAWLEY, J. P. (1965), *Research in Pesticides.* (Ed. Chichester, C. O.) Academic Press, London (p. 69)

FURMIDGE, C. G. L., HILL, A. C. and OSGERBY, J. M. (1966), *J. Sci. Fd Agric.,* **17,** 518

FURMIDGE, C. G. L. and OSGERBY, J. M. (1967), *J. Sci. Fd Agric.,* **18,** 269

GASSER, R. (1953), *Z. Naturf.,* **8(B),** 225

GYSIN, H. and MARGOT, A. (1958), *J. agric. Fd Chem.,* **6,** 900

HARTLEY, G. S. (1951), An address to the 15*th Internatn. Chem. Congr.,* New York, 11th Sept. 1951

HASSALL, K. A. (1965), *Brit. Vet. J.,* **121,** 199

HEATH, D. F. (1961), *Organophosphorus compounds,* Pergamon Press, Oxford

HOPF, H. S. and TAYLOR, R. T. (1958), *Nature, Lond.,* **182,** 1381

Insecticide and Fungicide Handbook for Crop Protection, (1963) (Ed. Martin, H.) Blackwell Publications, Oxford

MARGOT, A. and GYSIN, H. (1957), *Helv. chim. Acta,* **40,** 1562

METCALF, R. L. (1964), *Wld Rev. Pest Control,* **3,** (1), 28

Ministry of Agriculture, Fisheries and Food (1968), *Agricultural Chemicals Approval Scheme—List of Approved Products,* (A yearly publication)

Ministry of Agriculture, Fisheries and Food, loose leaf dossier. (For further details of this publication, see p. 22)

MITCHELL, J. W., SMALE, B. C. and METCALF, R. L. (1960), *Adv. Pest Control Res.,* **3,** 359

NEGHERBON, W. O. (Ed.) (1959), *Handbook of Toxicology, Volume* 3, *Insecticides,* W. B. Saunders Co., Philadelphia

O'BRIEN, R. D. (1960), *Toxic Phosphorus Esters,* Academic Press, London

O'BRIEN, R. D. (1962), *Wld Rev. Pest Control,* **1,** (1), 29

O'BRIEN, R. D. (1963), *J. agric. Fd Chem.,* **11,** 163

PIETRI-TONELLI, P. (1965), *Adv. Pest Control Res.,* **6,** 31

PRICE JONES, D. and EDGAR, E. C. (1961), *Outl. Agric.,* **3,** 123

RIPPER, W. E. (1952), 'Systemic Insecticides', *3rd Internatn. Congr. on Crop Protection,* September 17th, 1952, at the Sorbonne, Paris

SCAIFE, J. F. and CAMPBELL, D. H. (1959), *Can. J. Biochem. Physiol.,* **37,** 297

SHERLOCK, E. (1962), *Chemy. Ind.,* p. 715

SPILLER, D. (1961), *Adv. Pest Control Res.,* **4,** 249

WEIDHAUS, D. E. (1959), *J. Ass. off. agric. Chem.,* **42,** 445

6

OTHER INSECTICIDES AND RELATED COMPOUNDS

The organochlorine and organophosphorus compounds together account for a large percentage of the total tonnage of agricultural insecticides, but numerous other types of insecticides are employed on a smaller scale for specialist purposes. This chapter will describe a few of these other materials and also some closely related poisons which are used to control spider mites.

PLANT-DERIVED INSECTICIDES

Several thousand plants, in many plant families, contain toxic compounds. After elimination of those compounds which cannot be extracted profitably, and those which are not selectively toxic to insects, relatively few remain but, of these, some have proved valuable as insecticides. Certain writers who doubt the wisdom of using man-made insecticides on edible crops have raised few objections to the use of these 'natural' materials. In particular, plant-derived materials do not appear to induce the development of insect resistance so readily as do some, at least, of the synthetic materials.

NICOTINE

Nicotine (Fig. 6.1) and related materials occur in certain members of the Solanaceae, especially in various species of the genus *Nicotiana*. An isomeric substance possessing similar chemical and physiological properties occurs in *Anabasis aphylla*, a member of the Chenopodiaceae. It is called anabasine or neonicotine (Fig. 6.2) and is extracted commercially from *Anabasis* in the Soviet Union (West and Hardy, 1961). Nicotine is usually extracted from the leaves and roots of the tobacco plant, *Nicotiana tabacum*, by steam distillation. Its concentration in tobacco leaves may reach 2–5%. Natural nicotine is the laevo (−)isomer (the carbon atom in position 2 of the pyrrolidine ring being asymmetric). Nicotine itself was synthesised as early as 1904, and since then many nicotine-like substances have been prepared and screened for insecticidal activity. Racemic nicotine prepared synthetically is only about half as toxic as the natural material because the laevo isomer is much more insecticidal than its dextro counterpart. More recently, Kamimura *et al.* (1963) studied a series of 3-pyridyl methylamine derivatives and found that N-substituted materials with suitable basic properties, when tested against flies, had toxicities comparable to that of nicotine. This is of interest in view of Sexton's (1963) suggestion that, since the 1:2 bond of the pyrrolidine ring is labile *in vitro,* it is possible that a metabolic change could result in the formation of a substituted aliphatic amine. Yamamoto (1965), however, has provided evidence which throws

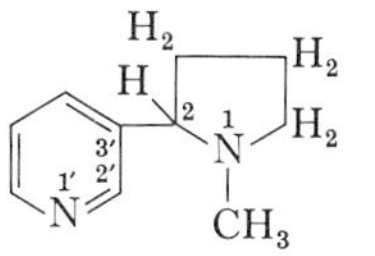

Fig. 6.1. Nicotine : (−) − 1–methyl–2 (3′–pyridyl) pyrrolidine

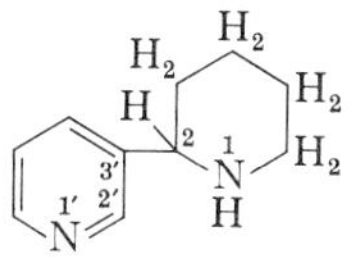

Fig. 6.2. Anabasine or neonicotine : (−) − 2–(3′–pyridyl) piperidine

some doubt on Sexton's suggestion. The possible biological significance of the absolute configuration of laevo-nicotine has been discussed by Barlow (1960).

Nicotine is a colourless and almost odourless liquid when pure, but it rapidly turns brown on ageing, especially in the presence of air, oxidising agents, light or traces of unsaturated materials. It should thus be stored in the dark and should not be used in conjunction with unsaturated detergents. Nicotine boils at 247°C and has a vapour pressure of about 0·04 mm at 25°C. It is miscible with water and is a weak base ($K_b = 10^{-6}$) which forms salts with both mineral and organic acids. The free base has been employed as a contact spray; it is probable that the vapour pressure, though low, is essential to its toxic action, for the principal method of entry into the insect appears to be as a vapour *via* the spiracles and trachea. By this means it gains ready access to the central nervous system. However, there is some evidence that it may be able to enter through the cuticle or by splashing into the insect's mouth, and in these cases the speed with which it acts appears to depend upon the proportion of undissociated molecules present—and the latter, in turn, depends on the way it is formulated.

Salts of nicotine, both soluble and insoluble, have been employed as insecticides. Soluble salts, because of their higher ionisation and lower vapour pressure, have difficulty in penetrating to their site of action, and therefore act more slowly than the free base, but they usually persist longer. Insoluble salts, such as the tannate, have been used as persistent (stomach) poisons, for they are resistant to wash-off by rain but are rendered soluble on ingestion by insects.

In all cases, the ultimate action is to block synapses or ganglia associated with motor nerves. Symptoms include stupefaction followed by a progressive motor paralysis, commencing at the rear and extending towards the brain. No adequate biochemical basis for these physiological symptoms has as yet been found, though there is some evidence that the active form is the nicotinium cation and that this ion bears a spatial resemblance to acetylcholine (Yamamoto, 1965). Nicotine induces the production of amplified and repetitive discharges in isolated nerve cords in a manner reminiscent of the effect of DDT (p. 71) but, unlike the latter substance, its distribution between oil and water is almost 1 : 1 at pH 7. It thus seems difficult to attribute its action to a *selective* absorption in the lipids of the nerve cells. Unexplained synergistic effects have been noted between nicotine and pyrethrin and between nicotine and potassium ions.

An official spectrophotometric method for the determination of nicotine has been described by Martin and Schwartzman (1964).

PYRETHROIDS

A second group of plant-derived insecticides comprises the pyrethroids, a set of at least six closely related compounds which occur to the extent of some 1–2% in the dried inflorescences of certain species of *Chrysanthemum*. The species *C. cinerariaefolium* is grown commercially in Kenya on account of the pyrethroid content of the achenes. The world production of pyrethroids, which was temporarily checked with the advent of the synthetic insecticides, has recently started to increase again and in 1961 some 10,700 tons of dried flowers were produced in Kenya alone (Kroll, 1964). This represents about two-thirds of the total world supply, the remainder being grown in Tanzania, Ecuador and New Guinea. Head (1963) and Kroll (1964) have described the cultivation and collection of the 'pyrethrum' flowers and the processing of the inflorescences.

Nowadays, the active principles are extracted from the dried inflorescences by treating them with kerosene or ethylene dichloride. The pyrethroids dissolve and the extract is concentrated by vacuum distillation. The four principal active substances present in the extract are all liquids of high boiling point, known respectively as pyrethrins I and II (Fig. 6.3) and cinerins I and II (Fig. 6.4). Jasmolins I and II also occur; they are very

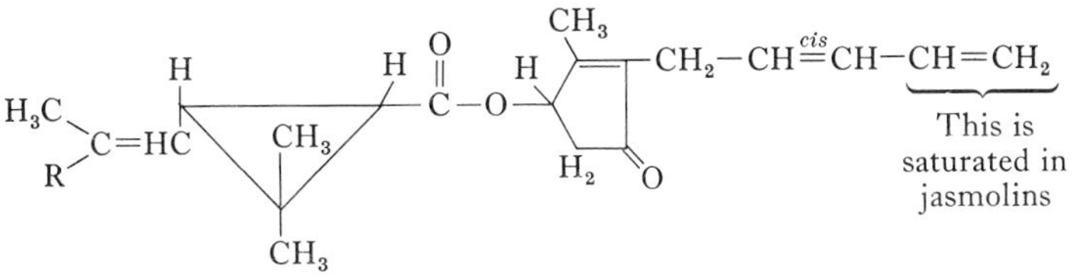

Fig. 6.3. The pyrethrins : in pyrethrin I, R = CH_3,
in pyrethrin II, R = $COOCH_3$

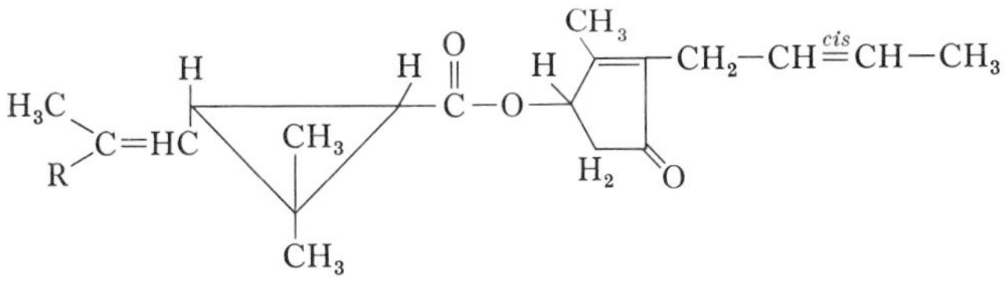

Fig. 6.4. The cinerins : in cinerin I, R = CH_3
in cinerin II, R = $COOCH_3$

similar to the pyrethrins except that the terminal $-CH = CH_2$ of the unsaturated side chain on the five-carbon ring is saturated ($-CH_2-CH_3$).

Pyrethrins, cinerins and jasmolins are all complex esters, consisting of one of two closely related acids united with one of three closely related alcohols. In the compounds designated by I, the acid is called chrysanthemic acid while in those designated by II the acid is called pyrethric acid. The difference between them is indicated in formulae given in Figs. 6.3 and 6.4. The three alcohols are termed pyrethrolone, cinerolone and jasmololone and the alcohol present determines the name of the ester. This is shown in Table 6.1, which also gives the approximate percentage of each of the six esters in a typical pyrethrum extract (Elliott, 1967).

Matsui and Meguro (1964) have reported investigations into the structure, isomerism and insecticidal action of the pyrethroids. Briefly, the acid component is theoretically capable of existing in *cis* and *trans* forms, and each of these as optical enantiomorphs (+ or −). The naturally occurring acid is the (+)-trans form and gives rise to esters which are more toxic than those formed from the other three stereo-isomers. Similarly, each of the alcohols can be made as a *cis* and *trans* form, each as an optical enantio-morph, but only the cis-(+) isomer occurs naturally. This geometrical

Table 6.1 COMPOSITION OF A TYPICAL PYRETHRUM EXTRACT

Alcohol	Acid	
	Chrysanthemic	Pyrethric
Pyrethrolone	Pyrethrin I (35%)	Pyrethrin II (32%)
Cinerolone	Cinerin I (10%)	Cinerin II (14%)
Jasmololone	Jasmolin I (5%)	Jasmolin II (4%)

isomerism occurs at the double bond marked in the formulae (Figs. 6.3 and 6.4), the asymmetric carbon atom being the one carrying the hydroxyl group when the alcohol is uncombined. None of the acids or alcohols is insecticidal until combined to form one of the esters.

All the natural pyrethroids have high insecticidal activity, possessing a remarkable 'knock-down' effect on flying insects. Under laboratory conditions it is possible to obtain resistant strains of organisms (Parkin and Lloyd, 1960; Fine, 1963) but there are very few reports of the development of serious resistance in the field. The 'knock-down' action, though rapid, is not necessarily fatal, and it is customary to include a slower acting but more certain killer, such as DDT, in many types of pyrethroid sprays and dusts. An advisory leaflet issued by the Murphy Chemical Company points out that pyrethroids often cause an initial burst of activity on the part of the insect and that this may lead to the insect picking up a lethal dose of the second poison. This is the principle underlying the use of pyrethroid-DDT mixtures in cockroach powders.

The pyrethroids have several major advantages when compared with organochlorine and some organophosphorus insecticides. They are, for instance, of very low toxicity to higher animals unless they are injected. Moreover, they are not persistent and so leave no harmful residues; perhaps for the same reason, they do not induce the rapid development of insect resistance. On the other hand, lack of persistence is a two-edged sword in crop protection, and the agricultural use of pyrethroids is almost exclusively as contact poisons. For the control of pests in stored food, however, their use is often preferable to that of, say, organochlorine insecticides, since in this circumstance pesticide persistence is undesirable and potentially harmful. They are also used for the control of household or industrial pests

—the careless and the foolish cannot harm themselves or others so readily with pyrethroids as they can with organochlorine compounds of high persistence or organophosphorus compounds of high acute toxicity.

Hydrolysis of the ester linkage, or minor variations in the structure of the very vulnerable side chains, results in the inactivation of pyrethroids. One or both of these changes occur quite readily within the gut and probably account for the fact that pyrethroids are of lower toxicity when given orally than when application is topical or by injection. For example, the LD_{50} when a pyrethroid is eaten by the American cockroach is over three times the LD_{50} for either of the other two routes of application (Negherbon, 1959, p. 641). Similarly, Warner (1963) considered that the use of pyrethroids on plants was limited by their instability to light and air. It is of interest that Glynne Jones (1960) observed that if chlorophyll is present in a crude pyrethroid extract, it is able to catalyse rapid photolysis of the active ingredients. Instability of pyrethroids to light can to some extent be decreased by protecting them in heavy oil sprays.

In view of this instability in the external environment (which includes the insect or mammalian gut)—an instability associated with double bonds and the ester linkage—it is of interest that some recent evidence (Casida and Yamamoto, 1967) suggests that degradation of pyrethroids which have gained access to the tissues is by a quite different pathway. The enzymes responsible for detoxication appear to be located in the microsomes and to be of the type often referred to as 'mixed function oxidases' or processing enzymes. The degradation of pyrethroids can thus be compared with the metabolism of appropriate organochlorine and organophosphorus compounds. According to the Berkeley workers mentioned above, oxidation occurs without initial hydrolysis. The major oxidation product of pyrethrin I,

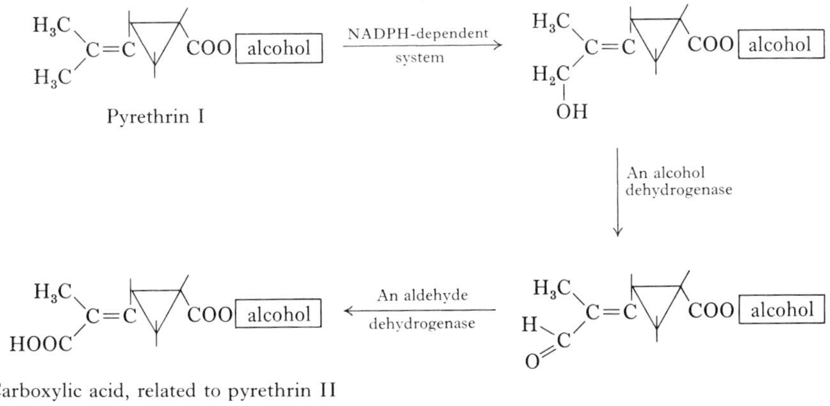

Fig. 6.5. *Microsomal oxidation of pyrethrin I*

using both liver homogenates and house fly abdomen homogenates, is the hydroxymethyl derivative of the chrysanthemic acid moiety depicted in Fig. 6.5. This primary oxidation product is formed in the presence of enzyme systems which are NADPH-dependent; being a primary alcohol, it is further oxidised enzymically *via* an aldehyde to a carboxylic acid. Since pyrethrin II is the methyl ester of the carboxylic acid so formed, it is possible that the biosynthesis of pyrethrin II from pyrethrin I in the 'pyrethrum' plant proceeds by this same route, followed by methylation of the product.

The rate of entry of pyrethroids into insects is correlated with the type of solvent in which they are dissolved, a longer time elapsing before the onset of toxic symptoms when the solvent is oily and of high boiling point. Wigglesworth (1942) explained these observations by suggesting that the pyrethroids gain access to the nervous system of the insect *via* the pore canals (p. 52). Chadwick (1963) concluded from their rapid action that response must occur after they have penetrated no more than a micron below the surface of the cuticle, a suggestion which implies that they need only to penetrate the thickness of the epicuticle.

Very little is known about how pyrethroids produce their toxic effect, although an obvious but incomplete conclusion is that the 'knock-down' must be occasioned by some sort of neurotoxic action. When applied to an isolated nerve, an amplified discharge takes place, followed by repeated trains of discharges which become progressively weaker. For a while the toxic effects can be reversed by washing the nerve free from pyrethroid, so it is possible that the toxic action does not demand a strong chemical attachment between the poison and its substrate. Alternatively, however, the pyrethroid might induce the release of a toxicant into the

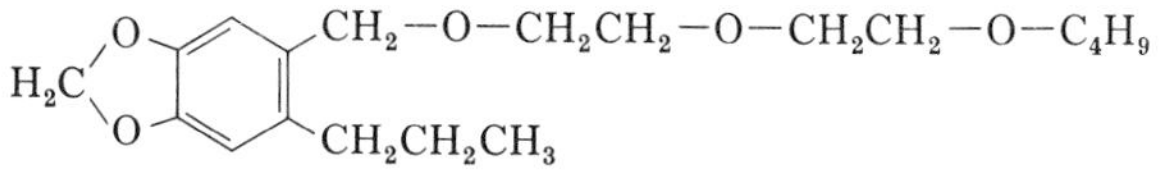

$$H_2C \underset{O}{\overset{O}{<}} \underbrace{}_{\begin{array}{l} CH_2-O-CH_2CH_2-O-CH_2CH_2-O-C_4H_9 \\ CH_2CH_2CH_3 \end{array}}$$

Fig. 6.6. Piperonyl butoxide

blood; one such possibility is that acetycholine may escape from the neuromuscular junctions (Winteringham and Lewis, 1959).

The pyrethroids are probably the most expensive of common insecticides (Chadwick, 1963) but fortunately substances are known which increase their toxicity when they are applied simultaneously. For example, one part of pyrethroid with two parts of piperonyl butoxide (Fig. 6.6.) produces a mixture which is as toxic as seven parts of the pyrethroid used alone. The synergised mixture has a lower 'knock-down' effect than the unsynergised material, but is somewhat more stable (Warner, 1963). Many other synergists have been studied (Chadwick, 1963; Incho and Odeneal, 1963), but few are as effective as piperonyl butoxide. On the other hand, many of them are cheaper to make, and in some cases reduced cost may offset their lower efficiency. The mechanism of action of pyrethroid synergists, like that of substances synergising the action of certain organochlorine and carbamate insecticides (pp. 96, 141) probably involves the inhibition of enzymes which would otherwise destroy the pyrethroid. The first step in the oxidative sequence shown in Fig. 6.5 would be the step most likely to be vulnerable to inhibition by synergists.

Once the structure and stereochemistry of the acids and alcohols which unite to give the natural pyrethroids had been elucidated, the way was open for the synthesis of related compounds of similar configuration. Early synthetic pyrethroids included the allethrins, which are as toxic to the housefly as are natural pyrethroids. Unfortunately, they are expensive to manufacture, have a weaker knock-down effect than have natural pyrethroids and do not respond dramatically to the presence of substances which are synergists for the natural pyrethroids. Barthel (1961, 1967) and Matsui and Meguro (1964) have reviewed the chemistry and toxic potential of these synthetic compounds.

Synthetic chrysanthemic acid is a racemic mixture of the (+) and (−) enantiomorphs of both *cis* and *trans* forms of the acid, but the separation of the (+)-trans form would be so costly that esters with synthetic alcohols are made without removing the three unwanted forms of the chrysanthemic acid. The first synthetic alcohol employed was allethrolone (Fig. 6.7a) and the synthetic esters were the allethrins mentioned above. Clearly, the allethrolone is an alcohol of the same order of complexity as cinerolone. In 1964, however, Japanese workers found that a fairly well known compound, N-hydroxymethyl tetrahydrophthalimide (Fig. 6.7b), could be

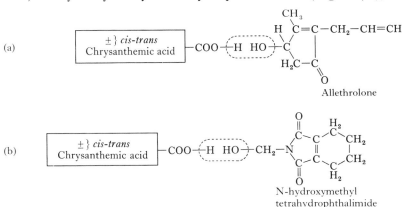

Fig. 6.7. (a) Allethrin; (b) Neopynamin; (partial formulae to show construction)

joined to the synthetic chrysanthemic acid to form an insecticidal chry-santhemate. It is of interest (whether or not it is coincidental), that a closely related phthalimide derivative is the active ingredient of the fungicide, captan (p. 179). The chrysanthemate has been marketed as Neopynamin (Fig. 6.7b), and is almost as effective against house flies as are the natural pyrethroids. Workers at Rothamsted Experimental Station have since dis-covered several other insecticidal chrysanthemates, prepared from alcohols containing the benzene (six-membered) ring instead of the natural cyclo-pentenolone (five-membered) ring. The most toxic compound of all synthesised by these workers, containing both a six- and a five-membered ring, is 5-benzyl-3-furylmethyl (+)-trans-chrysanthemate; this is over fifty times as toxic to house flies as are the natural pyrethrins. Perhaps the most significant aspect of this success is that the synthesis was based not so much upon the idea of closely copying the *chemical structure* of the natural pyrethrin I (although this also was taken into consideration) as it was upon copying the *molecular geometry* of the natural material. This point has been elegantly illustrated by Elliott (1967) by the diagrammatic superimposition of pyrethrin I and the synthetic chrysanthemate (see Fig. 6.8).

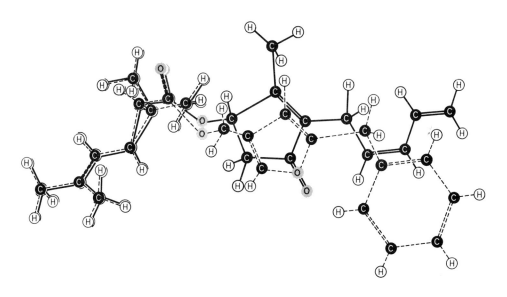

Fig. 6.8. Superimposition of pyrethrin I and a recently synthesised chrysanthemate of higher toxicity to flies than the natural material (Courtesy M. Elliott and SCIENCE JOURNAL, London). Continuous lines, pyrethrin I; dotted lines, synthetic chrysanthemate

Chromatographic techniques have been used to detect and estimate the pyrethroids. Smith (1960), for example, has described the preparation of the dinitrophenyl hydrazones of cinerins I and II and the chromatographic separation of these compounds.

ROTENOIDS

Rotenoids are insecticides present in the roots of certain genera of the *Leguminosae*. Species of *Derris* occur in several countries in the Far East and species of *Lonchocarpus* are native to South America. Long before their insecticidal properties were exploited, they were employed in tropical regions by local fishermen, who had discovered that macerated plants added to water paralysed the fish so that they floated to the surface. According to Gunther and Jeppson (1960) some 10 million lb of dried roots were imported into the United States in the peak year of 1946 but the figure had declined to about 6 million lb by 1955. About 90% of all United States imports of the root now originate from the South American plants.

The active principles can be extracted from the dried and ground roots by organic solvents or, for the preparation of 'derris dust', the ground roots are mixed with a clay diluent. In common with many other substances which are insoluble in water but soluble in oil, the rotenoids are usually sprayed after being dissolved in petroleum. The petroleum solution can be used as a homogeneous spray or, more often, it is first emulsified with water. Sometimes acetone or butyl phthalate is used as a co-solvent. In addition to these extracts of roots, Irvine and Freyre (1959) have suggested that the leaves of a species of *Tephrosia (T. Vogelii)* may be a suitable commercial source of rotenoids. The formulae of the three main

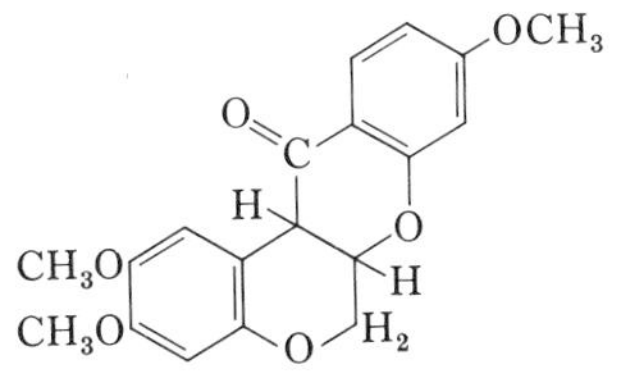

Fig. 6.9. Munduserone (the simplest rotenoid?)

members of the group—rotenone, deguelin and elliptone—are all complex and chemically very similar. The simplest of the rotenoids is possibly munduserone (Fig. 6.9). Its structure is regarded by Sexton (1963) as being close to the basic requirement for insecticidal activity in this group. The rotenoids were reviewed by Holman (1940) and their empirical formulae, structures and properties have been summarised in a publication by the United Nations Food and Agriculture Organisation (Anon, 1962). The reader is referred to one or other of these accounts for further chemical details.

In view of the complexity of their structure, it is not surprising that little is known about the mode of action of rotenoids, except that death follows after a period of paralysis. They probably interfere with oxidation, for they have been observed to affect glutamic acid dehydrogenase and succinoxidase (Roan and Hopkins, 1961). On the other hand, it remains uncertain whether the inhibition of these particular enzymes is the primary cause of toxicity when members of the group are used *in vivo*.

Derris is used primarily by horticulturists for the control of caterpillars, certain sawflies, wasps and the raspberry beetle. It may be sprinkled on the ground around the plants, or—for the control of aphids and red spider as well—it may be applied as a spray. A wettable powder is also marketed for earthworm control. In contrast to its high toxicity to most insects, derris is almost harmless to warm blooded animals unless it is injected (Table 3.1 p. 60). It is both of importance and of interest, however, that derris, in common with organochlorine and some other pesticides, is highly toxic to fish. Speaking very generally, it would seem that rotenone divides warm blooded creatures from many cold blooded ones, rather than Vertebrates from Invertebrates.

RYANODINE

Ryanodine and related alkaloids are present in the stems and roots of *Ryania speciosa,* a tree which is a member of the tropical family *Flacourtia-ceae* of the order *Bixales.* The rock-roses (family *Cystaceae*) are distantly related to it. The stems are ground up and used as an insecticide which is effective both as a contact and as a stomach poison. It has found special use against fruit tree pests in Canada. The *Lepidoptera* are particularly susceptible to it and codlin moth has been controlled successfully, with no serious effect upon the population of parasites and predators (Pickett, 1962).

CARBAMATE INSECTICIDES

It has long been known that physostigmine and certain other naturally occurring carbamates possess powerful anti-cholinesterase activity. Physostigmine occurs in the calabar bean, extracts from which were used in some parts of Africa in trials by ordeal—the fate of the accused apparently depending more upon his ability to respond to the emetic qualities of the concentrate than upon the extent of his guilt.

Pharmacologically active substances such as physostigmine (eserine) and carbamylcholine are moderately strong bases, soluble in water and appreciably ionised around pH 7. Probably for these reasons, but possibly also on account of their low solubility in lipid, they are not very toxic to insects, even upon injection. It will be recalled (p.109) that neurotoxic substances of high toxicity to mammals may not be very toxic to insects if they are predominantly in the ionised form at pH 7; this is probably because they are unable to penetrate the ion-impermeable barrier surrounding the insect nervous system. The work of Metcalf, Fukuto and Winton (1963) appears to confirm this supposition, for they found that prostigmine inhibited to an equal extent samples of cholinesterase isolated from mice and flies, yet was of low contact toxicity to flies. In this case, the specific mammalian toxicity cannot be ascribed to any major difference in target susceptibility in the two species.

With these considerations in mind, attempts have been made by several groups of workers to retain the N-substituted carbamate part of the molecule but to attach to it a less basic and more lipid-soluble component than is present in such materials as physostigmine. The result has been the introduction of substances with a certain spatial resemblance to acetylcholine. They are all based upon N-methyl or N,N-dimethyl carbamic acid. Gysin (1954), for example, introduced a pyrazole derivative (Fig. 6.10) which was

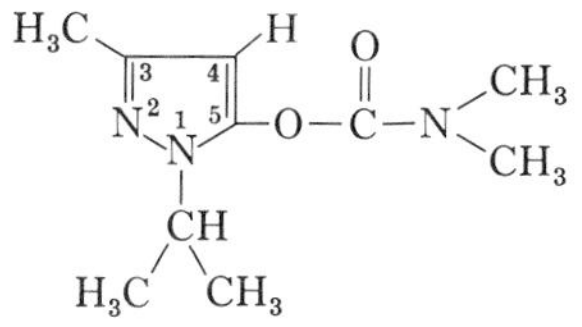

Fig. 6.10. 1–isopropyl–3–methylpyrazolyl–5–dimethyl-carbamate (trade name 'Isolan')

insecticidal, but which proved to be toxic to animals as well. The work of Haynes, Lambrech and Moorefield (1957) led to the marketing of a naphthyl carbamate, carbaryl (Fig. 6.11), which is relatively safe to mammals on ingestion and very safe when applied cutaneously. Indeed, as a mixture with piperonyl butoxide, it has been used for the control of lice on the human body. Carpenter and his collaborators (1961) ran a two year trial in which 200–400 ppm carbaryl were incorporated into the food of dogs and rats. They reported that no ill effects could be observed at the end of that time; parallel experiments with cancer-prone mice showed no evidence of any carcinogenic potential. In another trial, Claborn and his colleagues (1963) fed 50–200 ppm to steers for a period of 27 days. The animals were apparently unharmed at the end of the experiment and, one day after the end of treatment, no residue of carbaryl could be detected in the tissues.

Fukuto (1961) has summarised the earlier work on carbamate insecticides. Within the series of the N-methyl carbamates, the ability to inhibit cholinesterase *in vitro* increases as the compounds in the series become more stable to hydrolysis. In this respect the carbamates differ somewhat from the organophosphorus compounds, where a degree of lability is desirable (p.107); Fukuto concluded that carbamates act by competition with a substrate (acetylcholine) for the surface of an enzyme (cholinesterase), rather than by forming a stable compound with the enzyme. Nevertheless, if carbamates prevent the natural substrate from attaching itself to the cholinesterase, they too must fit the surface geometrically, even though they may not unite with it chemically, and the precise role of the carbamates at the biochemical level remains uncertain. Their mode of action has been discussed by Casida (1963) and by Metcalf (1964).

The *in vivo* toxicity of a carbamate insecticide cannot be predicted merely from a knowledge of the extent to which it inhibits cholinesterase *in vitro*, for factors affecting access and others leading to detoxication must also be taken into consideration. Since, for example, an ion-impermeable sheath surrounds the nervous system of insects, strongly polar materials may have difficulty reaching their site of action; it is possibly for this reason that when carbaryl (Fig. 6.11) is hydroxylated in position 4 of the naphthalene

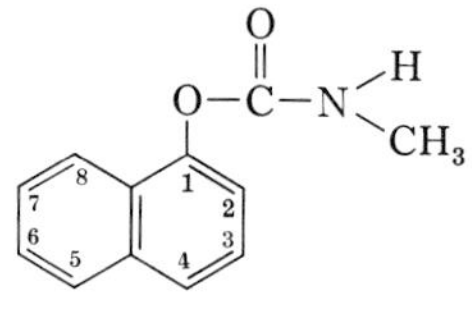

Fig. 6.11. Carbaryl: 1 naphthyl N–methylcarbamate (trade name 'Sevin')

ring it loses much of its toxicity to insects yet retains high cholinesterase activity *in vitro*.

Mechanisms leading to the detoxication of carbamates have been investigated intensively and the results collated and examined by Metcalf (1967). It would appear that even within the *Insecta*, the pattern varies considerably. Sometimes, hydrolysis precedes oxidation; in such cases sesamex (p. 97), an inhibitor of some microsomal oxidases, has little synergistic action. In other species, oxidation appears to precede hydrolysis, rather as it does for the pyrethroids.

The degradation of carbaryl in the cockroach is an example where some (but not all) of the evidence suggests that hydroxylation precedes hydrolysis. Microsomal enzymes can convert the N-methyl group to N-hydroxymethyl; they can also hydroxylate the naphthalene ring in position 4 or position 5. The hydroxylated carbamates so formed are far less stable than the original carbaryl, and carboxyesterases hydrolyse them to phenolic and acid derivatives; the acid fraction then probably undergoes further oxidation or decarboxylation. The importance of carboxyesterases in one part of the total detoxication process has been demonstrated by experiments in which house flies were pretreated with tri-orthocresyl phosphate, a specific inhibitor of carboxyesterases. It was found that the LD_{50} of carbaryl was 36 times as great when used against flies not pretreated with the cresyl phosphate as it was when used against pretreated flies in which the detoxifying esterases had been inhibited.

It is of interest that piperonyl butoxide and other methylene dioxyphenyl derivatives which synergise the pyrethroids also have a marked synergistic action with certain carbamates. Thus Fukuto and his colleagues (1962) showed that synergists increased the effectiveness of the *less toxic* carbamates up to 420 times against some test organisms, whereas they had only a small synergistic action when used with carbamates *highly toxic* to such species. The inference to be drawn is that, in all probability, the less toxic materials are not less toxic because they have a lower intrinsic ability to compete with acetylcholine at the site of action but rather that they are readily inactivated within the insect. It can thus be concluded that the route of degradation may depend upon the individual carbamate and upon the species of organism employed, but that the oxidative systems responsible for degrading many different types of pesticides are the same or similar.

The subject of insect resistance is linked closely to that of detoxication, for detoxication systems are determined genetically and often become more effective when breeding occurs under 'insecticide pressure', (Georghiou, 1965). Georghiou and Metcalf (1962), using homogenates prepared from house flies, have demonstrated that breakdown of carbamates is more rapid in resistant species than it is in susceptible ones but that the presence of a synergist suppresses this breakdown. Moreover, and presumably for the same reason, insects do not readily develop resistance to carbamates in the presence of a synergist whereas some species can become extremely resistant in as little as ten generations when certain carbamates are used on their own.

Much still remains to be discovered concerning the action of synergists, for El Sabae, Metcalf and Fukuto (1964) have demonstrated that synergism is shown not only by methylene dioxyphenyl derivatives, but also by quite different materials, including certain organic thiocyanates.

A colorimetric method of analysis suitable for the determination of carbaryl has been described by Miskus, Gordon and George (1959). It depends upon diazotisation followed by chromatographic separation.

The Ministry of Agriculture, Fisheries and Food (1968) states that carbaryl has been recommended for the control of caterpillars and earwigs, and Beesley (1964) has mentioned the use of certain carbamates as acaricides in relation to veterinary hygiene.

ARSENICAL STOMACH POISONS

Arsenic compounds have been used as insecticides for over a hundred years. Paris green, which is a copper aceto-arsenite, was used for the control of codlin moth before the turn of the century, but has the disadvantage that the composition varies somewhat from batch to batch. In addition, it decomposes fairly readily, and when it was used on foliage often proved phytotoxic. It is still sometimes used, despite its danger to higher animals, as an insect bait; for this purpose the arsenite is mixed with bran.

Calcium and lead arsenates are the two most common inorganic stomach poisons employed in agriculture at the present time. The primary function of the metal (whether or not it also contributes cations toxic to the insect), is to act as a regulator governing those properties of stability and solubility which determine how rapidly the materìal decomposes; by so doing, it generates soluble, toxic, arsenical compounds. If solubility is too high, or hydrolysis too rapid, soluble arsenical compounds will damage foliage. Symptoms of phytotoxic action are an initial wilting, followed by the leaves turning brown and shrivelling at their edges. On the other hand, if the compound is too stable, it may not undergo adequate decomposition during the relatively short time that it is within the insect gut; being insoluble, it would in such a circumstance act virtually as an inert mineral and be voided almost unchanged. An analogy may be drawn between the role of the metal in these compounds and the role of metals in determining the solubility and stability of carbonates; thus sodium carbonate is soluble and stable to heat, zinc carbonate is insoluble, while aluminium carbonate is so unstable that it does not exist at room temperature. In the case of arsenates, lead and calcium salts of appropriate composition provide the optimal balance of properties for achieving adequate persistence, successful stomach action and minimal phytotoxic action.

Arsenates can exist in a number of acidic or basic forms. The lead arsenate often used as an insecticide approximates to the composition $PbHAsO_4$. This 'acid' arsenate is almost insoluble in water and is normally sold as a powder, either alone or mixed with an organomercury fungicide. It is employed primarily in orchards for controlling caterpillars of codlin, tortrix and winter moths; when mixed with organomercury compounds, the mixture can be used to control apple and pear scab as well. In the United States of America, preparations containing calcium arsenate are often preferred to lead in view of the high intrinsic mammalian toxicity of the latter. This is perhaps wise, for environmental contamination by lead (but *not* lead of pesticide origin) presents a problem, especially at the sub-acute toxic level, which merits far more attention than it has in fact received. The disadvantage of calcium arsenate as an insecticide, however, is that it is hydrolysed somewhat too rapidly, and to reduce the danger of foliage damage, preparations of calcium arsenate usually contain excess of lime; this restricts its use because some plants are alkali-shy.

The mode of action of soluble arsenical compounds is often assumed to involve the inactivation of the sulphydryl ($-SH$) groups of enzymes, of which certain oxidoreductases are particularly important examples. An alternative, but not necessarily entirely distinct, suggestion is that the arsenate ion masquerades as a phosphate ion in such a way that the energy released during oxidative phosphorylation is squandered as heat instead of being trapped in the (terminal) high energy phosphate linkage of adenosine triphosphate.

HYDROCARBON OILS AND SUBSTITUTED DINITROPHENOLS

Compounds within these two groups are employed as herbicides as well as insecticides. Since there is reason to believe that the mode of action of substances within each group is broadly the same whether they are used as insecticides or herbicides, they will be discussed later (chapter 9).

INSECT CONTROL—FUTURE PROSPECTS

The large-scale use of insecticides has focused attention on four major problems which may be associated with their use. The problem of high acute toxicity to higher animals has, in practice, proved less serious than many people feared, while that of long term persistence has proved more serious, especially in relation to the organochlorine insecticides. The development of insect resistance on exposure of a population to non-eradicating doses is particularly troublesome when the compound is highly persistent. The fourth problem, the decimation of the predators and competitors of the pest, leading to an upsetting of the usual steady state existing between species, can occur for contact and persistent poisons alike. It may be found when a contact poison is non-selective in its action, while persistent materials of low selectivity can in addition prevent beneficial organisms re-establishing themselves by infiltration from unsprayed areas.

The general trend in the development of conventional insecticides is therefore likely to be away from compounds of very high persistence, and towards materials of moderate persistence on plants, in animal tissues and in the soil. Organophosphorus compounds and carbamates are therefore likely to become increasingly important in the next decade, while the use of organochlorine compounds will probably decline. With an increasing awareness of the biochemical implications of synergism and the knowledge that the processing enzymes in different organisms may be quantitatively or even qualitatively different, it is to be expected that such differences will be exploited to achieve selectivity of action. The problem of insect resistance, insofar as it occurs on account of highly developed detoxifying systems, may be simultaneously mitigated, although no rapid, single or easy solution of this problem is likely.

Selective control of insects vis-à-vis competitors can be, and already is being, achieved by timing applications correctly, by using systemic poisons and by employing materials of moderate to low persistence. The objective is not to avoid the deaths of all predators and competitors, but to bring about the maximal kill of the pest species with the minimal damage to beneficial organisms; clearly, a compromise of some sort is necessary, especially when the insecticide is of low selectivity. In the past, too much weight has often been placed upon the need to eradicate a species completely. In fact, the principal requirement is to reduce the food losses to acceptable levels; beyond a certain point, increasing the amount of material applied per acre increases the cost, increases the damage to beneficial insects and increases the hazard to worker and consumer. This is the point of diminishing returns, for eradication almost always fails and the final state of affairs may be worse than the original. At least until highly specific pesticides are available, there will always be a certain level of pests, for only by allowing some pests to survive can the beneficial insects be preserved and the problem of insect resistance minimised. Eradication as a policy has in any case failed—there are few, if any, records of a pest species being eliminated from a large land mass purely as a result of the action of an eradicant insecticide. On the other hand, the use of pesticides to prevent the development of serious outbreaks is both profitable and desirable; if the numbers in the population of a particular pest hàve reached epidemic proportions, nature has lost control of its customary steady state, and the insecticidal spray as an emergency prophylactic is the logical and sometimes the only counter-move open to man.

Instead of considering an insect-controlling agent as a killer—as the word insect*icide* implies—it may be possible in the future to use chemicals in a different way. The whole life cycle of an insect is conditioned chemically, whether it be feeding, migration, breeding, oviposition or the relation between it and its host plant. It may be possible to use some of these conditioning chemicals, with or without the simultaneous use of conventional insecticides, to disorientate the behaviour of the pest species and so place it in some way at a disadvantage in its environment. Various methods of control, exploiting insect sex attractants, food attractants and oviposition attractants have been studied for many years (Green, Beroza and Hall, 1960) and many of the highly species-specific chemicals involved have been isolated and several of them have been synthesised (Potter, 1965; Jacobson, 1965). Success in the field has so far been limited, though the Mediterranean fruit fly was eradicated from Florida in 1956 using a food bait consisting of protein hydrolysates to which malathion was added.

Another method, on the diffuse frontier where chemical and biological disciplines meet, involves the sterilisation of insects, usually the males, by the use of chemosterilants (Bertram, 1964) or of physical sterilants such as X-rays. Insects treated in captivity are liberated in large numbers and by competing with untreated males for the available females, lead to unsuccessful mating, decrease in egg production and consequently a fall in population numbers (Ascher, 1964). Such a method has the advantage that there is no possibility of resistance developing, and it leaves open the possibility that the whole population may indeed be eradicated. For, if the population number falls below a certain level, fertile males may never be able to find females to mate with. Another dual method of control is to mix with an insecticide the viable spores of some pathogen which has a very highly specific action on one or more species of insects: in Russia, for example, certain fungi have been found to increase the susceptibility of an insect to an insecticide. Norris (1967) has reviewed the work which has been done on the use of bacteria and viruses, and Angus (1968) has described the culture and use of *Bacillus thuringiensis* for the control of insect pests.

If successful, such methods of control as sterilisation, lures and repellents may eventually make large scale application of pesticides to edible crops an unusual event. Since their development will require close collaboration between biologists and chemists, it is to be hoped that the present dichotomy between those favouring biological and those favouring chemical means of insect control will automatically disappear, to the ultimate benefit of all. The part cannot be greater than the whole, and, from a long term point of view, integrated pest control must surely provide the soundest and safest solution.

ACARICIDES

The introduction of organic insecticides led at first to an alarming increase in the number of red spider mites in some regions which had been subjected to spraying. There were several inter-related reasons for this, the principal one probably being that selectively *insecticidal* compounds tended to kill the insect predators of phytophagous (plant-sucking) mites, so enabling surviving mites to multiply freely (Edgar, 1956). Since the life cycle of the spider mite is completed in about three weeks, a few surviving organisms are able to produce prodigious numbers of offspring in the few months between spring spraying and harvesting in autumn.

For the same reason, control measures could not be limited to the destruction of over-wintering eggs by the use of such conventional winter washes as petroleum, for complete eradication and prevention of re-infestation is a practical impossibility. Control measures must therefore be

Fig. 6.12. Basic molecular pattern of many acaricides

carried out during the summer, the target of such sprays being summer eggs, nymphal stages or adults. Various insecticides were at first used for this purpose. They frequently proved to be unsatisfactory, not so much because they lacked acaricidal power, but rather because they were often toxic either to beneficial insects or to crop plants. It is of interest that in veterinary entomology, where these two limiting factors do not apply, Beesley (1964) reported that certain carbamate and organophosphorus insecticides have considerable acaricidal potential.

A search was consequently made for new chemicals which would control phytophagous mites, and compounds possessing the basic molecular pattern shown in Fig. 6.12 soon proved to be of interest. Many acaricides are of this type, with the phenyl rings frequently substituted with chlorine in one or both *para* positions. Most acaricides are insoluble in water but moderately soluble in oil. They are fairly stable and usually of moderate persistence. According to the nature of the substance, the genus of the pests, and the environment, the amount per acre which must be applied each season ranges from 0·5 to 2·5 lb of undiluted material, though this is not necessarily applied all at one time.

The work leading to the development of modern acaricides started along two quite separate lines and provides an interesting example of convergent evolution of ideas. Azobenzene (Fig. 6.13) was used from about 1945 for

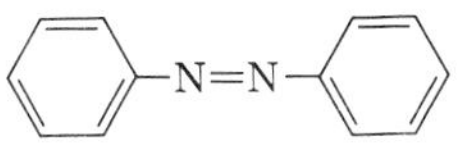

Fig. 6.13. Azobenzene

the control of the glasshouse red spider mite, but proved to be unsatisfactory for outdoor use against fruit tree spider mites (which belong to different genera from the glasshouse variety). However, early investigations, summarised by Eaton (1949), soon demonstrated that the azo-group was not in itself essential to toxicity, but could be replaced by a variety of other bridging groups. While this work was proceeding, other groups of workers were investigating the possibility of modifying the structure of DDT—a compound regarded at that time as a highly successful insecticide—so as to make it less insecticidal but more acaricidal. As will be seen later (p. 149), the modifications were indeed successful, but were so profound that the resulting compounds can only be regarded as special forms of the bridged ring structure (Fig. 6.12). March (1958) has reviewed the chemistry and mode of action of acaricides.

The studies originating with azobenzene led to the marketing of diphenyl sulphone ($C_6H_5 . SO_2 . C_6H_5$). This appears to have failed because, unlike later compounds, it possesses low persistence and little quasi-systemic

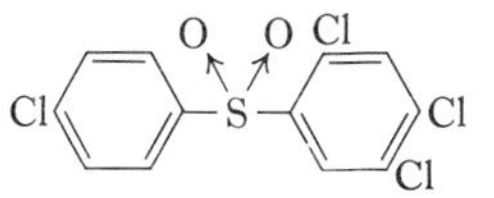

Fig. 6.14. Tetradifon : tetrachlorodiphenyl sulphone
(trade name 'Tedion')

activity (p. 114). A tetra-chlorinated derivative, tetradifon (Fig. 6.14), has, however, found considerable commercial application (Meltzer and Jacobs, 1961), possibly because the chlorine atoms confer a greater solubility in lipid and increased chemical stability. Cassil and Fullmer (1958) found that the concentration of tetradifon in citrus fruit did not diminish greatly for at least thirty-six days after application; the work of McBride (1959) indicated that it might persist for two or three months in the peel of citrus fruits, but that little of the substance was present in the pulp or juices. Ascher (1964) mentioned that tetradifon, in common with chlorbenside

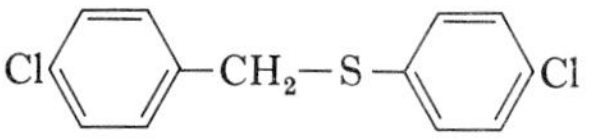

Fig. 6.15. Chlorbenside: p–chlorophenyl p–chlorobenzyl sulphide (trade name 'Chlorocide')

(Fig. 6.15) and some other acaricides, could affect the oviposition pattern of insects.

The sulphonate linkage can act as a bridge between phenyl or chlorinated phenyl rings to form a molecule which has acaricidal properties. *Para*-chlorophenyl benzene sulphonate (fenson) and its chlorinated derivative, chlorfenson (Fig. 6.16) have been used commercially in Britain. Such compounds, like tetradifon, are primarily toxic to the hatching eggs and nymphal stages of the mite; they are less toxic to the adults. Since they are compatible with derris and certain organophosphorus compounds, a combined wash may be employed when it is imperative to obtain immediate control of the adults. Phytotoxic effects are sometimes evident in the form of a cracking of the epidermis of fruit or a scorching of the leaves of fruit trees. These compounds are toxic to cucumbers (compare DDT).

A very successful acaricide, chlorbenside (Fig. 6.15), has sulphur as the linking atom, the bridge being 'extended' by a methylene group. Its chemistry and uses have been described by Cranham, Higgons and Steven-

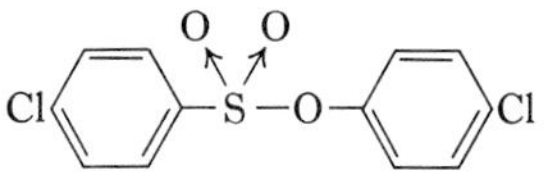

Fig. 6.16. Chlorfenson: p–chlorophenyl p–chlorbenzene sul-phonate

son (1953) and by Cranham (1956). Like the other acaricides mentioned above, it is an insoluble solid. It is generally stable, but can be oxidised *via* the sulphoxide to the sulphone. Since it is soluble in lipid, it diffuses across leaves in the same manner as the quasi-systemic insecticides. The oxidised forms, if produced after the sulphide has penetrated the leaf, may assist toxic action by ensuring a longer duration of persistence, for their

148

vapour pressures are lower than that of the sulphide. Their principal toxic action appears to be on the hatching eggs or nymphal stages, although an indirect effect—a reduction in the number and viability of the eggs laid by poisoned adults—has also been observed. Because the effect is indirect, a period of two or three weeks may elapse after spraying before there is any marked diminution in the numbers of phytophagous mites. More recently, preliminary work has been carried out on the acaricidal properties of heterocyclic sulphides (Van Zwieten, Meltzer and Huisman, 1962).

The second line of approach to specific acaricides involved modifying the structure of DDT. Of the many compounds discovered in this way, dicofol (Fig. 6.17) and chlorbenzilate (Fig. 6.18) serve as examples.

Dicofol or Kelthane is like DDT except that the solitary ethane hydrogen of the DDT molecule is replaced by a hydroxyl group. This modification

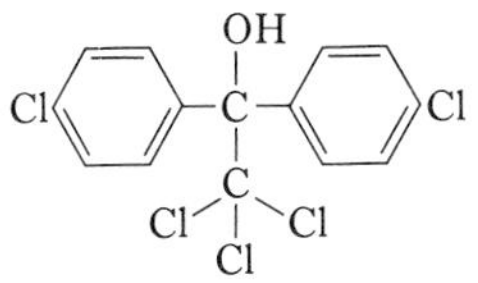

Fig. 6.17. Dicofol : p,p′–dichloro (trichloromethyl) benzhydrol (trade name 'Kelthane')

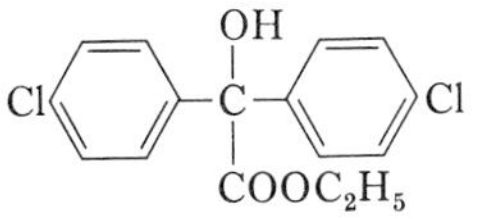

Fig. 6.18. Chlorbenzilate : ethyl p,p′–dichlorobenzilate

greatly decreases toxicity to insects (p. 88) but increases acaricidal power. The ability of dicofol to penetrate into leaves has been discussed by Cooke (1963). The same author refers to several papers dealing with the ability of various acaricides to diffuse through leaves and to kill mites feeding on the untreated undersurfaces.

Chlorbenzilate (Fig. 6.18) is an example of a substance in which the central part of the DDT molecule has been modified almost beyond recognition, leaving only a complex bridge between chlorinated rings. According to Horn, Bruce and Paynter (1955) the toxicity of chlorbenzilate to mammals is moderate, it is rapidly excreted, and it is not stored to any great extent in animal tissues. A technical document by the Geigy Chemical Company (Anon, 1956) describes its chemistry, toxicology and phytotoxicity, and refers to work carried out to investigate the problems of residues and the possibility of tainting of food.

149

Because of the very rapid life cycle of phytophagous mites and the tendency of acaricides (including acaricidal insecticides) to be moderately persistent, the situation is highly favourable to the development of resistance. Brown (1958a), who summarised the information available on this subject up to 1957, reported one case where *Metatetranychus citri* had developed a 7,000-fold resistance to parathion in California and another where *Metatetranychus ulmi* has been observed to become resistant to chlorbenside. In laboratory experiments, *Tetranychus urticae* rapidly developed resistance to chlorbenzilate when bred selectively under chlorbenzylate 'pressure'. The same author (Brown, 1958b) has dealt more fully with the subject of insect resistance to pesticides in a monograph issued by the World Health Organisation.

Finally, it should be mentioned that a rather interesting correlation sometimes exists between acaricidal and fungicidal potential. A well known example is that of dinocap (p. 187), a substituted dinitrophenol, which was first employed in 1945 as an acaricide. It was later found to have valuable fungicidal properties, and is now employed mainly for the control of powdery mildews. More recently, Fox and his colleagues (1963) have described the experimental use of azobenzene derivatives as fungicidal seed protectants for the control of *Pythium* and *Tilletia*. Conversely, the Ministry of Agriculture, Fisheries and Food (1968), in its *List of Approved Products,* classifies several materials, including lime sulphur, binapacryl and quinomethionate, as fungicides with acaricidal properties.

NEMATICIDES

There are few reliable estimates of the damage done by eelworms, but Strickland (1965) considered that approximately 1% of pest damage to cereals was attributable to root eelworms. In view of the vast acreages involved and the importance of cereals to mankind, this figure is not inconsiderable, and, with increasing intensity of crop production, the eelworm problem is likely to become more serious. Another important nematode, the potato root eelworm, causes losses of up to 2 tons per acre on severely infected land in southern England, and the sugar beet eelworm is also of economic importance.

Cultural, physical and chemical methods of control have all been investigated (Cathie, 1963); few dramatic successes have been reported, and it appears increasingly likely that the most promising long term approach will involve the integration of all three methods in the light of local circumstances (Oostenbrink, 1964). It is known, for instance, that the effectiveness of chemicals depends not only on the susceptibility of the pest, but also on such factors as soil texture and structure, porosity, temperature, moisture content and organic matter content (Peachey, 1962; Hague and Call, 1962).

Very little systematic work on agricultural nematicides has been carried out, and most substances possessing some nematicidal action were introduced initially for other purposes. Many nematicides have a fumigant action—i.e. they are liquids or solids with an appreciable vapour pressure and so volatilise in the soil after application by injection, by sprinkling or drenching, or by rotary cultivation. Some of the newer materials, however, are relatively involatile solids. In either case a certain solubility in water is desirable to facilitate their dispersion in soil water from the loci of application, while some solubility in organic solvents is necessary to enable the substance to penetrate into the nematodes (Peacock, 1960). The similarity of these requirements to those for systemic insecticidal action will be apparent (p. 111) and several organophosphorus insecticides have, in fact, found some use in the control of soil-inhabiting nematodes. Additionally, an intricate balance must be struck between factors leading to stability and those causing instability, since the nematicide must persist in the (living) soil until it reaches the nematode, yet must not be inert within the pest; this situation recalls the specifications for a stomach insecticide such as lead arsenate (p. 142).

Several organic halides of moderate to high volatility have found use as nematicides. These include methyl bromide, chloropicrin, ethylene dibromide and 1,2-dibromo-3-chloropropane, although the best known is 'DD'—a mixture of 1,2-dichloropropane and 1,3-dichloropropene. Moje (1960) has discussed the balance of physical and chemical characteristics likely to favour the nematicidal activity of halides. He concluded that those with nucleophilic centres were candidate nematicides and postulated that they might act by alkylating thiol groups of nematode enzymes. Brown and Dunn (1965) showed that labelled ethylene dibromide was taken up along the whole length of the nematode's body and that it did not accumulate preferentially in any particular body organ.

Thionazin is an organophosphorus compound which has shown some promise as a nematicide (Fraser and Lindley, 1961). It is O,O-diethyl, O-2 pyrazinyl phosphorothionate. Fair control of potato root eelworm was obtained by band application in the furrow; a secondary beneficial effect, arising from its systemic activity, was a reduction in the number of aphids on the leaves of the crop. It is noteworthy that both aphids and nematodes can act as vectors for viruses; consequently nematicides, like aphicides, could possibly play a role in diminishing the spread of virus disease (Cadman, 1961). Other organophosphorus compounds employed to control stem, bulb and root eelworms include malathion, demeton-methyl and demeton (Chapter 5).

Dithiocarbamates and related compounds are best known as fungicides, but certain members of the group have been found to have nematicidal action. Metham-sodium (p. 174) and dazomet (tetrahydro dimethyl thia-diazine thione) are currently employed for this purpose. Metham-sodium decomposes in the soil to methyl isothiocyanate, and it is probably this material which is the active toxicant—methyl isothiocyanate is, in fact, sometimes applied directly to the soil. Guile (1964) used metham-sodium and dazomet for the control of potato root eelworm and reported that each of these substances reduced the nematode population by 95%. Jones (1966) used dazomet for the control of cereal root eelworm.

REFERENCES

ANGUS, T. A. (1968) *Wld Rev. Pest Control*, **7**, (1), 11

Anon (1956), Geigy Agricultural Chemicals, Chlorobenzilate Technical Bulletin No. 56–1. (89 Barclay Street, New York 8)

Anon (1962), *Pl. Prot. Bull. F.A.O.*, **10**, 67

ASCHER, K. R. S. (1964), *Wld Rev. Pest Control*, **3**, (1), 7

BARLOW, R. B. (1960), *Biochem. Soc. Symp:* 19, 'Steric aspects of biochemistry', p. 46

BARTHEL, W. F. (1961), *Adv. Pest Control Res.*, **4**, 33

BARTHEL, W. F. (1967), *Wld Rev. Pest Control*, **6**, (2), 59

BEESLEY, W. N. (1964), *Ann. appl. Biol.*, **53**, 175

BERTRAM, D. S. (1964), *Trans. R. Soc. trop. Med. & Hygiene*, **58**, (4), 295

BROWN, A. W. A. (1958a), *Adv. Pest Control Res.*, **2**, 351 (see p. 395)

BROWN, A. W. A. (1958b), *W.H.O. Monograph* 38: *Insecticide Resistance in Arthropods*, Geneva. H.M.S.O.

BROWN, K. F. and DUNN, C. L. (1965), *Nematologica*, **11**, 353

CADMAN, C. (1961), *N.A.A.S. Quart. Rev.*, **13**, 52

CARPENTER, C. P., WEIL, C. S., PALM, P. E., WOODSIDE, M. W., NAIR, J. H. and SMYTHE, H. F. (1961), *J. agric. Fd Chem.*, **9**, 30

CASIDA, J. (1963), *A. Rev. Ent.*, **8**, 39

CASIDA, J. E. and YAMAMOTO, I. (1967), *Abstracts 6th Internatn. Congr. Crop Prot.*, Vienna, 1967, p. 233

CASSIL, C. C. and FULLMER, O. H. (1958), *J. agric. Fd Chem.*, **6**, 908

CATHIE, L. S. (1963), *Wld Crops*, **15**, 460

CHADWICK, P. R. (1963), *Pyrethrum Post*, **7**, (1), 25

CLABORN, H. V., ROBERTS, R. H., MANN, H. D., BOWMAN, M. C., IVEY, M. C., WEIDENBACH, C. P. and RADELEFF, R. D. (1963), *J. agric. Fd Chem.*, **11**, 74

COOKE, V. A. (1963), *Ann. appl. Biol.*, **51**, 485

CRANHAM, J. E. (1956), *J. Sci. Fd agric.*, **7**, Suppl. p. s.93

CRANHAM, J. E., HIGGONS, D. J. and STEVENSON, H. A. (1953), *Chemy Ind.*, p. 1206

EATON, J. K. (1949), *Proc. 2nd Internatn. Congr. Crop Prot.*, p. 119

EDGAR, E. C. (1956), *Outl. Agric.*, **1**, 16

ELLIOTT, M. (1967), *Sci. J.*, March, **3**, 61

EL SABAE, A. H., METCALF, R. L. and FUKUTO, T. R. (1964), *J. econ. Ent.*, **57**, 478

FINE, B. C. (1963), *Pyrethrum Post*, **7**, (2), 18

FOX, H. M., GEOGHEGAN, M. J., SILK, J. A. and SUMMERS, L. A. (1963), *Ann. appl. Biol.*, **52**, 33

FRASER, W. D. and LINDLEY, C. D. (1961), *Proc. Brit. Insecticide Fungicide Conf.*, **1**, 27

FUKUTO, T. R. (1961), *A. Rev. Ent.*, **6**, 313

FUKUTO, T. R., METCALF, R. L., WINTON, M. and ROBERTS, P. (1962), *J. econ. Ent.*, **55**, 341

GEORGHIOU, G. P. (1965), *Adv. Pest Control Res.*, **6**, 171

GEORGHIOU, G. P. and METCALF, R. L. (1962), *J. econ. Ent.*, **55**, 125

GLYNNE JONES, G. D. (1960), *Ann. appl. Biol.*, **48**, 352

GREEN, N., BEROZA, M. and HALL, S. A. (1960), *Adv. Pest Control Res.*, **3**, 129

GUNTHER, F. A. and JEPPSON, L. R. (1960), *Modern Insecticides and World Food Production,* Chapman and Hall, London

GUILE, C. T. (1964), *Plant Path,* **13**, 178

GYSIN, H. (1954), *Chimia*, **8**, 205, 221

HAGUE, N. G. M. and CALL, F. (1962), *Nematologica*, **7**, 186

HAYNES, H. L., LAMBRECH, J. A. and MOOREFIELD, H. H. (1957), *Contr. Boyce Thompson Inst. Pl. Res.,* **18**, 507

HEAD, S. W. (1963), *Pyrethrum Post,* **7**, (2), 3

HOLMAN, H. J. (1940), *A Survey of Insecticidal Materials of Vegetable Origin,* Imperial Institute, London

HORN, H. J., BRUCE, R. B. and PAYNTER, O. E. (1955), *J. agric. Fd Chem.*, **3**, 752

INCHO, H. H. and ODENEAL, J. F. (1963), *Pyrethrum Post,* **7**, (2), 37

IRVINE, J. E. and FREYRE, R. H. (1959), *J. agric. Fd Chem.*, **7**, 106

JACOBSON, M. (1965), *Insect Sex Attractants,* Interscience Publ. Co.

JONES, F. G. W. (1966), Rothamsted Exptl. Stn. Ann. Rep.

KAMIMURA, H., MATSUMOTO, A., MIYAZAKI, Y. and YAMAMOTO, I. (1963), *Agric. Biol. Chem.*, **27**, 684

KROLL, U. (1964), *Outl. Agric.*, **4**, 177

MCBRIDE, J. J. (1959), *J. agric. Fd Chem.*, **7**, 255

MARCH, R. B. (1958), *A. Rev. Ent.*, **3**, 355

MARTIN, R. and SCHWARTZMAN, G. (1964), *J. Ass. off. agric. Chem.*, **47**, 303

MATSUI, M. and MEGURO, H. (1964), *Agric. Biol. Chem.*, **28**, 27

MELTZER, J. and JACOBS, K. F. (1961), *Proc. Brit. Insecticide Fungicide Conf.*, **2**, 499

METCALF, R. L. (1955), *Organic Insecticides,* Interscience Publ. Inc., New York

METCALF, R. L. (1964), *Wld Rev. Pest Control,* **3**, (1), 28

METCALF, R. L. (1967), *Ann. Rev. Entomol.*, **12**, 229

METCALF, R. L., FUKUTO, T. R. and WINTON, M. (1963), *J. econ. Ent.*, **55**, 889

Ministry of Agriculture, Fisheries and Food (1968), *List of Approved Products for Farmers and Growers,* (A yearly publication)

MISKUS, R., GORDON, H. T. and GEORGE, D. A. (1959), *J. agric. Fd Chem.*, **7**, 613

MOJE, W. (1960), *Adv. Pest Control Res.*, **3**, 181

NEGHERBON, W. O. (1959), *Handbook of Toxicology, Vol. III. Insecticides,* W. B. Saunders Co., Philadelphia, U.S.A.

NORRIS, J. R. (1967), *Chemy. Ind.,* November 18th, p. 1941

OOSTENBRINK, M. (1964), *Nematologica*, **10**, 49

PARKIN, E. A. and LLOYD, C. J. (1960), *J. Sci. Fd Agric.*, **11**, 471

PEACHEY, J. E. (1962), *N.A.A.S. Quart. Rev.*, **57**, 34

PEACOCK, F. C. (1960), *Ann. appl. Biol.*, **49**, 381

PICKETT, A. D. (1962), *Wld Rev. Pest Control,* **1**, (2), 19

POTTER, C. (1965), *Sci. Progr.*, **53**, 393

ROAN, C. C. and HOPKINS, T. L. (1961), *A. Rev. Ent.*, **6**, 333

SEXTON, W. A. (1963), *Chemical Constitution and Biological Activity,* E. & F.N. Spon Ltd., London

SMITH, H. J. (1960), *J. Sci. Fd Agric.*, **11**, 172

STRICKLAND, A. H. (1965), *J. Royal Soc. Arts* No. 5102, **113**, 62

VAN ZWIETEN, P. A., MELTZER, J. and HUISMAN, H. O. (1962), *Recl. Trav. chim. Pays-Bas Belg.*, **81**, 616

WAIN, R. L. (1963), *Nature, Lond.*, **200**, 28

WARNER, J. L. (1963), *Pyrethrum Post,* **7**, (1), 34

WEST, T. F. and HARDY, J. E. (1961), *Chemical Control of Insects.* Chapman and Hall, London

WIGGLESWORTH, V. (1942), *Bull. ent. Res.*, **33**, 205

WINTERINGHAM, F. P. W. and LEWIS, S. E. (1959), *A. Rev. Ent.*, **4**, 303

YAMAMOTO, I. (1965), *Adv. Pest Control Res.*, **6**, 231

7

INORGANIC FUNGICIDES

TYPES AND USAGE

In earlier chapters it has been shown that insecticides may be divided conveniently into those which kill an already established pest and those whose action is primarily protective. The fact that many modern insecticides perform both functions to a greater or lesser degree does not lessen the fundamental distinction between these two types of action. But for most fungicides (the case of a potential systemic fungicide being excluded), the distinction becomes blurred because of the almost unlimited capacity of fungal mycelium to regenerate from surviving strands of hyphae.

Some fungi are ectoparasites, and these are more vulnerable to contact sprays than are endoparasites. Nevertheless, even the former possess nutritive branches, called haustoria, which penetrate into plant cells, and which may survive when the external mycelium is destroyed. Thus, although the growth of mycelium may be checked to a great extent by a contact poison, and the rate of spreading from one plant to another diminished by destruction of reproductive branches, eradication of an already established infection is usually difficult. In practice, therefore, the majority of successful fungicides possess a protective action, being most effective when applied prior to the arrival of the infection. While such fungicides may also possess a contact (eradicant) action, a poison which acts exclusively by contact is unlikely to be a good fungicide. Consequently, some degree of persistence is a primary characteristic of fungicides at the present time, and will remain so until good systemic materials with a powerful eradicant action on hyphae *within* the plant have been developed.

There is, however, an important additional use to which certain fungicides can be put. Sometimes the spores of fungi are carried on the surface of seeds, or a dormant mycelium is present within the seed. In either case, the mechanism ensures that infection is passed on from one generation of crop plant to the next. Of particular importance in this respect are the spores of smut, bunt and rust of cereals, for grain contaminated with them germinates to give infected seedling plants. Fungicidal seed dressings, and especially organomercury compounds, are of great value in the control of diseases transmitted in this way.

There are three main groups of fungicides, based on metals, sulphur and carbon. Gayner (1961) stated that in 1958, 275,000 tons of sulphur were used in world agriculture. The corresponding figures for copper and organic compounds were 56,000 tons and 12,000 tons respectively. The copper compounds have become less popular with the advent of high pressure and of low volume spraying equipment, partly because copper is more phytotoxic if it is blasted into the leaf surface. The increasing price of metallic copper has also contributed to the decline, by rendering copper fungicides less competitive with others on a cost basis.

In Britain, inorganic sulphur fungicides still have a wide but declining use in horticulture and agriculture. Strickland (1966) pointed out that the usage of lime sulphur, for example, had decreased to 25% of its 1957 level and that the 1957 level was in turn only 85% of the level in 1953. He tabulated both the tonnage of various fungicides applied and the number of 'spray-acres' covered by each of them. (Because some areas receive each year more than one application of a fungicide, the number of spray-acres is greater than the actual land area, or basic acreage, treated with certain compounds). Strickland's figures show that the tonnage of inorganic sulphur compounds used in Britain is several times the tonnage of copper compounds (expressed as elemental copper), while the tonnage of the latter (468 tons) is some twenty times the tonnage of mercury applied in the form of organic or inorganic mercury compounds. Nevertheless, when considered from the viewpoint of the number of spray-acres to which the materials were applied, copper, at 471,000 spray-acres was, in the period 1960–64, used more than inorganic sulphur compounds (318,000 spray-acres). On the other hand, 13·4 tons of mercury in the form of seed dressings were used on no less than six million acres; clearly, according to the criterion adopted to express usage, very different pictures emerge regarding the extent to which each type of compound is employed.

A sulphur spray programme consists classically of several separate applications. Nowadays, although sulphur is still used widely for washes early in the season, it is becoming common practice to replace later lime sulphur washes by organic fungicides. Moreover, certain crops, especially varieties of bush and top fruit, are 'sulphur-shy', suffering damage which varies in intensity with the variety, the temperature and the amount of sun-shine at the time of spraying. Damage may thus vary with district—in general, 'sulphur-shyness' is less of a problem in the west of Britain than in the east. These disadvantages can be minimised by using elemental sulphur as a wettable powder instead of applying it in the form of soluble polysul-phides (lime sulphur), but powders are extravagant in the use of sulphur, sometimes costly, and less effective than lime sulphur against the mildews.

A severe but temporary shortage of sulphur occurred at the time of the Korean war and brought additional impetus to the work already progressing on organic fungicides. This work originated from a desire to repeat in the field of fungicides the success already achieved with organic insecticides, and has continued because it is now clear that many fungi will not be controlled adequately till *systemic* fungicides have been discovered which match in effectiveness the systemic insecticides already in use.

PENETRATION OF SUBSTANCES INTO FUNGI

Surprisingly little appears to be known about the barrier surrounding cells and spores of fungi or about its permeability characteristics. Horsfall (1956), who summarised the earlier literature, assumed that typical semi-permeable lipoprotein membranes lying within the cell wall were responsible for selectivity of uptake from the external medium, the rigid cell wall probably acting as a non-selective physical barrier. It is probable that enzymes governing the selective permeability of cells are present in the lipoprotein membrane (Zalokar, 1965).

It has long been known that cell walls of some fungi contain chitin but, as was observed on p. 51, chitin itself is probably penetrated readily by aqueous solutions. More recently, Bartnicki-García (1963) has described the composition of the cell walls of a species of *Mucor.* The major com-ponents were chitosan (30%) and phosphate (22%), though 6–10% each of chitin, proteins and lipids were also present. In other fungi, cellulose, callose and nucleic acid derivatives are present (Aronson, 1965). Cellulose is hydrophilic in nature but lipids and callose, a lignin-like substance, if suitably deposited, could be essentially hydrophobic in nature.

Considerable variability in composition has been noted, not only between the cell walls of different species of fungi, but even between the cell walls of one species grown under different conditions. Electron microscope studies of the conidia of *Botrytis* have demonstrated the existence of a double-layered wall, the outer layer of which is thin but electron-dense, the inner being thick but electron-transparent (Hawker and Hendy, 1963). On germination, only the outer layer appears to rupture, for the inner elastic layer surrounds the emerging germ tube. No sub-structure to either layer has so far been demonstrated.

It may tentatively be assumed that the rigid spore wall, through its lipid and callose components, exerts a general physical barrier to permeation, for spores usually become more susceptible to fungicides at the time of emergence of the germ tube. The cell membranes of spores and hyphal cells are probably typical semi-permeable membranes. This situation recalls the relationship of leaf cuticle to the underlying epidermal cells (Chapter 2) and of insect cuticle to internal semi-permeable barriers (Chapter 3).

COPPER FUNGICIDES

Copper ions in solution are toxic to all plant life. Selective fungicidal action can therefore be achieved only by applying copper to foliage in the form of an insoluble compound. Copper oxychloride, copper carbonate, cuprous oxide and Burgundy mixture are amongst the many insoluble materials which have been, or are, used as fungicides. Bordeaux mixture is, however, the best known of all copper fungicides and this material will therefore be chosen to illustrate some of the characteristics and problems associated with the copper fungicides.

BORDEAUX MIXTURE

The principal use of copper sprays in Britain today is for the control of potato blight. In conjunction with petroleum, they are also employed against powdery mildews of fruit. It is frequently recommended that the Bordeaux precipitate should be made by the addition at room temperature of a concentrated solution of copper sulphate to a suspension of fresh calcium hydroxide in the remainder of the water, though some investigations by Somers (1959) throw doubt upon whether this is always the most satisfactory method. Nevertheless, it is certain that care must be exercised in the preparation of the precipitate, for the preparative method influences such physical properties as the fineness of the precipitate, the ease of dispersion and the degree of retention of the deposit on the crop. The fungicidal efficiency of Bordeaux precipitate declines on storage, probably because of minor changes in physical characteristics, and for this reason Bordeaux mixture is one of the few pesticides which is best prepared by the grower himself, the manufacturer providing the correct proportions of the two ingredients.

The fungicidal component of the precipitate is not copper hydroxide, for if a suspension is boiled it does not turn black, whereas copper hydroxide suspension does. It is probably a basic copper sulphate approximating to the complex [$CuSO_4 . 3Cu(OH)_2$]. After deposition on the leaf, the precipitate acts as a reservoir from which copper ions can be mobilised. It is believed that mobilisation is followed by transportation and deposition on the fungal spore.

There is much evidence suggesting that the mobilisation of the copper from the Bordeaux mixture involves the formation of complexes rather than the production of cupric salts. An early idea, the oligodynamic theory (*oligo* = few, little), suggested that although the deposit was extremely insoluble, equilibrium adjustment following uptake of ions by spores might cause toxic amounts of copper ions to enter solution. The theory now has few adherents. Similarly, although carbon dioxide and oxygen cannot be proved to be without effect under field conditions, controlled experiments show that such 'weathering' effects are not an essential aspect of the dissolving process. The two remaining possibilities are that the host plant, or the fungal spore, produces some material which acts upon the insoluble precipitate; again, although the first may well be a contributory factor under field conditions, experiments with spores on microscope slides demonstrate that the presence of the host plant is not essential to the effective functioning of Bordeaux mixture. A theory has thus become accepted which supposes that the germinating spores exude materials which dissolve the Bordeaux precipitate, so enabling it to exert a fungistatic or fungicidal effect.

It is a well known fact that copper readily forms complexes by dative covalency with numerous organic materials. Amongst these are amino- and keto-acids, and many workers believe that small but measurable amounts of these substances are exuded by germinating fungal spores. If this happens, such materials could dissolve copper from the Bordeaux precipitate, giving rise to organic complexes, probably of a type in which the copper is present in the negative radical (Fig. 7.1).

The complex is represented in the figure as octahedral, although its exact stereochemistry is unknown; it is possible that the third amino acid group behaves as a monodentate ligand and is attached only through its amino group (Martell and Calvin, 1952). Many amino- and keto-acids are present in exudates and could form such complexes, though, in practice, glycine is the potential ligand produced in largest amount.

The probable importance of spore exudates in the 'solubilisation' of

Bordeaux deposit has been discussed by Wain (1959), but the 'suicide theory' has its critics. Tröger (1958), for example, could not confirm that substances which contained nitrogen were exuded by fungal spores in the *absence* of copper, and concluded that the production of such substances in the presence of copper and other heavy metals was a *result* of the action of the metal rather than a cause of its mobilisation. The evidence relating to the toxicity of complexes formed between copper and amino acids is also ambiguous. Tröger (1960a) considered that such complexes were non-toxic to the spores of *Fusarium,* a conclusion apparently supported by Arakatsu (quoted from Horsfall, 1957) who noted that a strain of yeast,

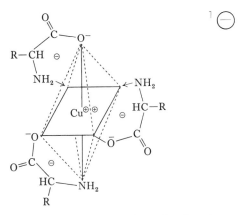

Fig. 7.1. Probable structure of complex anion formed between copper and amino acids

which was resistant to copper, synthesised more glutamic and aspartic acid than did a non-resistant strain. The possibility exists that the stability of the complex may determine whether it is an effective carrier of copper or whether it inactivates the copper. The latter could occur if the complex were *more* stable than the complex which the copper is presumed to form with chemical constituents of the spore. The importance of the relative stabilities of complexes, including those formed by copper within the spore, has been discussed by Tröger (1960b). The same author concluded that spores which produced gelatinous and hygroscopic substances in their cell walls were more susceptible to copper than were those which did not, because the swollen material presented a larger surface of contact to solid Bordeaux deposit.

The mode of action of copper within the spore is still uncertain. It is initially fungistatic, inhibiting the germination of spores rather than killing them. This important observation was made at the turn of the century, when Herzeberg, Tubeuf and Volkart observed independently that fungal spores treated with copper sulphate (used instead of Bordeaux mixture to reduce the practical difficulties) do not germinate in water, yet exhibit normal germination on gelatin or in soil. In both cases the probable explanation is that these media contain various complexing agents which have greater affinity for copper than have the vital binding sites within the spore. Hecke showed shortly afterwards that almost all the copper in poisoned fungal spores could be removed easily by washing with dilute acid, and that the spores were then able to germinate normally. He also observed that spores had the ability to accumulate large amounts of copper even when the concentration in the suspension medium was exceedingly low. In other words, the factor deciding the amount of copper absorbed from solutions of copper salts is not the concentration as such, but the total amount present in the medium. When copper ions are absorbed from copper sulphate solution by spores, the sulphate ions do not accompany them into the spore, and work by Bodnar and his co-workers between 1927 and 1932 showed that cations left the spore to restore the electrical balance.

For many years it was believed that the uptake was a simple case of cation exchange. It now seems probable that such uptake is accompanied by an increase in the permeability of the cell membranes, with the result that salts originally stored within the cells tend to seep outwards. This seepage can result in the appearance of a large excess of equivalents of cations in the external medium over the equivalents of copper absorbed by the cells. Using algal cells, McBrien and Hassall (1965) found that, in particular, a large proportion of the cellular potassium was lost on treatment of cells with copper.

Several factors can influence the amount of copper taken up by spores and other types of cells. As would be expected from what was said above, the amount of copper absorbed becomes less as the hydrogen ion concentration of the medium increases. Horsfall (1957) has suggested that the resistance of many fungi to copper fungicides could be attributed to their secreting enough hydrogen ions to render the medium appreciably acidic. In addition, several workers have observed that some reagents which form stable complexes with copper may reduce both the uptake and the toxic effect of copper. EDTA (trisodium ethylenediamine tetra-acetate), a well-known complexing agent, was found by Müller and Biedemann (1952) to reverse the inhibition of the germination of *Alternaria* spores pretreated with copper. Various sulphydryl compounds, including glutathione, cysteine and B.A.L. (British Anti-Lewisite) have the same effect. It should be added that copper complexes sometimes penetrate living tissue more readily than ionic copper, but neither the total amount of copper absorbed nor the ultimate toxic effect is necessarily greater than when ionic copper is employed.

There is still controversy about whether copper exerts its ultimate toxic effect in the cuprous or the cupric form. Parker-Rhodes (1941), on kinetic grounds, and Lowry, Sussman and von Böventer (1957), on unspecified experimental evidence, considered that cuprous copper was the toxicant. Most other workers, including Wain and Wilkinson (1943) and Tröger (1958) support the alternative view. Unpublished work of the writer has demonstrated that copper absorbed on dead algal cells is replaced by silver ions almost quantitatively on an equivalent-for-equivalent basis, if the copper is assumed to be divalent. This demonstrates that the over-whelming majority of copper ions absorbed are present in the form of cupric ions or cupric complexes, but the possibility cannot, of course, be excluded that in living cells a small but important percentage may be present as cuprous complexes at a relatively few vital sites.

Evidence has been accumulating which shows that copper is very toxic when applied to various micro-organisms under anaerobic conditions. Grumbach (1949) noticed that both cupric and cuprous ions were more toxic to aerobic bacteria within the anaerobic zone of growth than they were within the aerobic zone. Hassall (1963) reported that when copper is applied to *Chlorella vulgaris* under anaerobic conditions, subsequent aerobic respiration is markedly reduced compared with the respiration of cells treated with the same amount of copper aerobically. It was also noticed that, for a fixed amount of copper applied to cells, slightly more copper is absorbed by the cells under anaerobic conditions than under aerobic conditions (Fig. 7.2)—but the increased uptake of copper cannot, of itself, account for the greater respiratory inhibition. Somewhat similarly, Somers (1963) observed that spores of *Neurospora* absorb 25% more copper under anaerobic conditions than when air is present.

McBrien and Hassall (1967) demonstrated that algal cells exposed to copper under aerobic conditions suffer drastic respiratory inhibition if, after removing excess copper, the cells are then exposed to a period of anaerobiosis. It was concluded that an internal redistribution of copper occurs at the onset of anaerobiosis and that the extra sites, which only became available or vulnerable under anaerobic conditions, could be sulphydryl groups. The protective effect of sulphydryl reagents, such as B.A.L., and complexing reagents, to which reference was made earlier, is of interest in this respect, although the precise significance of these ob-servations is not yet clear. Hassall (1967) has also demonstrated that, while copper applied aerobically has no immediate effect on the respiration of algae, it nevertheless strongly inhibits respiration when it is administered aerobically but with fluoride present at suitable concentrations. If, as is generally assumed, fluoride inhibits enolase and hence the glycolytic pathway, it is possible that copper ions block some part of the pentose phosphate pathway, a well known 'alternative' pathway by which sugars can be oxidised. Although this possibility has not yet been fully explored,

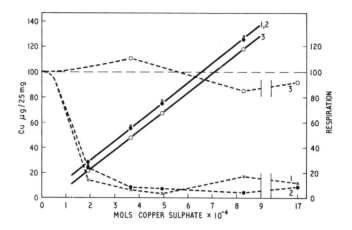

Fig. 7.2. *Respiration and copper in cells when copper sulphate is applied under aerobic and anaerobic conditions*
Abscissa: initial copper concentration, Mols $\times 10^{-4}$/litre (3 ml used)
Right Ordinate: respiration, corresponding control = 100
Left Ordinate: μg copper/25 mg dry weight of cells after 5 hrs' contact.
Continuous lines, cell copper content. Broken lines, respiration from 4 until 4½ hrs after addition of copper
1. Cells shaken in flasks flushed with hydrogen for first 2 hrs
2 Cells with copper in stationary tubes for first 2 hrs
3 Cells in flasks shaken in air
(Note: Results between 9 and 17 have been omitted)

it would account for the greater susceptibility of photosynthesis than of respiration to the effects of copper in the presence of air. The toxic role of copper in various micro-organisms appears to be very similar and work on algae and bacteria is consequently of importance in relation to the fungitoxic properties of copper ions.

The evidence outlined in the last few paragraphs, and the fact that, of all metals tested, only copper led to the difference in response in the absence of air, does not support the commonly held view that the action of copper is *exclusively* one of a non-specific precipitation of proteins of the type occasioned by all heavy metals. Nevertheless, there is often a general relationship between the toxicity of metal ions and certain of their physical characteristics;

copper may be no exception if a broad fungitoxic or phytotoxic effect, rather than inhibition of respiration, is taken as the index of toxicity. For example, the toxicity becomes greater the lower the metal is in the electrochemical series—copper, silver and mercury are all powerfully toxic to fungi and green plants. This relationship was illustrated by the work of Hassall (1963). However, the ease with which metal atoms form ions can only be related indirectly to the strength of the forces binding copper, probably by complex formation, at the site of action. Danielli and Davies (1951) considered that the degree of polarity of the bonds which one element forms with another is a suitable index of the tendency of metals to form strong covalent bonds with cell constituents. The physical measure of this polarity is termed electronegativity. Somers (1961) tested the validity of this idea using spores of *Alternaria* and *Neurospora,* and demonstrated a relationship between the logarithm of the toxic concentration of the metal ions and a quantity which was derived from the electronegativity.

OTHER COPPER FUNGICIDES

Soluble copper compounds are too phytotoxic for use as fungicides on plants but, besides Bordeaux mixture, a variety of insoluble copper compounds has been used for seed treatment, for pre-emergence treatment of the soil in seed boxes and for direct foliage spraying.

Basic copper chloride approximates to the composition $[CuCl_2.3Cu(OH)_2]$ and is thus related chemically to the active principle of Bordeaux mixture. Often referred to as copper oxychloride, it can be purchased both as a dispersible powder and as a colloid. The colloidal formulation must be used with a surfactant—the spray mixture is usually constituted by adding the colloidal concentrate to the wetting agent dissolved in enough water to provide the correct dilution of the active ingredient. For use on some crops, basic copper chloride is mixed with a high grade petroleum oil instead of a wetting agent. This wash has the advantage of checking infestations of red spider mite as well as acting as a fungicide, but it may be phytotoxic if applied under humid conditions or in direct sunshine.

Burgundy mixture is a basic copper compound prepared by adding a small excess of sodium carbonate to a solution of copper sulphate. The sodium carbonate thus replaces the calcium hydroxide used in the preparation of Bordeaux mixture. Upon addition of the sodium carbonate, some carbon dioxide is produced and this reduces the alkalinity (and hence the phytotoxicity) of the mixture by converting the excess sodium carbonate to sodium bicarbonate.

Cuprous oxide has been used both for seed treatment and for the control of blight. It is made by the reduction of cupric salts in alkaline solution and by the electrolytic oxidation of metallic copper. Cupric phosphate, cupric silicate and cupric oxide have all been used from time to time, while a double chromate of copper and zinc has proved effective for disease control on tomatoes, curcurbits and peanuts (Martin, 1953). All these substances are necessarily of low solubility in water (p. 157).

Inorganic copper compounds are employed to control blight of potato and tomato as well as many leaf and fruit diseases of horticultural crops. Some formulations are used specifically for the control of downy mildew of hops (Ministry of Agriculture, Fisheries and Food, 1968). Often, powdery mildew control requires the addition of petroleum to the copper fungicide in powder form, whilst damping-off often succumbs to colloidal or other suspensions of the solid. Copper has the disadvantage of being occasionally phytotoxic, typical symptoms being leaf scorch and russetting on fruit trees and bushes. The phytotoxic hazard is increased after rain or heavy dew, but can be reduced by the addition of cotton seed oil.

Various organic derivatives of copper have been used as fungicides both in crop protection and for the protection of industrial products. The copper derivatives of a mixture of aromatic carboxylic acids derived from petroleum are collectively called copper naphthenates. These substances are viscous liquids and have been employed as wood preservatives and to prevent the rotting of hemp and fabric. They are insoluble in water, soluble in many organic solvents and extremely phytotoxic. Clearly, their use in agriculture is of a vicarious nature—to preserve wooden sheds or fences, wooden seed boxes and greenhouse benches.

Other organic compounds of copper used as fungicides are the complexes formed between copper and 8-hydroxyquinoline, and between copper and 3-phenyl salicylic acid. However, by no means all copper complexes are fungicidal, in spite of the apparent advantage of lipid solubility conferred by complex formation. If the complex is so stable that the copper cannot readily escape from it (and perhaps some form of competition for the copper takes place between the material used in the fungicide and biological complexing agents) then the complex may prove to be of very low fungitoxicity. Wain (1959) refers to several complexes apparently of this type, including copper salicylaldoxime, cuprous thiocyanate and copper phthalocyanine.

For further information on the chemistry and toxic action of heavy metals, including copper, the reader is referred to the reviews of Horsfall (1957), McCallan and Miller (1958) and McBrien (1964), and to the articles by Somers (1961, 1963) and by Hassall (1963).

INORGANIC MERCURY FUNGICIDES

Several inorganic mercury compounds have been used for seed treatment and soil disinfection, but their use has decreased with the advent of organo-mercury fungicides.

Mercuric chloride, $HgCl_2$, is more soluble, more poisonous to animals and more phytotoxic than calomel, Hg_2Cl_2, but it may give some protection against diseases which are carried over in the form of dormant mycelium within the seed (e.g., loose smuts of barley and wheat).

Mercuric chloride is effective against clubroot of brassicas, and was once used as a solution to water-in newly transplanted seedlings. Nowadays it has been largely replaced for this purpose by mercurous chloride or calomel. Although of low solubility, calomel is very phytotoxic and cannot be employed as a fungicide on foliage other than grass. It is rapidly decomposed by, and hence is incompatible with, lime and other alkalies. It is formulated as a 4% dust for the control of clubroot and turf disease, but it is also used undiluted as a root dip. Both mercurous and mercuric chloride have insecticidal as well as fungicidal action and are sometimes useful against soil-dwelling larvae such as those of the cabbage root fly, which gain access to the roots of crop plants from the surrounding soil.

The mode of action of mercury compounds is uncertain. It has been suggested that mercurous chloride may be toxic because of the mercury formed as it slowly decomposes. On the other hand, the toxic action of mercuric chloride when added to spores can be reversed by thiol reagents such as cysteine. It is thus possible that thiol groups within the cell form complexes with mercury compounds, and that these complexes dissociate in the presence of reagents which unite more firmly with the fungicide or with one of its decomposition products.

SULPHUR

To those interested in the chemistry of crop protection, sulphur presents some intriguing dilemmas. The tonnage of sulphur employed for fungicidal purposes in 1958 was some four times that of all other fungicides combined, yet today we are little nearer understanding its striking selectivity as a fungicide than was Forsyth who, in 1803, first described the use of a sulphur spray for fruit trees. Some theories suggest that it is oxidised to an active material, while others suggest that it is reduced to one. Sempis proposed as early as 1932 that it might act in the elemental state; it now seems that this, the simplest of all possibilities, may be the correct explanation.

Although flowers of sulphur have been used in dusts and sprays, use of sulphur in this form is inefficient and wasteful. Sulphur dusts are therefore usually prepared by controlled grinding rather than by sublimation, and contain about 95% sulphur. Elemental sulphur to be used for spraying may be formulated in two ways—as a wettable powder (specified officially as dispersible sulphur), and as a paste (officially termed colloidal sulphur).

Dispersible sulphur must, according to the Ministry of Agriculture specifications, contain not less than 70% sulphur. Moreover, since particle size is of great importance in determining fungicidal effectiveness, the official specification also requires that not less than 40% of the sulphur should be in particles of 6μ or less in diameter. Since pure sulphur particles tend to aggregate, a dispersing agent or diluent, such as kaolin or zinc oxide, is usually added; this largely accounts for the remaining 30% of a dispersible sulphur preparation. The composition of colloidal sulphur pastes and the distribution of the sizes of their particles are similarly subject to official specification in Britain. A paste must contain 40% or more sulphur, and not less than 90% of the particles should be less than 6μ diameter.

The stringent official specifications, as well as the interests of both manufacturer and grower, have demanded the establishment of reliable analytical techniques not only for total sulphur content but also for other attributes including the distribution of particle size in a sample of product. The Food and Agriculture Organisation (FAO) has provided detailed instructions for the determination of sulphur in colloidal sulphur and for determining the distribution of particle sizes in colloidal and dispersible sulphurs (Anon, 1961).

An alternative method of applying sulphur in water is in the form of lime sulphur, in which the sulphur is in true solution as soluble poly-sulphides. Lime sulphur is considered in more detail below, as the main example of a sulphur fungicide.

The Ministry of Agriculture, Fisheries and Food (1958) has issued a technical bulletin in which analytical details and specifications for lime sulphur and other pesticidal materials have been described.

Sulphur is only slightly hydrolysed by water in accordance with the reversible equation:

$$3S + 3H_2O \rightleftharpoons 2H_2S + H_2SO_3$$

but in the presence of alkalies the hydrolysis proceeds readily from left to right:

$$3S + 3Ca(OH)_2 \rightarrow 2CaS + CaSO_3 + 3H_2O$$

When an excess of sulphur is present, as when a suspension of lime is boiled with flowers of sulphur, the additional sulphur reacts with calcium sulphide to give calcium polysulphide and with calcium sulphite to produce calcium thiosulphate:

$$CaS \xrightarrow{xS} CaS.S_x \qquad\qquad CaSO_3 \xrightarrow{S} CaS_2O_3$$

The polysulphide sulphur, S_x, can be regarded as a solution of sulphur. An analogy is provided by the complex KI_3 (formed when iodine is shaken with a solution of potassium iodide), which acts as though it were a solution of iodine in water. Experience has shown that it is the polysulphide content of a lime sulphur wash, rather than the total sulphur content, which provides the best index of fungicidal efficiency in the field.

Lime sulphur is a clear orange-coloured solution which, for the official specification, should contain at least 24% weight/volume of polysulphide sulphur. It is alkaline in reaction and deposits elemental sulphur on exposure to air. Because of its alkalinity and the high availability of sulphur when applied as a true solution, it is often a more efficient fungicide than sulphur suspensions of equal sulphur content. On the other hand, many plants are 'sulphur-shy', including some highly prized varieties of apples and other top fruit. It has been found that over-spraying with lime sulphur on warm days (above 26°C) is particularly liable to cause phytotoxic symptoms. Acute damage is visible as marginal burns on the leaves. Chronic damage takes the form of the development of premature abscission layers which result in early drop of both leaves and fruit.

Lime sulphur is particularly useful against apple scab, although it has a wider anti-fungal 'spectrum' than most organic fungicides and offers some control of powdery mildews (Horsfall, 1957). A full lime sulphur programme for scab may require the application of four sprays of lime sulphur: an early one of high concentration (up to 2·5%) is applied at the 'green cluster' stage of growth; a second and less concentrated spray at the 'pink bud' stage; a third, dilute one at petal fall and a fourth one at the fruitlet stage. The first application is now sometimes omitted and, as was mentioned earlier, one or more of the later applications may be replaced by sprays containing organic fungicides. It should be noted that lime sulphur, because of its alkalinity, its content of calcium ions and its reactivity, is incompatible with many other pesticides and some supplements. It is never compatible with soap and, on arsenic-sensitive plants, is incompatible with lead arsenate (since toxic thio-arsenates are formed). Neither is it compatible with readily hydrolysable organophosphates or with petroleum oils (which greatly accentuate its phytotoxicity). Meyer (1960) found that several metals, including copper, acted as synergists when they were added to sulphur.

At first sight, lime sulphur appears to disobey the general rule that a persistent material must be both stable and insoluble, but this is not so. Instead, it illustrates another generalisation—that materials which undergo non-harmful chemical changes after spraying may thereby become more firmly bound to the leaf surface. The principal chemical change is probably the precipitation of polysulphide sulphur following the action of carbonic acid, but the hydrolytic and oxidative changes shown in Fig. 7.3 may also

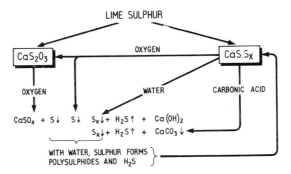

Fig. 7.3. *Possible cyclic changes, involving precipitation and re-dissolving, occurring after lime sulphur is sprayed. The original components are shown in frames*

occur. This precipitation may itself be part of a cyclic process, for it is possible that the sulphur so deposited may tend to redissolve to some extent in the presence of moisture. The hydrogen sulphide liberated is believed by some authors to be fungicidal; it was, for a time, regarded as the actual toxic substance, but it has since been shown that colloidal sulphur is, according to the nature of the fungus, from five to fifty times more fungitoxic than an equal number of moles of hydrogen sulphide (McCallan and Miller, 1958). Nevertheless, spores of many fungi have a remarkable capacity to reduce sulphur—some spores can take up nearly 2% of their own weight of sulphur and then convert most of it into hydrogen sulphide within two hours. Consequently, whether or not this gas is itself fungitoxic, it seems very probable that the biochemical processes which lead to its formation must lie very near the centre of the problem relating to the toxicity of elemental sulphur.

Work with radioactive sulphur in a sulphur fungicide preparation applied to *plants* has shown that internal sulphur compounds become rapidly labelled; as in fungi, it was found that the main labelled end-product was hydrogen sulphide (Miller, 1956). McCallan and Miller (1957) demonstrated an equimolar relationship between carbon dioxide and hydrogen sulphide produced under anaerobic conditions.

Work on fungi and plants alike thus demonstrates that elemental sulphur is certainly not biologically inert and that it probably becomes entangled in one or more biochemical redox systems. Horsfall (1957) ascribed the toxicity of sulphur to its structural resemblance to the natural metabolite, oxygen—the two elements are, of course, members of group 6 of the Periodic Table. Such a theory does not in itself explain the apparently *specific fungicidal* action of sulphur—which unlike copper and many organic fungicides, is almost non-toxic to higher animals (Table 7.1). It is possible that some redox system exists which is only important in fungi, or that, by the sulphur attacking some particular dehydrogenase or electron-carrier, the normal oxidative pathway is deflected in a manner which does not occur in higher organisms. However, Horsfall (1957) appears to prefer the alternative suggestion that the apparently highly selective action of sulphur may be another example of differential availability at the site of action. He suggested that lipid-rich fungi, such as powdery mildews, might retain more sulphur than other types of organisms.

Table 7.1 ACUTE ORAL AND DERMAL TOXICITIES OF SOME FUNGICIDES

Substance	Oral LD_{50} (rat) mg/kg body weight	Dermal LD_{50} (rat) 24 hr contact; mg/kg body weight	Volatility mm Hg
Ethyl mercury salts	30	200	Sometimes high; serious toxic hazard
Mercuric chloride	37	—	$1.4 \times 10^{-4}/35°C$
Phenyl mercury acetate	60	—	$9 \times 10^{-6}/35°C$
Triphenyl tin acetate	106*	—	Negligible
Mercurous chloride	210	—	Negligible
Pentachlorophenol	280	150*	Sufficient to provoke intense sneezing
Copper salts	300*	>1000	Negligible
Thiram	375*	—	Negligible
Dinocap	980*	>9400	Negligible
Dodine acetate	1000*	—	Negligible
Zineb (and similar bis-dithiocarbamates)	1000*	>1000	Negligible
Dicloran	1500*	—	$1.2 \times 10^{-6}/20°C$
Quintozene	1650*	—	Negligible
Chloranil	4000	—	Very low
Captan	9000	—	Negligible
Sulphur and polysulphides	Apparently non-toxic		Negligible

Table compiled from data collected by Edson, Sanderson and Noakes (1966) and from information given in the *Insecticide and Fungicide Handbook* (Anon, 1965).
*signifies that the lowest of several recorded values has been given here.
>signifies that the highest dose tested was less than the LD_{50}.

REFERENCES

Anon (1961), *Pl. Prot. Bull. F.A.O.,* **9,** pp. 80, 83, 103

Anon (1965), *Insecticide and Fungicide Handbook,* (2nd Ed.) (Ed., Martin, H.), Blackwell Publications, Oxford

ARONSON, J. M. (1965), *The Fungi,* Vol. 1, pp. 49–76, (Ed. Ainsworth, G. C. and Sussman, A. S.), Academic Press, New York

BARTNICKI-GARCÍA, S. (1963), *Bact. Rev.,* **27,** 293

DANIELLI, J. F. and DAVIES, J. T. (1951), *Adv. Enzym.,* **11,** 35

EDSON, E. F., SANDERSON, D. M. and NOAKES, D. N. (1966), *Wld Rev. Pest Control,* **5,** 143

GAYNER, F. C. H. (1961), 'Fungicides in Agriculture and Horticulture', *Soc. Chem. Ind. Monogr.* No. 15, 23

GRUMBACH, A. (1949), *Schweiz. Z. Pathol.,* **12,** 97

HASSALL, K. A. (1963), *Physiologia Pl.,* **16,** 323

HASSALL, K. A. (1967), *Nature, Lond.,* **215,** 521

HAWKER, L. E. and HENDY, R. J. (1963), *J. gen. Microbiol.,* **33,** 43

HORSFALL, J. G. (1956), *Principles of Fungicidal Action.* Chronica Botanica Co., Waltham, U.S.A.

HORSFALL, J. G. (1957), *Adv. Pest Control Res.,* **1,** 193

LOWRY, R. J., SUSSMAN, A. S. and VON BÖVENTER, B. (1957), *Mycologia,* **49,** 609

MCBRIEN, D. C. H. (1964), *Aspects of the Uptake of Copper and its Physiological Effects upon Chlorella vulgaris:* Ph.D. Thesis, Reading University

MCBRIEN, D. C. H. and HASSALL, K. A. (1965), *Physiologia Pl.,* **18,** 1059

MCBRIEN, D. C. H. and HASSALL, K. A. (1967), *Physiologia Pl.,* **20,** 113

MCCALLAN, S. E. A. and MILLER, L. P. (1957), *Contr. Boyce Thompson Inst.,* **18,** 497

MCCALLAN, S. E. A. and MILLER, L. P. (1958), *Adv. Pest Control Res.,* **2,** 107

MARTELL, A. E. and CALVIN, M. (1952), *Chemistry of the Metal Chelate Compounds,* Prentice-Hall (pp. 74–75)

MARTIN, H. (1953), *Guide to the chemicals used in crop protection,* Canadian Dept. Agric. loose leaf dossier

MEYER, H. (1960), *Arch. Mikrobiol.,* **37,** 28

MILLER, L. P. (1956), *Atomic Energy Commission Rpt. TID-7512,* p. 228 U.S. Govt. Printing Office, Washington 25, D.C.

Ministry of Agriculture, Fisheries and Food (1958), *Technical Bulletin No.* 1: *Specifications and Methods of Analysis for Certain Insecticides and Fungicides*

Ministry of Agriculture, Fisheries and Food (1968), *List of Approved Products for Farmers and Growers,* (A yearly publication)

MÜLLER, E. and BIEDEMANN, W. (1952), *Phytopath. Z.,* **19,** 343

PARKER-RHODES, A. F. (1941), *Ann. appl. Biol.,* **28,** 389

SOMERS, E. (1959), *J. Sci. Fd Agric.,* **10,** 68

SOMERS, E. (1961), *Ann. appl. Biol.,* **49,** 246

SOMERS, E. (1963), *Ann. appl. Biol.,* **51,** 425

STRICKLAND, A. H. (1966), *J. appl. Ecol.,* **3,** (Supplement—Pesticides in the Environment and their Effects on Wildlife), p. 3

TRÖGER, R. (1958), *Arch. f. Mikrobiol.,* **29,** 430

TRÖGER, R. (1960a), *Arch. f. Mikrobiol.,* **37,** 341

TRÖGER, R. (1960b), *Phytopath, Z.,* **40,** 91

WAIN, R. L. (1959), 'Some Chemical Aspects of Plant Disease Control', *Roy. Inst. Chem. Lectures, Mongr. and Repts.,* No. 3

WAIN, R. L. and WILKINSON, E. H. (1943), *Ann. appl. Biol.,* **30,** 379

ZALOKAR, M. (1965), *The Fungi,* Vol. 1., pp. 377–426, (Ed. Ainsworth, G. C. and Sussman, A. S.), Academic Press, New York

8

ORGANIC FUNGICIDES

Organic substances of many kinds have been used as fungicides. The arbitrary classification in Table 8.1 indicates the variety of materials which has found application in the field, though the list is far from complete.

Nine of the twenty-four organic fungicides mentioned in the Ministry of Agriculture *List of Approved Products* (1968) consist of, or contain,

Table 8.1   CLASSIFICATION OF ORGANIC FUNGICIDES

A. *Sulphur-containing materials*	
1. Non-cyclic	Dithiocarbamates
2. Cyclic	Captan and analogues
B. *Usually without sulphur*	
1. Carbocyclic	Organometal compounds (mercury and tin) Nitro compounds Chlorine-substituted aromatic compounds
2. Non-cyclic or Heterocyclic	Alkyl guanidine salts Alkyl imidazoline salts
C. *Compounds which by systemic action limit attacks of fungi*	
1. Antibiotics	
2. Synthetic systemic 'fungicides'	

derivatives of dithiocarbamic acid. With the exception of the organomercury seed dressings, the dithiocarbamates are the most widely used fungicides in Britain when spray-acreage is the criterion of usage. However, if considered in terms of the tonnage applied, there was in the period 1962–4 (Strickland, 1966) little difference in usage between dithiocarbamates and

Table 8.2 FUNGICIDE USAGE, ILLUSTRATING THE LOW TONNAGE-TO-ACREAGE RATIO OF SEED DRESSINGS IN COMPARISON TO FOLIAGE SPRAYS (AFTER STRICKLAND, 1966)

Chemical substances and crops treated	Basic acreage (in thousands of acres)	'Spray-acres'*	Tonnage employed in the U.K. per year
Dithiocarbamates			
Potatoes, sugar beet	184	547	244
Fruit and hops	41	120	70
Thiram seed dressings	454	454	$\frac{1}{2}$
Organomercury			
Potatoes	10	30	4
Fruit	38	95	$2\frac{1}{2}$
Cereal and sugar beet seed dressings	6000	6000	$13\frac{1}{2}$
Captan			
Fruit	48	288	321
Seed dressings	137	137	$11\frac{1}{2}$

*The difference between basic acreage and 'spray-acres' is explained on p. 155.

captan. The great conservation of pesticide—and consequent saving in cost and reduction in consumer hazard—when seed treatment can be used instead of foliage spraying, is demonstrated for dithiocarbamates, organo-mercury compounds and captan by the figures of Strickland quoted in Table 8.2.

FUNGICIDAL DITHIOCARBAMATES

The uses of dithiocarbamates and their derivatives as fungicides have been excellently reviewed by Ludwig and Thorn (1960) and by van der Kerk (1959) and Thorn and Ludwig (1962).

CLASSIFICATION

Fungicidal dithiocarbamates fall into two major groups. The principal chemical difference is that members of the first group do not have a hydrogen atom linked directly to the nitrogen, whereas those in the second group do (compare Figs. 8.1 and 8.2). When this hydrogen atom is present, it is

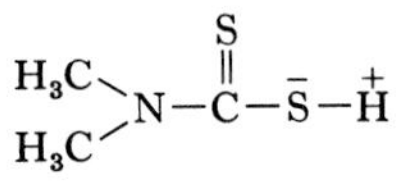

Fig. 8.1. Dimethyl dithiocarbamate (Group 1) 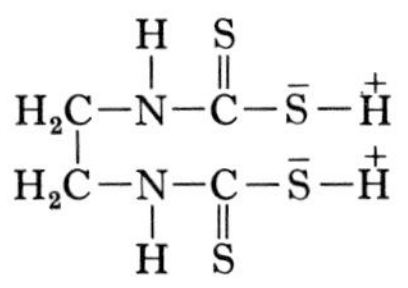   *Fig. 8.2. Ethylene bis-dithiocarbamate (Group 2)*

reactive, a fact which probably accounts for the somewhat different range of organisms killed by substances in the two groups. It may also be responsible for another biological difference—namely, that only members of the first group are more toxic to germinating spores than they are to established mycelium. It is possible, though unlikely, that compounds in the two groups have entirely different modes of action.

Carbamic acid is aminoformic acid, $H_2N.COOH$. The fungicides in the first major group are all derivatives of dimethyl dithiocarbamic acid, although two sorts of derivatives have been used. The first are metallic derivatives, those containing zinc and iron being particularly useful. These metallic compounds are complexes rather than salts. The zinc complex contains two molecules of acid united with one divalent metal ion (Fig. 8.3), while the iron complex contains the ferric ion. The second type of

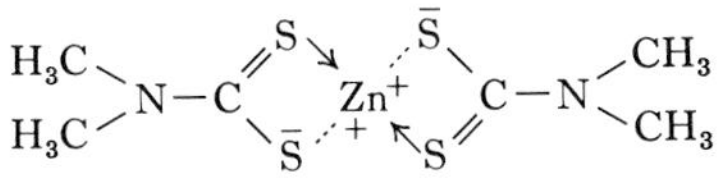

Fig. 8.3. The 1 : 2 complex between zinc and
dimethyl dithiocarbamic acid (Group 1)

derivative is a disulphide oxidation product called thiram (Fig. 8.4). The oxidation can be effected readily in the laboratory and occurs *in vivo* through the mediation of the cytochrome oxidase system. Conversely,

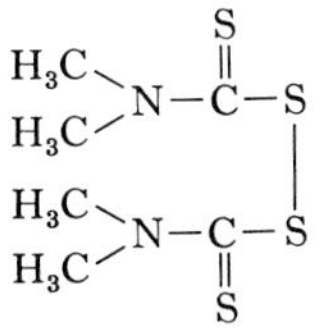

Fig. 8.4. Thiram : tetramethyl thiuram disulphide (Group 1)

micro-organisms are able to reduce the disulphide form back to sulphydryl, so it is probable that the oxidised and reduced forms are inter-convertible under biological conditions (see Fig. 8.5). The somewhat similar antifungal

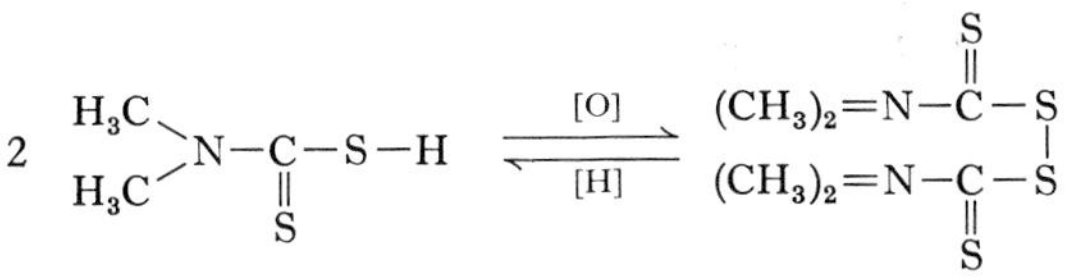

Fig. 8.5. Oxidation derivative of dimethyl dithiocarbamic acid

activity of the metallic complexes and of thiram is therefore to be expected. The alkylene bis-dithiocarbamates of the second major group are quite distinct from the dialkyl dithiocarbamates. First patented in 1943, ethylene bis-dithiocarbamate (Fig. 8.2) is used in the form of its sodium, zinc and manganese derivatives. Common names have been given to both dimethyl dithiocarbamate and bis-dithiocarbamate derivatives, to avoid use either of trade names or of complex chemical terminology. These are given in Table 8.3.

Table 8.3   CLASSIFICATION AND COMMON NAMES OF DITHIOCARBAMATE FUNGICIDES

Type of compound	Type of derivative	Common name
Group 1. The dialkyl dithiocarbamates	(a) Metal derivatives	
	Sodium salt	(none)
	Zinc complex	Ziram
	Ferric complex	Ferbam
	(b) Oxidation Product	Thiram
Group 2 (a) The bis-dithiocarbamates	Metal derivatives	
	Sodium salt	Nabam
	Zinc complex	Zineb
	Manganese complex	Maneb
	Complex of zinc and maneb containing 20% Mn, 2·5% Zn	Mancozeb
(b) Mono-methyl dithiocarbamate	Sodium salt	Metham—sodium

PENETRATION OF SPORES

It is probable that dithiocarbamates of both groups usually enter the fungal spore as unionised molecules, either of the weak acid, its oxidation product, or of one of its covalent complexes. Nabam, for example, which is soluble in water and highly ionised, is of low toxicity to spores of *Monilia* if environmental conditions are such that oxidation cannot occur; conversely, the water-insoluble and lipophilic zinc complex is toxic under these conditions. Once at the site of action, however, it may be essential to the toxic mechanism that an ionic form is readily assumed, for it has been observed that the stable methyl ester of dimethyl dithiocarbamic acid is of low toxicity in spite of its lipid solubility.

MODE OF ACTION OF DITHIOCARBAMATES

Sodium dimethyl dithiocarbamate, and probably other members of group I, exhibit a remarkable phenomenon termed 'inversion of toxicity'. As the dosage increases, it is found that at first the mortality of fungal spores increases in the normal manner, but eventually a concentration is reached after which increasing concentration diminishes the mortality. When the dimethyl dithiocarbamate concentration has increased some twenty fold above this point of inversion, the mortality again commences to

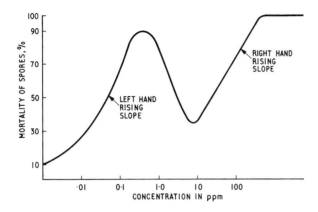

Fig. 8.6. Bi-modal curve, pH 7, for sodium dimethyl dithio-carbamate

rise. Such a dose-response relationship is represented by what is termed a bi-modal curve (Fig. 8.6).

It has long been suspected that the 'cancelling out' effect associated with an increase in concentration in the centre part of the curve might be due to the formation of a new molecular species at the site of action. One theory supposes that the *free dithiocarbamate ion* is functional within the spore,

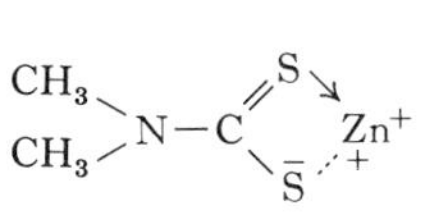

Fig. 8.7. The charged and resonating 1 : 1 complex formed between zinc and dimethyl dithiocarbamic acid (Group 1)

irrespective of which complex (or oxidation product) is applied externally. This dithiocarbamate ion then forms complexes with *internal* heavy metals, especially the trace elements zinc and copper. At low concentrations of dithiocarbamate a univalent resonating complex is formed containing one metal 'ion' to one dithiocarbamate molecule (Fig. 8.7). According to the theory, this complex is toxic, perhaps because it unites with some vital (but un-named) enzyme and its formation may account for the left hand rising portion of the bi-modal curve. At higher concentrations of dithio-

175

carbamate, the stable complex has two dithiocarbamate molecules united to the metal and is the same sort of complex (Fig. 8.3) as that in the formulated product, ziram. At the site of action, this complex is non-toxic and its formation *internally* accounts for the descending part of the bi-modal curve. As the concentration of internal dithiocarbamate rises, a point is eventually reached at which all the internal heavy metal has been converted to the 1:2 complex; thereafter, further increase in external dithiocarbamate causes free dithiocarbamate ions to accumulate internally. This ionic species is believed to be toxic in its own right, perhaps by uniting with a sulphydryl-containing enzyme.

This theory may be satisfactory so far as the much studied sodium dimethyl dithiocarbamate is concerned, but experience with other types of fungicides does not suggest that insolubility in water, either externally or (as for the 1:2 complex encountered here) at the site of action, is necessarily correlated with biological inertness. Several substances, including histidine and certain imidazoles, antagonise the action of thiram and dimethyl dithiocarbamate derivatives. Various authors have attempted to explain this antagonism in terms of some aspect of the chemistry of the 1:1 complex mentioned above, but such theories of action seem only to explain how the left hand ascending limb of the bi-modal curve could be displaced to the right.

In relation to problems associated with the toxic action of thiram, it will be recalled that it can be reduced *in vivo* to the sulphydryl form. Now, thiram has also been found to have a bi-modal dosage-response curve, and one theory of action suggests that the left hand ascending portion of this curve could be due to dithiocarbamate formed on reduction, while the right hand ascending portion is ascribed to the *disulphide* itself. There is, however, something a little unsatisfactory about attempting to explain so rare an event as a bi-modal curve in two different ways for closely related compounds. Admittedly, the left hand section ascribed to sulphydryl compounds could be brought into line with the 1:1 metal complex theory above. But a redox relationship appears to replace the theories which were called upon to explain the central and right hand sections of the response curve of sodium dimethyl dithiocarbamate. Another theory suggests that the dithiocarbamate formed by reduction is the only active form. If this is so, it is odd that heavy metals appear not to alter the toxicity of thiram in the manner to be expected if heavy metal complexes are indeed formed.

Of considerable interest, and of possible relevance to the discussion of the preceding few paragraphs, is the observation that thiram is approximately *twice* as toxic as the 'monomeric' sulphydryl form (Lindahl, 1962). It may be coincidental, but it is potentially of even greater interest, that

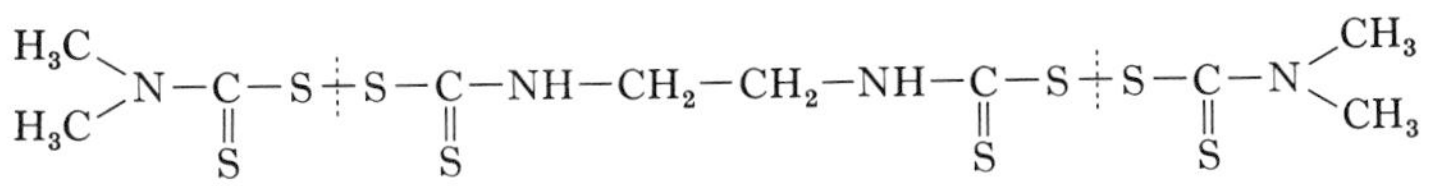

$$H_3C \diagdown N - C - S \dotplus S - C - NH - CH_2 - CH_2 - NH - C - S \dotplus S - C - N \diagup CH_3$$

Fig. 8.8. The 'tri-mer' formed from two molecules of dimethyl dithiocarbamate and one molecule of ethylene bis-dithiocarbamate

the 'tri-mer' formed from two molecules of dimethyl dithiocarbamate and one of ethylene bis-dithiocarbamate is *three* times as toxic as the 'monomers' (Thorn and Ludwig, 1962) (see Fig. 8.8).

Weed, McCallan and Miller (1953), using S^{35}-labelled ferric dimethyl dithiocarbamate (ferbam) had earlier observed that decomposition occurred to give carbon disulphide and that the rate of decomposition was increased by reduced glutathione; oxidised glutathione had no effect. Since glutathione and cysteine partially reverse the toxic action of ferbam, it is possible that the fungitoxic action of dithiocarbamates involves interference with cell constituents important in redox reactions.

Chemistry and mode of action of ethylene bis-dithiocarbamate

The sodium salt of ethylene bis-dithiocarbamate is soluble and ionised. Since it is readily oxidised in dilute solution and on exposure to air, it is seldom used as a fungicide. It is, however, sold by the manufacturers for conversion in the spray tank to zinc or manganese derivatives by the addition of soluble salts of these metals. Zineb prepared in the spray tank is often said to be more effective than that purchased ready made from the manufacturers, but for maneb the opposite is claimed to be the case.

On only two occasions have bi-modal curves been attributed to ethylene bis-dithiocarbamate and its derivatives, but there are other ways in which the biological action of the members of this second group differs from that of the first. It has been shown, for example, that histidine is not able to antagonise their action. Also they kill a different range of fungi from the members of the first group and they are equally toxic to both the spores and mycelium of any one fungus. Since the members of the first group more readily kill spores than mycelium, the implication seems to be that, for the first group, this special toxic action on spores is the one affected by histidine, and that it is represented by the metal-dependent, left hand rising portion of the bi-modal curve. An important practical consequence of the difference in fungicidal 'spectrum' is that, whereas the dimethyl dithio-carbamate derivatives only control early blight of potatoes, ethylene bis-dithiocarbamate derivatives control both early and late blight.

It has been known for a long time that bis-dithiocarbamates (and certain others which have a hydrogen atom attached to the nitrogen) can be oxidised *in vitro* to toxic isothiocyanates, but the corresponding *in vivo* conversion was not suspected till about 1951 (Lloyd, 1962; Cathie, 1963). This is shown in Fig. 8.9.

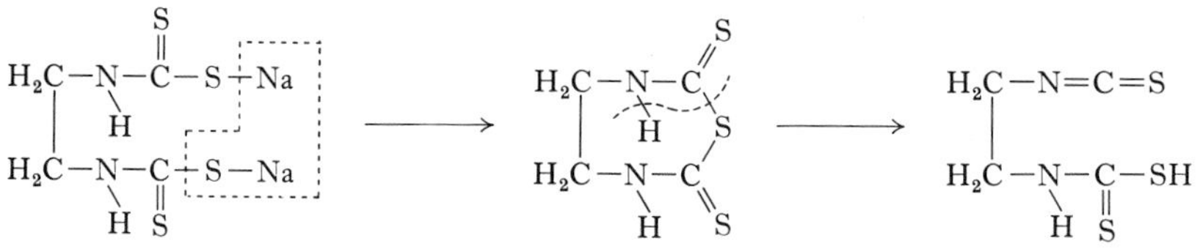

Fig. 8.9. Conversion of bis-dithiocarbamates to isothiocyanates

Whilst there is some biological evidence that an isothiocyanate could be the actual toxicant at the site of action when bis-dithiocarbamates are used, it is difficult to see how a mechanism working through a mono-sulphide could be applicable to the dialkyl dithiocarbamates of the first group; once again, this would lead to the somewhat unconvincing expedient of postulating alternative modes of action for dithiocarbamate fungicides belonging to different groups.

Wedding and Kendrick (1959), investigating the respiration and permeability of the mycelium of *Rhizoctonia,* could find no evidence that N-methyl dithiocarbamate acted *via* an isothiocyanate decomposition product. They concluded that fungicidal effectiveness was more likely to be related, at least in part, to a reaction of dithiocarbamate with the outer surface of living membranes in such a way as to alter their permeability characteristics.

SOME PRACTICAL USES OF THE DITHIOCARBAMATES

Various zinc, manganese and iron derivatives are used as foliage sprays against scabs and rots of fruit and against potato blight. They persist for a shorter time than insoluble copper fungicides, a property which is disadvantageous in seasons when conditions favour potato blight, because more frequent spraying is essential. Zineb, as remarked earlier, is particularly well known for its use against potato blight; it is also employed against several other fungal diseases of potato, tomato, hop, onion, lettuce and mushrooms. It is not usually applied to top fruit, and is being partly replaced on vegetables by the manganese compounds maneb and mancozeb, since these sometimes give superior control.

Ferric dimethyl dithiocarbamate, ferbam, has been used very successfully for the control of apple scab, but gives poor control of powdery mildews. It is, therefore, sometimes employed with elemental sulphur as a double spray. A disadvantage of ferbam is that it leaves an unsightly black deposit on the fruit, a deposit which is only removed with difficulty when the fruit is washed after harvesting.

Thiram is employed more frequently as a seed protectant than as a foliage spray (Table 8.1). Its effectiveness can be attributed partly to the fact that certain soil bacteria, which suppress pathogenic fungi, multiply more rapidly in its presence; as a secondary effect, it can reduce the numbers of some phytophagous soil insects.

Metham-sodium is used as a soil sterilant for the control of potato eelworm and weed seedlings, as well as for controlling soil borne fungi.

METABOLISM AND ANALYSIS OF DITHIOCARBAMATES

There is much evidence to suggest that dithiocarbamates are metabolised rapidly in animals, plants and micro-organisms. The DuPont Company (1951) reported that rats fed for fifteen weeks on diets which contained up to 500 ppm thiram showed the same growth patterns as the control animals. Robbins and Kastelic (1961) studied the fate of thiram when it was fed to lambs. Micro-organisms in the rumen degraded it rapidly; only six hours after feeding, 78% of the ingested dose had been decomposed. The same authors quoted references which suggest that most animals can probably tolerate at least 200 mg/kg body weight. Sijpesteijn and Kaslander (1964), investigating the metabolism of sodium dimethyl dithiocarbamate in plants and micro-organisms, concluded that it was converted, at least in part, to beta-glucosides and to derivatives of amino acids.

Methods of analysis for thiram and other dithiocarbamates are mentioned by Schechter and Hornstein (1957) and later methods have been discussed by Bontoyan (1963).

CAPTAN

Captan is a valuable fungicide derived from phthalic acid, $C_6H_4(COOH)_2$. The acidic hydrogen atom of the imide of this acid can be replaced by metal ions, which in turn can be used as a means of attaching chlorinated mercaptans to the ring. This is illustrated in Fig. 8.10 for the reaction of trichloromethyl mercaptyl chloride with potassium tetrahydro-phthalimide,

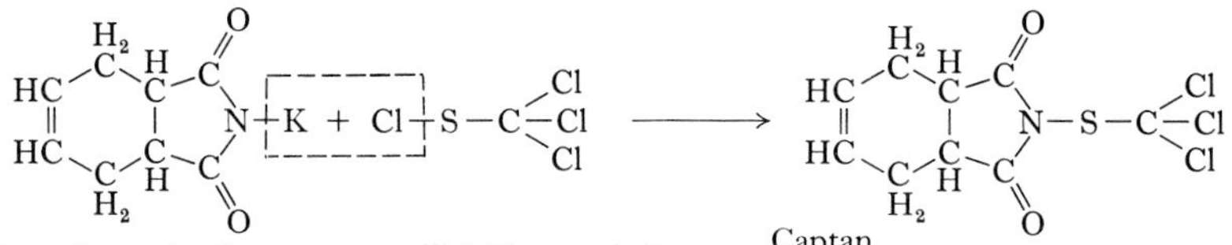

Potassium salt of
tetrahydro phthalimide

Trichloromethyl-
mercaptyl chloride

Captan
(N-trichloromethyl thio-
tetrahydro-phthalimide)

Fig. 8.10. Formula and preparation of captan

when the product is captan. Its fungicidal powers were first recognised in 1952, since when it has been shown that many substances possessing the $= N-S-CCl_3$ and $-O-S-CCl_3$ groups are fungicides (Wain, 1959; Richmond, Somers and Zaracovitis, 1964).

Captan is a white solid of low vapour pressure, insoluble in water and not very soluble in oil. Its oleyl alcohol/water partition coefficient is about 140. It is of moderate stability except under alkaline conditions.

Two formulations are available: a wettable powder containing 50% captan for application as a spray suspension, and a 10% dust. A useful summary of its practical uses and limitations has been issued by the Murphy Chemical Company (Anon, 1955). Captan controls apple and pear scab, grey mould on strawberries and lettuces, as well as blight on potatoes and tomatoes. In comparison with a normal spray programme based on sulphur (especially when the crop is sulphur-shy), captan decreases fruit damage and increases yields of apples and pears. It does not control powdery mildews on any crop, so should not be used in orchards where mildew is already established. At spray dilution, phytotoxicity under British conditions is slight or absent, although minor damage has been reported in other countries. In 1955, the Murphy publication reported the cost of a full schedule of eight applications at fortnightly intervals during the season to be some four times that of a conventional lime sulphur or mercury programme, but in almost all cases, the additional yield amply paid for the increased cost.

Captan is of low mammalian toxicity and presents few hazards to man so long as the powder is kept away from the skin. In common with many other pesticides, it is highly toxic to fish. It possesses a novel residue problem in that it accelerates the corrosion of cans, a complication which can lead to tainting. Klayder (1963) reported that if canning is accompanied by the customary heat processing, most of the captan deposited on fruit is destroyed. Nevertheless, the Ministry of Agriculture, Fisheries and Food (1968) recommends that it should not be used on fruit grown for canning or for quick freezing. The effect of this and other fungicides on the quality and taste of several varieties of fruit and on the corrosion of metal containers has been studied by Crang and Clarke (1961).

Little definite information exists as to why captan is toxic to fungi. The observation of Hochstein and Cox (1956) that it disrupts the thiamine pyrophosphate-decarboxylase system was initially received with some enthusiasm, but it has since been possible to demonstrate that captan can, in the right circumstances, inhibit the action of a wide range of enzymes. For details, reference should be made to articles by Richmond and Somers (1963) and by Montie and Sisler (1962). Hence this, like many other pesticides, embarasses the investigator by having too *many* demonstrable biological effects rather than too few. Consequently, research workers— and their readers—must proceed circumspectly, for mere evidence that some enzyme system can be disturbed does not constitute proof that it is the primary target of the pesticide *in vivo*. Moreover, even after taking into consideration the question of availability of toxicant at the site of action, it is difficult to reconcile the involvement of so universal a system— one involving coenzyme A as well as thiamine—with the fact that captan is selectively fungicidal.

On the other hand, the current trend of opinion favours the view that captan may inactivate sulphydryl groups in enzymes or coenzymes. Opinion is divided as to how this blocking may occur, but it appears to be nonspecific, in the sense that any exposed sulphydryl group may be attacked. Lukens and Sisler (1958), who have postulated a mechanism of attack, considered that amino and carboxyl groups may also be inactivated. Since the decarboxylase system studied by Hochstein and Cox (also susceptible enzymes like phosphoglyceraldehyde dehydrogenase) depend on sulphydryl groups, the sulphydryl-inactivation theory has won fair acceptance.

Richmond and Somers (1963) observed that spores pretreated with thiol-inactivating agents did not absorb so much captan as untreated spores, yet were equally susceptible to the poison. Extending their work to various species of fungi, they observed a correlation between the amount of captan absorbed by spores and their sulphydryl content, but no correlation between the sulphydryl content and susceptibility to captan. From these and other observations they concluded that much captan was inactivated or destroyed at (non-vital) sulphydryl sites, and so prevented from reaching a vital receptor site. If, as seems likely, captan attacks thiols indiscriminately, there is no reason why this work of Richmond and Somers should necessarily be in conflict with the concept that the vital site is itself a sulphydryl compound. It does, however, demonstrate that there may be many inactive or inactivating thiol sites for each one of physiological importance.

By pretreatment of cells of *Neurospora* with iodoacetic acid, a reagent which reacts preferentially with soluble thiol compounds, Richmond and Somers (1966) have provided evidence that soluble cell thiols can, in general, be regarded as detoxifying agents for captan, whereas the less numerous insoluble thiols may be the sites of toxic action. An analogy exists here with the competition between general body lipids and essential lipids which can influence the toxic action of organochlorine insecticides. Thus, if soluble cell thiols are blocked by pretreatment with iodoacetic acid, captan becomes much more toxic on a spore-weight basis—a situation recalling the way in which organochlorine insecticide residues in higher organisms become more toxic under starvation conditions—so long as allowance is made for the difference between (temporary) physical in-activation in fat and permanent chemical detoxication.

Captan is a highly selective fungicide, but if the criterion of toxicity is the amount needed to effect a toxic response, calculated as the amount absorbed per gram of spore substance, it cannot be regarded as being very toxic. This has been well illustrated by Somers (1962). Whereas such substances as atropine, penicillin and organophosphates can exert their toxic effects on various types of organisms within the range of $0.5–2.0\mu g/g$ body weight, the toxic dose of captan (and many other organic fungicides) is frequently within the range of $10^3–10^4\mu g/g$ spore weight. It is the ability of fungi to absorb organic fungicides from dilute external media which makes these substances appear to be very toxic. Their low inherent toxicity, coupled with their relatively non-specific mode of action, may account, at least in part, for the fact that resistant strains of fungi have not so far developed in the field. Resistance is, in fact, extremely difficult to induce even in the laboratory.

The experimental work referred to above demonstrates that the external toxic dose can sometimes be a poor criterion of toxic effectiveness, especially if comparative toxicities of closely related substances are being investigated. The explanation is, of course, that phase distribution between the external medium and the (lipophilic) components of the fungal spore intervenes and may give a false impression of both absolute and relative toxicity. In a classic paper describing the thermodynamic basis of physical toxicity, Ferguson (1939) pointed out that the relative saturation of the external medium was sometimes a more adequate index of toxicity than such things as the amount or the concentration applied. Although this approach, in theory, can only be applied when an equilibrium exists between the amount of toxicant present in the internal and external phases (p. 227), in practice it is often applied to cases of chemical toxicity where a steady state exists between the processes of uptake and those of degradation.

Richmond and Somers (1962) examined the evidence concerning the relative saturations at which captan and some closely related substances operated, and concluded that 'the high levels of uptake of the compounds required to inhibit spore germination, and the high levels of their relative saturations, suggest unspecific mechanisms of toxicity and possible detoxication of the fungicides before they reach vital cellular sites'.

Although phase distribution, and therefore lipid solubility, is an important factor in relation to the apparent toxicity of captan and its analogues, extremely large partition coefficients in favour of oil do not necessarily favour high fungitoxicity. Richmond, Somers and Zaracovitis (1964) could obtain no evidence that lipid solubility, as assessed by the partition coefficient between water and oleyl alcohol, was directly correlated with either protectant or eradicant toxicity. Indeed, the better eradicants amongst the captan analogues tested had, as might have been predicted, somewhat higher aqueous solubilities than the other substances.

ORGANOMERCURY COMPOUNDS

These materials were first introduced as seed dressings some fifty years ago and since then have found limited use as foliage sprays. The general formula of fungicidal organomercury compounds is:

$$R-Hg-X$$

where R may be a substituted or unsubstituted aryl or alkyl group. The group X is frequently, but not always, derived from an acid.

Phenyl mercury chloride, PMC, probably the best known of these fungicides, was introduced as a foliage spray for the control of apple scab in 1942. Many seed dressings in current use contain active ingredients of greater molecular complexity, the acidic group sometimes being acetate, silicate or phosphate, the organic group R ranging from phenyl and cresyl to alkoxy-substituted ethyl ($ROCH_2CH_2$). Specific examples are:

cresyl mercury acetate, $C_6H_4(CH_3)-Hg-O.CO.CH_3$
ethyl mercury phosphate, or EMP
phenyl mercury urea, $C_6H_5-Hg-NH.CO.NH_2$
methoxyethyl mercury silicate, $CH_3OCH_2CH_2-Hg-SiO_3$

Most of the alkyl and alkoxy derivatives of small molecular weight are somewhat soluble in water and appreciably volatile, but some aryl compounds such as phenyl mercury chloride are almost insoluble. The relative extent of eradicant, vis-à-vis protective action possessed by any one member of the group, probably depends upon differences in solubility, volatility and chemical stability. The alkoxyalkyl derivatives are much less stable to hydrolysis than are the aryl compounds, but alkyl compounds are usually the most stable of all. The volatilities of aryl mercury compounds have been investigated by Phillips, Dixon and Lidzey (1959), who reported that there was some correlation between volatility and chemical constitution. Techniques suitable for the analysis of organomercury fungicides have been reviewed by Schechter and Hornstein (1957), but absorptiometric techniques and techniques such as neutron activation analysis are now often employed to assess total mercury rather than organic mercury.

Organomercury seed dressings have been used widely for the control of bunt of wheat and to protect oats and barley from smut. The seeds may either be steeped in a suspension of the poison or they may be dusted with the dry powder. In the latter case the seeds can first be coated with an adhesive, which assists the toxic material, diluted with an inert carrier, to stick to the seed coat. The properties of the carrier are known to influence the retention of the toxic substance—one worker concluded that the best carrier had an average particle size of approximately 10μ. According to the type of dressing (solid or liquid) and the nature of the poison, the mercury content may be as low as 0.5% or as high as 2%. In addition to their use on grain (where they are often the fungicidal component of an insecticide plus fungicide dressing) their possible use for the control of seed borne infections of potatoes and peas has been investigated. In particular, Gates (1959) and Byford (1963) have investigated the possibility of using them to control black-leg disease of potatoes.

Seed treatment has obvious application whenever plant disease is seed borne. Organomercury compounds, unlike most organic fungicides, also possess a limited eradicant action when sprayed on foliage, so long as the infection is not too firmly established. The presence of the organic group almost certainly confers a degree of lipid solubility, which facilitates penetration into both leaf and seed, while the nature of the group X may determine aqueous solubility and hence such properties as phytotoxicity and the ease of translocation. Clearly, a delicately poised balance must be established between these opposing properties if the compound is to be a successful eradicant fungicide. In addition, their low but not always negligible vapour pressure may determine to what extent a seed protectant, acting within the confines of the soil, is able to act as a fumigant.

From the point of view of safety to man and animals, the method of seed treatment has considerable advantages over foliage application. It is economical in the use of poison—in the case of organomercury compounds only a few ounces are needed per acre. Moreover, seed treatment is now usually carried out by the seed merchant, not the grower (a most desirable practice since all reputable merchants will have adequate equipment, as well as technicians trained in the handling of highly toxic chemicals). Thus, when seed treatment is possible, it is not necessary for the grower to handle or dilute dangerous concentrates, and the hazard both to himself and to people and animals in the vicinity is greatly diminished. On the other hand, all treated grain must, of course, be sown; it must never be employed for the preparation of food products for either men or animals. Equally essential is the safe storage of sacks of treated grain prior to sowing, to ensure that it is inaccessible to children and farm animals.

Treated seed is also a hazard to birds, particularly in springtime, and especially when organochlorine insecticides are also present in the dressing; the more voracious devourers of farmers' newly-sown seed may pay dearly for their activities, to the dismay of nature lovers. This complication is a most unfortunate one (Hassall, 1965) for it has unjustifiably brought into disrepute a method of pest control which, when it is applicable, is perhaps the most efficient, economic and—for man himself—the safest, way of applying chemicals which has yet been devised. The problem should, however, be kept in perspective for, in Britain, where phenyl mercury compounds are much more widely employed as seed dressings than are alkyl mercury compounds, few cases of mercury poisoning in birds have been reported on agricultural land. Moreover, the commonest alkyl mercury compound used in Britain is the ethyl derivative; although this is much more persistent than many aryl mercury compounds, probably on account of its greater stability to hydrolysis, it is nevertheless much safer to wild life than is its methyl counterpart. Thus, in Sweden, where methyl mercury compounds are still employed extensively as liquid seed dressings, lethal effects upon grain-feeding birds and their predators have been reported frequently (Borg, Wanntorp, Erne and Hanko, 1966).

If the farmer should for some reason need to apply dry organomercury dressings himself (liquid dressings are not made available to him in Britain), he must proceed with the greatest caution, for the compounds are often skin irritants and some of them are highly poisonous if inhaled. It is, therefore, essential that forearms and hands should be covered by protective clothing, and that some form of respirator should be worn. All the precautions of elementary hygiene (such as washing before eating or smoking) should also be conducted with more than usual rigour. In practice, however, seed dressing is nearly always done by seed merchants. To obviate the risk of treated grain being consumed by accident, it is conventional to colour the seed dressing, the colour of dusted grain acting both as a warning and a code to the nature of the substance in the dressing.

In comparison with their use as seed dressings, the use of organomercury compounds as foliage sprays is of much less importance. They have, however, been employed for the control of such diseases as scab and canker of apple, despite the fact that their field performance depends upon climatic conditions. Phenyl mercury chloride, the one most used for this purpose, is both more effective and more phytotoxic in wet summers than in dry ones. Furthermore, different varieties of fruit show varying tolerance to mercury, and considerable care must therefore be exercised in the application of the correct amount of material. Certain commercially prized varieties, such as Cox's Orange apples, are particularly susceptible. Spray residue problems potentially exist when these stable water-insoluble materials are applied to trees during the growing season—the perceptible eradicant action of phenyl mercury compounds presumably indicates a degree of internal transportation. On the other hand, Beidas and Higgons (1959) investigated the magnitude of residues on apples after spraying the trees with an organomercury compound, and found little evidence of accumulation in fruit. Of 33 samples of apples investigated, 29 had residues of less than 0·01 ppm and the remainder of less than 0·10 ppm. Nevertheless, it is advisable that in Britain these substances should not be used to spray fruit trees after the end of July, and that at least six weeks should elapse between the last application and the time when the fruit is picked. The Ministry of Agriculture, Fisheries and Food (1968) states that at least two weeks must elapse after spraying before animals and poultry are allowed into the treated area.

Phenyl mercury acetate, PMA, is somewhat more soluble than the chloride, and although it has also been used as a foliage spray, it is, as would be expected, of limited persistence. On the other hand, it has a more pronounced eradicant action. It is extremely toxic to animals.

Mercury, like several other heavy metals, is known to affect respiration by attacking sulphydryl groups of enzymes. However, it is not certain whether organomercury compounds are toxic in their own right, or whether they merely act as vehicles by means of which toxic mercury ions are conveyed through lipid barriers to some vulnerable site; consequently, little purpose is served by discussing the biochemical effects of these substances further. Their physiological effects, on the other hand, are of great importance and are of several types. Their tendency to irritate and blister the skin has already been mentioned. Secondly, Hook, Lundgren and Swensson (1954) reported that certain alkyl (not phenyl) mercury compounds produced severe brain lesions in animals. The possibility of destruction of nervous tissue, with its attendant horrors in the case of man, cannot therefore be ignored. Thirdly, some organomercury compounds hydrolyse, and others presumably undergo metabolic decomposition, to give inorganic mercury salts; these are powerful cumulative poisons, tending to concentrate especially in the kidneys (Barnes, 1957; Stolman and Stewart, 1960). All in all, it seems reasonable to question the advisability of using organomercury compounds except as seed dressings, and to recommend that they should not be employed as pesticides at all when less toxic alternatives exist.

ORGANO–TIN COMPOUNDS

As well as mercury compounds, numerous other organo-metallic derivatives have been investigated from time to time. Perhaps the most interesting are the organo-tin compounds which have been studied and marketed in recent years. The principal use of such substances at the present time is for the control of potato blight.

Pieters (1962) reported that in 1950 the Institute for Organic Chemistry at Utrecht commenced work to investigate the possible agricultural uses of organo-tin compounds. It was found that alkylated tin compounds of the general types $RSnX_3$, R_2SnX_2, R_3SnX became more toxic to fungi as the number of alkyl groups increased up to three, but that the nature of the group X (chloride, hydroxide, acetate) was of less importance. Of the alkyl groups, those with three and four carbon atoms conferred highest fungicidal activity. However, when used on plants, the trialkyl tin derivatives were highly phytotoxic at fungicidal concentrations and interest, so far as agricultural use was concerned, switched to the corresponding triphenyl tin derivatives. Although of lower toxicity to fungi, the latter are of low solubility—triphenyl tin (fentin) acetate is soluble in water to the extent of about 20 ppm—and are tolerated by some plants at concentrations well above those necessary to control fungi. For further information, the articles by Hartel (1962) and Lloyd, Otaci and Last (1962) should be consulted.

DINOCAP

Dinitrophenol derivatives are pesticides of great versatility. One member of the group was being employed in Germany as a moth-proofing agent as early as 1892. Their ovicidal properties had been demonstrated by 1925 and a French patent was filed in 1932 to cover the use of two of them (dinitrophenol and dinitro-ortho-cresol, DNOC) as herbicides. Dinocap, dinitrocapryl phenyl crotonate (Fig. 8.11), is the most successful fungicide in this group. First introduced in 1934 as a result of a systematic study of dinitrophenol derivatives of low phytotoxicity, its acaricidal and general fungicidal properties had been recognised by 1945. Sprague (1949) observed that it was particularly effective against the powdery mildews,

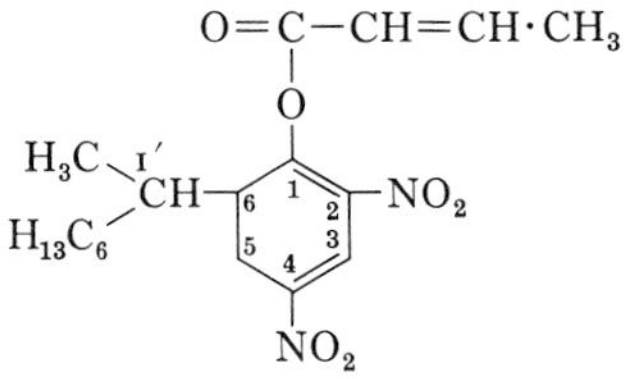

Fig. 8.11. Dinocap : 2,4–dinitro 6–(1'–methyl–n–heptyl)
phenyl crotonate

and his work was confirmed and extended by Yarwood (1951), who applied 73 potential fungicides to bean and cucumber mildews, and, except for an antibiotic, actidione, found dinocap to be the most toxic compound tested.

The discovery of dinocap was to prove of unusual importance, for most organic fungicides have since been found to be somewhat selective in the way they combat fungi, destroying rots and scabs of fruit trees more readily than they attack mildews. The unexpected opposite direction of the selectivity of dinocap has enabled growers to achieve simultaneous control of scabs and mildews on top fruit by applying both dinocap and captan (or some similar material) in their spray programme, especially on apples and hops. This procedure, although costly, has enabled lime sulphur to be replaced by organic materials for the control of fungi on sulphur-shy varieties of fruit.

The mildews are the only important pathogens with mycelium principally on the surface of the aerial part of the host plant. Moreover, they are xerophytic and may sometimes be injured by water as well as by the toxicants suspended in it. Consequently, it might be considered, as Yarwood (1951) apparently did, that they should be susceptible to attack by eradicant as well as protective fungicides, but in practice this has not proved to be the case. This is regrettable, for according to Kirby (1963), the greatest problem associated with the control of (apple) mildew by a protective poison arises from the need to apply the fungicide sufficiently frequently to give protection to newly emerging foliage. The problem is aggravated by the fact that the rate of appearance of new foliage reaches its peak at about the time of the onset of infection.

188

The correct chemical name for dinocap (Fig. 8.11) is 2,4-dinitro, 6-(1'-methyl-n-heptyl) phenyl crotonate, but the substitution in the 6-position is sometimes called '2-octyl' or 'capryl'. Dinocap is an ester, insoluble in water; in it, the phenolic hydroxyl group is combined with crotonic acid, $CH_3.CH = CH.COOH$. Being rapidly hydrolysed by alkalies, it is incompatible with lime sulphur and other alkaline spray toxicants or supplements. In common with many other non-ionised dinitrophenols it is somewhat soluble in oil. Solutions of toxicants in oil are frequently more toxic than aqueous solutions or suspensions, and since dinocap is no exception, it should not be employed in conjunction with hydrocarbon oils. It is of low volatility and—somewhat unexpectedly in view of the toxicity of most derivatives of dinitrophenol—it is not very toxic to animals. The oral LD_{50} for rats has been reported as 980 mg/kg body weight, in contrast to 25–40 mg/kg for DNOC, the commonest member of the group (Table 9.1, p. 213). Dinocap can, however, be irritant to the skin, eyes and nose.

Dinocap is usually formulated as a 25% wettable powder, or, for low-volume application, as a 50% emulsifiable liquid. It is also used occasionally as a dust. Its action is both protective and eradicant, the latter action being increased by those factors affecting penetrability, such as the use of an oily emulsion or of much spreading agent. According to Yarwood (1951), the powder is less effective than the liquid formulation when used as an eradicant, but ten times as effective as a protectant.

The primary use of dinocap on food crops is for the control of powdery mildews on apples, pears, gooseberries and cucumbers. For reasons of cost, lime sulphur is probably, in most circumstances, still the best spray to employ on sulphur-tolerant crops, but should be replaced by dinocap, with or without supplementation by another fungicide, whenever the use of lime sulphur is inadvisable.

The mode of action of dinocap, and in particular the precise contribution of the crotonic acid part of the molecule, is still in doubt. This is somewhat surprising, since the biochemical effect of simple dinitrophenol derivatives is better understood than that of almost any other group of pesticides. Their mode of action is described elsewhere (p. 225) but, briefly, they are known to uncouple oxidation from phosphorylation in the cytochrome system within the mitochondria (Simon, 1953). *A priori,* dinocap might be expected to act similarly. If so, the various substituents in different dinitrophenol derivatives act as carrier groups—or 'shaped charges', as Horsfall (1956) has described similar groups in other molecules—and their task would then be to assist the active or 'toxophoric' dinitrophenol group to reach its site of action. Each type of organism has its own peculiar envelope or surface layer and therefore different carrier groups could be expected to differ in their effectiveness in different organisms. Nevertheless, it is only in recent years that the dinitrophenolic moiety has been suspected of being the toxic centre in the particular case of dinocap.

Bates, Spencer and Wain (1962) found that the benzoate ester of DNOC was not as toxic to spores on slides as it was to spores on the host plant, and in this respect it strikingly resembles the behaviour of dinocap. They also proved that no chemical change occurred to the ester on the slide, but that it was hydrolysed to dinitrocresol on the plant. They thus appear to have demonstrated by a direct method, for a substance of a similar chemical type to dinocap, that the material increases in toxicity *after* a chemical trans-formation has taken place. Kirby (1963) has similarly produced evidence that, in the case of dinocap itself, it is the dinitrophenolic portion of the molecule that is responsible for both its eradicant and protective activity against at least two mildews.

Few investigations have been reported which have dealt with the effect of dinocap upon flavour and quality of bottled, canned or frozen foods, although the general problem of off-flavours has been studied at the Fruit and Vegetable Canning Research Association's laboratories at Chipping Campden, Gloucestershire. In a study by Crang and Clarke (1961), dinocap seemed to be one of the most satisfactory fungicides tested from the point of view of flavour control. At 10 ppm, it could not be detected in fruit syrup and had no effect on cans although corrosion was caused by captan and thiram. In limited trials, no taint of fresh or frozen strawberries and, with one exception, of fresh or frozen gooseberries, was detected. Differences in

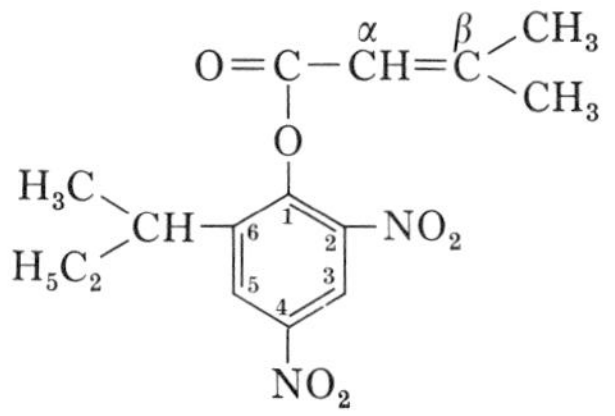

Fig. 8.12. Binapacryl: β—methyl crotonic acid ester of 2,4–dinitro 6 (sec–butyl) phenol

texture of canned fruit were noted in certain trials but it is not clear whether such differences can be attributed to treatment with the fungicide.

Binapacryl (Fig. 8.12) is closely related to dinocap, and has been intro-duced as a fungicide for the control of powdery mildews and red spider mites on apples and on other crops. When binapacryl was first introduced, it was officially recommended that four weeks should elapse between spraying and harvesting an apple crop, but more recently binapacryl has been brought into line with dinocap, and the minimal interval now recommended is seven days (Ministry of Agriculture, Fisheries and Food, 1968). Live-stock must, however, be excluded from the treated area for at least four weeks, a precautionary measure not mentioned in relation to dinocap.

OTHER CHLORINE-SUBSTITUTED AROMATIC FUNGICIDES

DICLORAN

This material (Fig. 8.13), 2,6-dichloro-4-nitroaniline, was first marketed by a British firm in 1959 and has found application in the control of species of *Botrytis* which attack lettuce, tomatoes and strawberries (Clark and

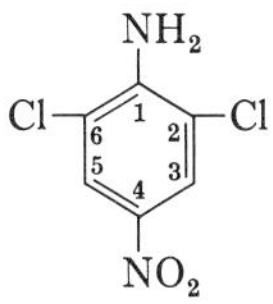

Fig. 8.13. Dicloran : 2,6–dichloro–4–nitroaniline

Hams, 1961). Its use has been extended to the control of organisms which cause post-harvest fruit decay. Thus Ogawa, Lyda and Weber (1961) reported that post-harvest fungal attacks on stone fruits could be sup-pressed by applying dicloran after harvesting but before storage. Ogawa, Boyack, Sandeno and Mathre (1964) have also studied its effect on *Rhizopus* and *Monilinia* spp when applied, not to the stored fruit, but to the tree before fruit is harvested. They found that the 'half-life' of the residue depended on the amount originally applied to the fruit trees and on the time before harvesting at which the material was applied; generally, however, it was some four to eight days.

Dicloran is a solid, insoluble in water, and sufficiently stable to be compatible with most other fungicides, including lime sulphur. Its stability, combined with low volatility, renders it slightly persistent, and the Ministry of Agriculture, Fisheries and Food (1968) recommends that three weeks should elapse between final application (to lettuce) and harvesting. It is used mainly as a 4% dust but it is also formulated as a wettable powder. Phytotoxicity is low, as is mammalian toxicity, the LD_{50} for rats being upwards of 1,500 mg/kg body weight.

A colorimetric determination of dicloran has been described by Roburn (1961). Two procedures for its analysis by gas chromatography are described by Beckman and Bevenue (1962); one of these methods will detect the chlorine in as little as 0·3μg of dicloran.

QUINTOZENE AND TECNAZENE

The fungicidal properties of quintozene (Fig. 8.14), PCNB or pentachloro-nitrobenzene, were known a quarter of a century ago, but it excited little interest until 1956, when it was observed that quintozene could control

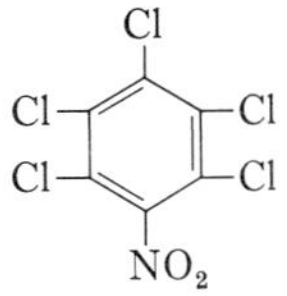

Fig. 8.14. Quintozene : pentachloronitrobenzene

many pathogenic fungi in soil. It is now employed principally to control certain soil or seed-borne fungal diseases (Rose, 1963), including bunt of wheat and damping-off of brassicae. It has also been used against *Botrytis* on lettuce and *Rhizoctonia* spp.

Tecnazene (Fig. 8.15), TCNB or 1,2,4,5,-tetrachloro-3-nitrobenzene, with one chlorine atom per molecule less than quintozene, was introduced in 1947, mainly for use against *Fusarium* dry rot of potatoes. However, it

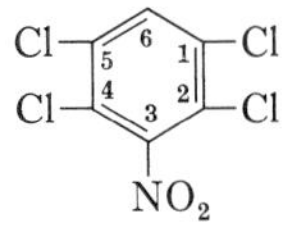

Fig. 8.15. Tecnazene : 1,2,4,5–tetrachloro–3–nitrobenzene

also depresses the growth of angiosperms, and is used as a dust to inhibit the sprouting of stored potatoes (British Insecticide and Fungicide Council, 1965, p. 54). It is less safe than quintozene for use on lettuce, and can both delay hearting and stunt growth.

Quintozene is a colourless, odourless solid, almost insoluble in water but readily soluble in benzene. It is stable and of low volatility, and it is formulated as a 20% dust. Tecnazene is similar, but, being of lower molecular weight, is somewhat more volatile. It is marketed as a 6% dust, as an emulsifiable concentrate and as a smoke formulation. The persistence of these two chlorinated nitrobenzenes in an enclosed space, such as soil, is an inverse function of volatility, hence quintozene is the more persistent.

Both tecnazene and quintozene are of low toxicity to man and animals. Phytotoxicity is also usually low, but cucumbers and tomatoes are susceptible and should neither be sprayed with them nor planted in soil recently treated with them.

A related material, 1-chloro,2,4-dinitronaphthalene, has been reported to be more toxic than either captan or dithiocarbamates to certain pathogenic fungi under laboratory test conditions.

CHLORINATED PHENOLS

If a hydroxyl group is substituted for the nitro-group in the formula of quintozene (Fig. 8.14), pentachlorophenol (Fig. 8.16) is obtained, a substance well known for its herbicidal properties. Although also strongly fungicidal, it has only limited and indirect uses in agriculture, for it is too

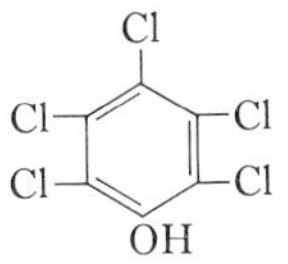

Fig. 8.16. Pentachlorophenol

phytotoxic to be employed on foliage. However, it is used on the farm to preserve timber in fences, barns and mushroom houses. In addition, it has wider uses for the protection of wool and textiles against fungal and insect attack (Waterhouse, 1958).

Pentachlorophenol is usually formulated as its sodium salt. This forms a colourless solution which can be brushed on to timber, or into which timber can be dipped. It is of moderate toxicity to animals, the LD_{50} for rats being about 210 mg/kg, but the solution, even at a concentration of only 1%, may cause skin irritation and the vapour induces severe sneezing (British Insecticide and Fungicide Council, 1965, p. 52).

Several attempts have been made to reduce the phytotoxicity of pentachlorophenol while retaining its antifungal action. Woodcock (1959) reported work by himself and Byrde in which an attempt was made to achieve this result by 'disguising' the hydroxyl group, usually by converting it into an ester. The acetic ester was much less phytotoxic than the parent

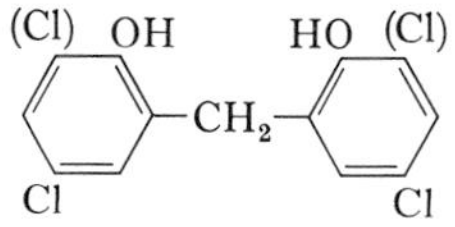

Fig. 8.17. Fungitoxic bisphenols

phenol, but still too damaging for safe use on plants except in the absence of foliage. Other workers have noticed that if the hydroxyl group is 'disguised' by producing a stable ether rather than an unstable ester, fungitoxicity is almost lost. This fact suggests that enzymes in fungi hydrolyse acylated phenols.

Several authors have reported that bisphenols are fungitoxic, both as mildew preventives on fabric and when used against plant pathogens. Thus Corey and Shirk (1955) found a di- and a tetra-chlorinated bisphenol (Fig. 8.17) to be extremely effective in inhibiting the growth of *Aspergillus niger*.

CHLORINATED QUINONES

Two of these, chloranil (Fig. 8.18) and dichlone (Fig. 8.19) have found some use as agricultural fungicides. Chloranil, tetrachloro-1,4-benzoquinone, was first seriously investigated as a fungicide in 1938, although it had been patented for this purpose much earlier (Horsfall, 1956, p. 187).

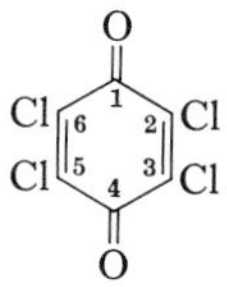

Fig. 8.18. Chloranil : tetrachloro–1,4–benzoquinone

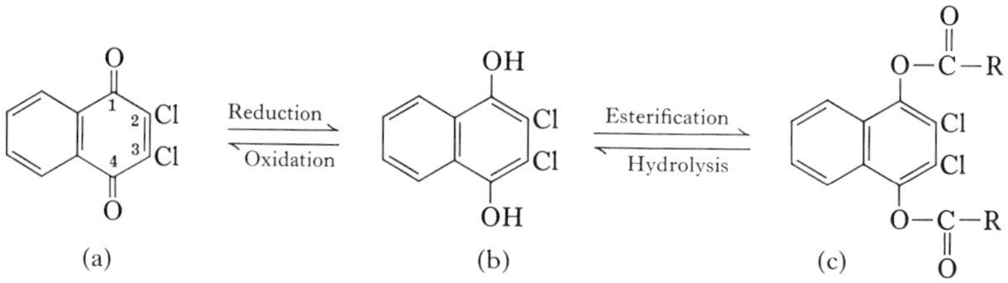

Fig. 8.19. Dichlone : 2,3–dichloro–1,4–naphthoquinone (a) and its relation to dichloro–naphthohydroquinone (b) and its esters (c)

Curiously, like the dithiocarbamates, chloranil was a well known pro-oxidant in the rubber industry before its fungicidal potential was recognised.

Chloranil is used mainly as a protectant for seeds and bulbs. It is particularly useful for seeds of legumes; some 3 ounces per 100 lb pea seeds, for example, will protect them against damping off (Rose, 1963, p. 136). It has also been used as a foliage spray, especially against downy mildew of brassicae, although it tends to be phytotoxic. Moreover, in the presence of light, chloranil is readily oxidised to a more soluble compound, a fact which may account for its low fungitoxicity on foliage.

Unchlorinated quinone has some anti-fungal activity, but halogenation increases toxicity, probably by decreasing aqueous solubility and increasing solubility in oil. However, the chlorine atoms may do more than merely alter the physico-chemical attributes of the molecule, for a probable detoxication mechanism involves the combination of molecules in the presence of a polyphenol oxidase to give rise to a melanin type of pigment of high molecular weight. Such a polymerisation does not seem to occur if the positions ortho to the quinone group are occupied by chlorine atoms.

Dichlone (Fig. 8.19), is 2,3-dichloro-1,4-naphthoquinone. It appeared in 1943, and although often used as a seed dressing, it can also be applied to leaves (McCallan, 1957, p. 87). As a foliage spray, it has been used against apple scab and late blight of potatoes. It is incompatible with oil, and is highly phytotoxic when dissolved in covalent solvents. As a seed dressing, dichlone is sometimes 4 to 8 times as effective as chloranil in the protection of seeds of legumes. It has the advantage over mercury seed dressings of being far less toxic to man, although it can cause skin irritation. It is formulated as a 50% wettable powder for use both as a foliage spray and as a seed dressing.

Attempts to reduce the phytotoxicity of dichlone led to the investigation of the corresponding hydroquinone and of many of its esters. The hydroquinone is fungitoxic, probably because it is readily oxidised *in vivo*, but it also possesses high phytotoxicity. Its esters are somewhat less phytotoxic, and possess a toxicity to fungi which is roughly correlated with the ease with which they can be hydrolysed. This is another example of how hydroxyl groups can be 'disguised' by forming a compound which is more or less readily converted back to the active form (in this case, first to the hydroquinone and then the quinone) by the action of enzymes.

Dichlone is taken up rapidly by fungal spores and is, on the basis of weight absorbed by unit weight of fungal spores, amongst the most effective of organic fungicides. The dose for 50% inhibition of germination is of the order of 500μg per g spore weight, compared with many thousands of μg for most organic fungicides (p. 182).

GUANIDINE AND IMIDAZOLINE DERIVATIVES

DODINE

Dodine, or n-dodecyl guanidine acetate (Fig. 8.20), was introduced in America in 1956. It has found considerable use in the control of apple scab in seasons when the incidence of infection is high, although Byrde, Clarke

$$C_{12}H_{25}-NH-\underset{\underset{NH}{\parallel}}{C}-NH_3^+\cdots\cdots{}^-OOC\cdot CH_3$$

Fig. 8.20. Dodine : n–dodecyl guanidine acetate

and Harper (1962) found it no more effective than captan in seasons when the incidence was low. It probably also checks mild attacks by mildews. There is some evidence that, as well as being a protective fungicide against scab, it may be able to eradicate recent (although not well established) scab infections. Its ability to protect foliage against apple scab increases with the frequency of spraying, but even three applications will often give excellent control. It is also used for the control of pear scab and of certain diseases of cherry and strawberry.

Dodine is a cationic surfactant and is incompatible with many anionic detergents. It is soluble in hot water, has a low volatility, and, being a strong base ($pK_b = 1\cdot5$), it is almost fully ionised within the pH range of biological importance. It is formulated as a 65% wettable powder. Salts other than the acetate have more recently been patented as fungicides.

Dodine is of low mammalian toxicity, the LD_{50} for rats being above 1000 mg/kg body weight. Although it can be irritant to the skin, it is not regarded as a hazard to operators and is not in the Agriculture (Poisonous Substances) Regulations. It may be used on any growing edible crop without danger to the consumer (Ministry of Agriculture, Fisheries and Food, 1963) and apples can be picked within one day of the final application. Dodine has been reported as being slightly phytotoxic to some varieties of apples, though this was not observed in extended trials at Long Ashton (Byrde, Clark and Harper, 1962). Pears, however, may occasionally be damaged when the weather is cold.

The toxicity of dodine to fungi varies with the pH of the external solution. Thus, Brown and Sisler (1960) found that, for a given toxic effect, the toxic dose was twenty times as great at pH 5·1 as at pH 7·8. This was ascribed to the effect of pH upon the ionisation of those anionic sites, present within the fungal cell, with which the (fully ionised) guanidine cation was believed

196

to react. The uptake of dodine by spores is very rapid, at least 85% of the dose ultimately taken up being removed from the external solution within one minute of contact. It is apparently attached to anionic cell constituents such as (insoluble) phosphate and carboxyl, for whereas washing dead spores treated with captan results in the removal of this substance, similar spores treated with dodine acetate retain all the dodine they have absorbed (Somers, 1966).

The experiments of Hamilton and Szkclnik (1958) indicated that dodine was capable of a local movement within the leaves of sprayed plants, for when leaves were sprayed with it on their undersides prior to inoculating the upper surfaces with *Venturia,* the spores failed to develop. Nevertheless, any such movement is limited and is probably associated with the surface activity of the molecule; it is not a truly systemic effect. This is demonstrated by the work of Curry (1962), who labelled dodine on the guanidine carbon atom and repeatedly applied the labelled material to branches of apple trees throughout the growing season. Subsequent measurement of radio-activity indicated that only traces of breakdown products, representing less than 0·2% of the dodine applied, were to be found in the fruit, and chemical tests suggested that these products were innocuous materials such as creatine and amino acids.

Two groups of workers have investigated the connection between structure and toxicity within the guanidine series by varying the length of the alkyl side chain. Brown and Sisler (1960), using yeast and *Monilinia* as test organisms, found that whereas maximal fungitoxicity was obtained when the alkyl group contained 13–14 carbon atoms, the maximal phytotoxicity occurred when it contained only ten. Byrde, Clifford and Woodcock (1962) confirmed this work, using a series of thirteen alkyl guanidine acetates and employing *Venturia* as test organism. Maximal fungitoxicity occurred when the side chain contained 12–15 carbon atoms.

The only extensive study so far made of the mode of action of dodine at the biochemical level is that of Brown and Sisler (1960). They demonstrated that it altered the metabolic pattern in their two test organisms; for example, under anaerobic conditions, untreated yeast cells did not ferment pyruvate whereas treated ones did. Dodine also altered the permeability of the cells, causing loss of phosphorus compounds and of ninhydrin-positive substances. Both the effect of dodine on permeability and its dependence on pH are characteristic of the action of many other cationic surfactants, and it is of interest that Kirby and Frick (1963), in a study of surfactants, found that the fungitoxicity of cationic detergents was greater than could be explained by their wetting ability alone.

A method of analysis for dodine residues on fruit, capable of detecting down to about 0·2 ppm, has been described by Pasarela (1964). The extracted material is complexed with bromocresol purple, and the complex is separated and hydrolysed. Optical absorbence of an aqueous solution containing the salt of bromocresol purple is then measured at 590 mμ.

GLYODIN

Glyodin, or heptadecyl-2-imidazoline (Fig. 8.21) is the best known of the imidazoline (glyoxalidine) fungicides. It was discovered in 1946 and found use in the control of apple scab. It appears to have been largely superseded

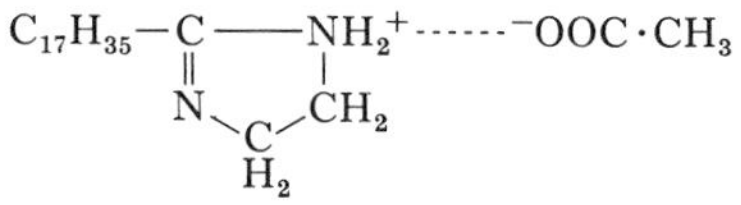

$$C_{17}H_{35}-\underset{\displaystyle N}{\overset{\displaystyle \parallel}{C}}\text{------}NH_2^+\cdots\cdots{}^-OOC\cdot CH_3$$

Fig. 8.21. Glyodin: heptadecyl–2–imidazoline

by dodine in Britain, for it appears neither in the Ministry of Agriculture *List of Approved Products* for 1968 nor in the Official Handbook of the British Insecticide and Fungicide Council (1965).

The imidazoline fungicides resemble the guanidines in two ways: first, compounds in both groups are alkyl-substituted bases formulated as their salts (usually acetates); secondly they are cationic surfactants. Glyodin, like dodine, is taken up rapidly by fungal spores and probably attaches itself to fixed anionic sites on or in the cell. The result is an absorption which appears to be a spectacular example of accumulation against the concentration gradient (McCallan and Miller, 1958). Such an appearance is, however, deceptive, for true accumulation is endergonic, and requires that the molecular species are the same on either side of some active 'membrane'; when molecules are removed from solution by attachment to a substrate, the apparent concentration gradient may be quite illusory.

In the imidazoline series, as in the alkyl guanidines, maximal fungitoxicity occurs higher in the series than does maximal phytotoxicity. In the case of the imidazolines, these occur respectively when there are 13–17 and 11–13 carbon atoms in the alkyl group (Martin, 1964, p. 137). Horsfall (1956, p. 72) ascribes the fungitoxicity of the heptadecyl analogue to its similarity with the length of the carbon chain of the fats in fungi. Unsaturated side chains attached to the imidazoline nucleus increase greatly the phytotoxicity in comparison with the toxicity of the corresponding alkyl compounds.

When in the form of the free base, heptadecyl imidazoline is slowly decomposed by water (an aliphatic amine being produced by the opening of the imidazoline ring), but its salts are much less readily hydrolysed. Moreover, the uncombined base is a soft waxy grease. For these reasons, the fungicide is normally formulated as a solution of the acetate in isopropyl alcohol. After dilution in the spray tank, the fungicidal base is liberated by the addition of lime.

Little is known of the mode of action of heptadecyl imidazoline, but West and Wolf (1955) consider that it is a competitive analogue of guanine. If this is the case, its action would appear to be quite different from that of dodine.

An analytical method resembling that described above for dodine, and dependent on bromophenol blue, has been described by Kleinman (1963).

Numerous series more or less closely related to the guanidines or the imidazolines have been tested as fungicides, often with quite striking results, at least in the laboratory. Compounds based upon pyrazole, which is similar to imidazole except that the two nitrogen atoms of the hetero-cyclic ring are adjacent, have proved outstandingly toxic against *Alternaria* and *Pythium*. Some aryl nitroso-pyrazoles have systemic properties but unfortunately, for reasons of phytotoxicity and perhaps of cost, they do not seem to be very useful in the field. Similarly, various alkyl-substituted pyrimidines, purines and oxazolines (which have an oxygen atom in place of one of the two imidazole nitrogen atoms) have been found to be power-fully fungitoxic in spore germination tests (McCallan, 1957; Martin, 1964).

SYSTEMIC COMPOUNDS WHICH LIMIT FUNGAL ATTACK

The successes of systemic insecticides and herbicides have led to strenuous attempts to develop systemic fungicides, and in view of the enormous losses of food caused by fungi, it is regrettable that these attempts have so far been poorly rewarded. The systemic fungicide would be the ideal way to attack plant pathogens, for translocation would enable internal mycelium and penetrating haustoria to be attacked directly, would overcome problems arising from the fact that even small pieces of surviving mycelium are capable of regeneration, and would reduce the present need to rely on highly persistent external protective poisons. Unfortunately, fungi and plants are more similar biologically than are insects and plants, and it is found that many compounds potently fungicidal *in vitro* cannot be used on plants because they are also very phytotoxic. Some progress has nevertheless been made and the present state of knowledge relating to systemic anti-fungal compounds has been comprehensively reviewed by Dimond (1965), by van der Kerk (1963), Goodman (1962), Cremlyn (1961) and by Dimond and Horsfall (1959).

A systemic antifungal compound is also often termed a therapeutant. Plant chemotherapy has been defined by Dimond (1959) as 'the control of plant disease by compounds that, through their effect on the host or the pathogen, reduce or nullify the effect of the pathogen'. It should be noted that such compounds are not necessarily fungicidal, or even fungitoxic, in the conventional sense, for their effect may be indirect. Indeed, the majority of systemic compounds at present known to check the spread of fungal infection probably act in an indirect manner. Although the nature of these indirect effects is by no means fully understood, there is evidence that some systemic compounds assist the plant to combat fungi by altering the metabolism of the plant, while others inactivate enzymes which are secreted by fungi to facilitate their attack on plant tissue. There is evidence that yet others may, in an unknown way, alter the plant-fungus relationship in favour of the plant (van der Kerk, 1963).

As with other types of pesticides, antifungal systemic compounds may enter the plant through the leaves or through the roots. The latter method of entry has been studied most extensively, although van der Kerk (1963) does not consider that compounds dependent on this path of uptake are likely to prove so valuable as those penetrating through the leaves—except, perhaps, for the control of vascular diseases and diseases of the root. Antifungal substances entering through the roots vary greatly in the extent to which they become attached to cellulose or other insoluble cell con-stituents, and it seems possible (Chapman, 1951) that those which are effective against root fungi are those which are attached strongly, whereas substances entering through the soil must be weakly fixed to components of root cells if they are intended to combat an infection in the shoot.

Downward movement of substances applied to leaves, although rare for substances so far investigated, has been noted in several instances. Oxine benzoate (see below), and certain protective poisons such as Bordeaux mixture and zineb (p. 174) have been observed to bring about a diminution in the fungal or bacterial populations in the soil surrounding the roots after being applied to leaves (Kendrick and Zentmyer, 1957). Although little is known about the mechanism of translocation after application to leaves, Brian (1956) has pointed out that it is the small movement from leaf surface to the vascular system, rather than the large movement thereafter, which probably demands a precise balance of physico-chemical properties in the molecule.

STREPTOMYCIN

Streptomycin, produced by *Streptomyces griseus,* is one of several antibiotic substances used for the control of plant diseases. It is primarily a bacteriostatic substance, and has found commercial use for the control of bacterial pathogens of plants. For example, it is superior to Bordeaux mixture or captan for the control of bacterial diseases of stone fruits (Brian, 1956). In addition, it is active *in vivo,* though seldom *in vitro,* against obligate parasites of the Order *Peronosporales,* and has been used commercially to eradicate 'blue mould' fungus on tobacco. In Britain, the Ministry of Agriculture, Fisheries and Food (1968) has suggested its use for early spraying against downy mildew of hops; at least eight weeks must elapse from the time of spraying to the time that the hops are picked.

There is no evidence to suggest that streptomycin undergoes metabolic activation within the plant and it is therefore possible that its low *in vitro* activity implies that it acts indirectly by inducing a change in the tissue of the host plant (Goodman, 1962). It has been suggested that streptomycin increases the activity of plant phenolases, enzymes which are believed to assist the plant indirectly to combat the spread of fungal infections.

Streptomycin is a basic substance with a molecular weight of 581. It is soluble in water and fairly stable to moderate heat and to a restricted range of pH, although it is destroyed by boiling with dilute acid or alkali. It is readily taken up by the roots of plants, but suffers from the disadvantage of a somewhat high phytotoxicity; it causes chlorosis by interfering with the synthesis of chlorophyll. It also appears to be able to enter through the leaves and even the stems of many plants, and has been detected in the pith, cortex and phloem of stems some time after being applied to the surface. Its apparent absence from the xylem is probably due to rapid upward translocation; conversely, its presence in the phloem of stems near the place of application would appear to confirm that downward translocation, if it occurs at all (it has been reported to occur when high concentrations are used) is a relatively slow process. The translocation of this and other antibiotics has been discussed by Mitchell, Smale and Metcalf (1960).

CYCLOHEXIMIDE

Cycloheximide, or actidione, is also produced by *Streptomyces griseus.* It is much less soluble in water than is streptomycin, a saturated solution containing only 20 g/l, but it is soluble in chloroform. Perhaps because of this greater solubility in lipids, it is more specifically antifungal in its action than streptomycin, and can eradicate cherry leaf spot and wheat stem rust. Its effectiveness in the control of plant fungal diseases has been reviewed by Ford, Klomparens and Hammer (1958). It appears to be translocated upwards after foliar application, for Lemin and Thomas (1961), using tritium-labelled cycloheximide, observed that it appeared in the stem and leaves above the point of application but that it did not enter the roots. This study, using pine seedlings, also suggested that the material is able to persist in a plant for many weeks without detectable degradation. As in the case of streptomycin, it is sometimes phytotoxic, though its effect appears to be primarily one of inducing necrosis rather than of inhibiting the production of chlorophyll (Cremlyn, 1961).

Cycloheximide has the distinction of being the most powerful fungicide known if the criterion of toxicity is the amount of absorbed poison having unit effect (rather than dose measured in terms of the external solution). The LD_{50} for cycloheximide is, in fact, only $0.4\mu g/g$ yeast cells (Somers, 1966) while the corresponding figures for most other organic fungicides is often many hundreds of micrograms. Its toxicity is possibly due to its ability to inhibit the transfer of amino acids from soluble RNA to ribosomal protein.

GRISEOFULVIN

Griseofulvin, produced by *Penicillium griseofulvum,* is one of the most interesting systemic antifungal substances. It has been marketed on a small scale in Britain, though it does not appear in the 1968 *List of Approved Products.* It is soluble in water but is of limited solubility in organic solvents and enters plants through their roots. It is fairly stable except at the extremes of the pH range.

Griseofulvin has a wide antifungal 'spectrum', as the work of Napier, Turner and Rhodes (1956) has demonstrated, but its use against *Botrytis* and *Alternaria,* especially on lettuce and tomato, is worth special mention. It is usually most effective against fungi with immature cell walls, causing hyphae to curl in a rather characteristic manner (Cremyln, 1961). It is of low toxicity to animals, presents no hazard to operators, and does not appear in the Agriculture (Poisonous Substances) Regulations. The official recommendation, however, is that at least four weeks should elapse between the last application to edible crops and harvesting.

Griseofulvin is less phytotoxic than most other antibiotics but it is much more readily absorbed and translocated in some plants than in others. The main movement within the plant is passive, the amount taken up being linearly related to the amount of water transpired. In short experiments griseofulvin is transported largely unchanged, and some passes into the non-vascular tissues of stem and root. In the bean, it has a half-life of about four days.

SYNTHETIC SYSTEMIC COMPOUNDS

Synthetic materials of many sorts have been tested experimentally as potential antifungal systemic compounds (the antibiotic substances already described were, at least initially, derived from living organisms). Insofar as the search has been carried out systematically, two lines of approach can be recognised. One of them has been to test biologically active compounds of many kinds after altering their molecules so as to minimise the undesirable phytotoxic side of their activity. The second has been to commence with non-systemic fungicides and to confer mobility upon them by suitable modification of the molecular structure. A few of the many materials which have been tested experimentally, and sometimes used commercially, are mentioned below.

Sulphonamides

The sulphonamides are the most interesting of the numerous medical drugs which have some systemic action in plants (Rudd Jones, 1956, Mitchell, Smale and Metcalf, 1960), although procaine derivatives have also been investigated (van der Kerk, 1963). The particular use of sulphonamides has been against rusts in cereals, but fairly large doses are needed and they tend to be toxic to the host plant. To check spores of rust, for example, concentrations of 100 $\mu g/g$ fresh weight of leaves may be necessary. Other disadvantages of sulphonamides include the fact that they are only effective against obligate parasites and also that they are only fungistatic; as soon as the treatment ceases the fungus is able to start growing again.

All the sulphonamides appear to have the same effect on the fungus, for they probably interfere with the synthesis of folic acid. Nevertheless, their systemic effectiveness varies (Brian, 1956). For example, sulphanilamide enters plants better than sulphaguanidine. Again, while sulphanilamide and sulphathiazole both enter plants readily, only sulphanilamide is rapidly transported away from the roots.

Oxine

Oxine (Fig. 8.22), which is 8-hydroxyquinoline (8-quinolinol) is an example of a conventional fungicide which, when suitably formulated, appears to possess some systemic action. In particular, the sulphate has been used to control *Rhizoctonia* and *Fusarium* on horticultural crops and the benzoate

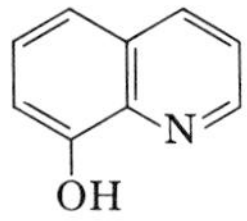

Fig. 8.22. Oxine : 8–hydroxyquinoline (8–quinolinol)

has been used against Dutch elm disease. There is some evidence that oxine can be translocated downwards.

One of the most striking chemical characteristics of oxine is its capacity to chelate with metals, and it was thought originally that its ability to remove trace metals might be the explanation of its fungitoxicity. But, contrary to the requirements of such a theory, at least in its simplest form, addition of heavy metal ions will not reverse the toxic action. Moreover, the copper chelate, which on this theory might have been expected to be inactive, is a potent fungicide, apparently because its lipid solubility confers upon it a greater penetrative power than is possessed by the hydroxyl-containing base. Indirect support for this interpretation comes from the work of Byrde, Clifford and Woodcock (1958), who synthesised alkyl derivatives of oxine and demonstrated that maximal fungitoxicity was achieved with the relatively lipid-soluble amyl and hexyl members of the series.

On the other hand, it is possible that two chelate complexes play a part in the overall toxic action. It has been suggested that a complex containing two oxine molecules joined to one copper ion enters the plant, but equilibrates there with another complex containing one oxine molecule attached to one copper ion; this second complex may then be the actual toxicant (Woodcock, 1959, p. 274). This proposed mode of action should be compared with that advanced for the dithiocarbamates (p. 174) and it is noteworthy that oxine shares with the dithiocarbamates the rare distinction of having a bi-modal dosage-response curve. The significance of the bi-modal curve and of the nearly irreversible action of oxine except in the presence of certain very powerful chelating agents, has been discussed in more detail by Horsfall (1957). The present writer shares the view expressed by Durkee (1958), that while the formation of metal complexes no doubt plays a part in the overall toxic action, the mere removal of trace metals by complex formation is not, in itself, sufficient to explain the toxicity of oxine; toxicity appears to be partially correlated with lipid solubility, with ability to chelate and with the strength of various chelation complexes.

Oxine is an excellent example of how difficult it is to draw a precise line between the conventional protective fungicide and a substance with systemic action. The free oxine would normally be regarded as a typical protectant, yet, as has been seen, it is widely accepted that lipid-soluble metal chelates are readily formed from it, and that it is these which penetrate into fungal spores. It seems highly likely, therefore, that such complexes can also penetrate into plants. Indeed, Woodcock (1959) considered that even the allegedly systemic oxine sulphate and benzoate are actually translocated within the plant in the form of metal complexes.

Phenyl thiosemicarbazide and phenyl thiourea

Phenyl thiosemicarbazide derivatives have been reported by van der Kerk (1963) to be of potential importance as antifungal systemic compounds. Some compounds of this group have high antifungal activity, are readily absorbed by both roots and leaves, and have been shown to control *Cladosporium, Venturia, Phytophthora* and *Botrytis* on plants.

Phenyl thiourea is an interesting example of a systemic compound which may favour the host by indirect action. There is evidence that it functions by inactivating a pectolytic enzyme secreted by the fungus to dissolve the middle lamellae of cells it is attacking. This evidence has been discussed by Kaars Sijpesteijn and Pluijgers (1962) and by van der Kerk (1963); the latter author has mentioned other materials, especially certain quinones, which may possess an indirect antifungal action by the operation of a somewhat similar mechanism. Wain (1960) has speculated that natural inhibitors of pectolytic enzymes may exist in plants, and that the efficiency of these inhibitors may sometimes be a factor contributing to resistance when a plant has a *natural* immunity to a fungal disease.

Phenoxycarboxylic acids

Phenoxycarboxylic acids are well known as plant growth regulators and as herbicides. Many attempts have been made to reduce the phytotoxicity of these systemic compounds while at the same time accentuating their antifungal activity. Since most of these substances are of low fungitoxicity *in vitro,* yet do not seem to be activated by the plant, it seems likely that the protection they confer on the plant is not due to a direct attack on the fungus, or even upon its exuded enzymes. Rather, they seem to change the metabolism of the plant so as to render the environment less favourable to the fungus. There is evidence, for example, that they alter the level of reducing sugars in the host (Kendrick and Zentmyer, 1957; Cremlyn, 1961).

As early as 1952, American workers had noticed that herbicides based on phenoxyacetic acid gave tomatoes some protection against *Fusarium.* Fawcett, Spencer and Wain (1955, 1957) carried out a systematic investigation of *in vitro* and *in vivo* activity using numerous aryloxy- and arylthio-alkane carboxylic acids. They found that certain derivatives of iso-butyric acid, and others of 2,6-di-substituted phenoxyacetic acid, were without activity as growth regulators, yet were highly antifungal *in vivo.* Indeed, these substances were often superior to the griseofulvin used as a standard. As has so often been observed within series tested as fungicides, it was found that, with few exceptions, the aryl-thio compounds were far more effective antifungal agents than were their aryl-oxy counterparts.

REFERENCES

Anon (1955), *Orthocide (Wettable* 50% *Captan).* Reports on trials conducted during 1954, Murphy Chemical Co., Ltd., Wheathampstead, Herts.
BARNES, J. M. (1957), *Adv. Pest Control Res.,* **1,** (1), 20
BATES, A. N., SPENCER, D. M. and WAIN, R. L. (1962), *Ann. appl. Biol.,* **50,** 21
BECKMAN, H. and BEVENUE, A. (1962), *J. Fd Sci.,* **27,** 602
BEIDAS, A. S. and HIGGONS, D. J. (1959), *J. Sci. Fd Agric.,* **10,** 527
BONTOYAN, W. R. (1963), *J. Ass. off. agric. Chem.,* **46,** 662
BORG, K., WANNTORP, H., ERNE, K. and HANKO, E. (1966), *J. appl. Ecol.,* **3** (Supplement). Pesticides in the Environment and their Effects on Wildlife, p. 171
BRIAN, P. W. (1956), *Proc. 2nd Internatn. Plant Protection Conf.,* Fernhurst, p. 143. Butterworths, London
British Insecticide and Fungicide Council (1965), *Insecticide and Fungicide Handbook,* (Ed. Martin, H.) Blackwell Publications, Oxford
BROWN, I. F. and SISLER, H. D. (1960), *Phytopathology,* **50,** 830
BYFORD, W. J. (1963), *Ann. appl. Biol.,* **51,** 41
BYRDE, R. J. W., CLARKE, G. M. and HARPER, G. W. (1962), *A. Rept. Agric. Hortic. Res. Sta.,* Long Ashton, Bristol, for 1961
BYRDE, R. J. W., CLIFFORD, D. R. and WOODCOCK, D. (1958), *Ann. appl. Biol.,* **46,** 167
BYRDE, R. J. W., CLIFFORD, D. R. and WOODCOCK, D. (1962), *Ann. appl. Biol.,* **50,** 291
CATHIE, L. S. (1963), *Wld Crops,* **15,** 460
CHAPMAN, R. A. (1951), *Phytopathology,* **41,** 6
CLARK, N. G. and HAMS, A. F. (1961), *J. Sci. Fd Agric.,* **12,** 751
COREY, R. R. and SHIRK, H. G. (1955), *Arch. Biochem. Biophys.,* **56,** 196
CRANG, A. and CLARK, G. M. (1961), *J. Sci. Fd Agric.,* **12,** 227
CREMLYN, R. J. W. (1961), *J. Sci. Fd Agric.,* **12,** 805
CURRY, A. N. (1962), *J. agric. Fd Chem.,* **10,** 13
DIMOND, A. E. (1965), Adv. Pest Control Res., **6,** 127
DIMOND, A. E. (1959), *Plant Pathology: Problems and Progress.* (Ed. Holton, C. S.), p. 221, Univ. Wisconsin Press

DIMOND, A. E. and HORSFALL, J. G. (1959), *A. Rev. Pl. Physiol.*, **10**, 257

DU PONT, E. I. DE NEMOURS (1951), *Dithiocarbamates and Thiuram Fungicides*

DURKEE, A. B. (1958), *J. agric. Fd Chem.*, **6**, 194

FAWCETT, C. H., SPENCER, D. M. and WAIN, R. L. (1955), *Ann. appl. Biol.*, **43**, 553

FAWCETT, C. H., SPENCER, D. M. and WAIN, R. L. (1957), *Ann. appl. Biol.*, **45**, 158

FERGUSON, J. (1939), *Proc. R. Soc.*, **127(B)**, 387

FORD, J. H., KLOMPARENS, W. and HAMMER, C. L. (1958), *Pl. Dis. Reptr.*, **42**, 680

GATES, L. F. (1959), *Ann. appl. Biol.*, **47**, 502

GOODMAN, R. N. (1962), *Adv. Pest Control Res.*, **5**, 1

HAMILTON, J. M. and SZKOLNIK, M. (1958), *Phytopathology*, **48**, 262

HARTEL, K. (1962), *J. agric. vet. Chem.*, **3**, 19

HASSALL, K. A. (1965), *Brit. vet. J.*, **121**, 105

HOCHSTEIN, P. E. and COX, C. E. (1956), *Amer. J. Bot.*, **43**, 437

HOOK, O., LUNDGREN, K. D. and SWENSSON, A. (1954), *Acta med. scand.*, **150**, 131

HORSFALL, J. G. (1956), *Principles of Fungicidal Action*, Chronica Botanica Co., Waltham, Mass., U.S.A.

HORSFALL, J. G. (1957), *Adv. Pest Control Res.*, **1**, 193

KAARS SIJPESTEIJN, A. and PLUIJGERS, C. W. (1962), *Meded. LandbHoogesch, OpzoekStns Gent*, **27**, 1199

KENDRICK, J. B. and ZENTMYER, G. A. (1957), *Adv. Pest Control Res.*, **1**, 219

KIRBY, A. H. M. (1963), *Wld Rev. Pest Control*, **2**, (1), 18

KIRBY, A. H. M. and FRICK, E. L. (1963), *Ann. appl. Biol.*, **52**, 45

KLAYDER, T. J. (1963), *J. Ass. off. agric. Chem.*, **46**, 241

KLEINMAN, A. (1963), *J. Ass. off. agric. Chem.*, **46**, 238

LEMIN, A. J. and THOMAS, R. C. (1961), *J. agric. Fd Chem.*, **9**, 254

LINDAHL, P. E. B. (1962), *Physiologia Pl.*, **15**, 607

LLOYD, G. A. (1962), *J. Sci. Fd Agric.*, **13**, 309

LLOYD, G. A. OTACI, C. and LAST, F. T. (1962), *J. Sci. Fd Agric.*, **13**, 353

LUDWIG, R. A. and THORN, G. D. (1960), *Adv. Pest Control Res.*, **3**, 219

LUKENS, R. J. and SISLER, H. D. (1958), *Phytopathology*, **48**, 235

MCCALLAN, S. E. A. (1957), *Proc. Pl. Prot. Conf.*, 1956, Butterworths, London

MCCALLAN, S. E. A. and MILLER, L. P. (1958), *Adv. Pest Control Res.*, **2**, 107

MARTIN, H. (1964), *Scientific Principles of Crop Protection*, (5th ed.) Edward Arnold, London

Ministry of Agriculture, Fisheries and Food (1963), sheet on dodine acetate in the loose leaf dossier issued by the Ministry's Safety, Health and Welfare Branch

Ministry of Agriculture, Fisheries and Food (1968), *List of Approved Products for Farmers and Growers* (A yearly publication)

MITCHELL, J. W., SMALE, B. C. and METCALF, R. L. (1960), *Adv. Pest Control Res.*, **3**, 359

MONTIE, T. C. and SISLER, H. D. (1962), *Phytopathology*, **52**, 94

NAPIER, E. J., TURNER, D. I. and RHODES, A. (1956), *Ann. Bot.* **20**, 461

OGAWA, J. M., BOYACK, G. A., SANDENO, J. L. and MATHRE, J. H. (1964), *Hilgardia*, **35**, 365

OGAWA, J. M., LYDA, S. D. and WEBER, D. J. (1961), *Pl. Dis. Reptr.*, **45**, 636

PASARELA, N. R. (1964), *J. Ass. off. agric. Chem.*, **47**, 300

PHILLIPS, G. F., DIXON, B. E. and LIDZEY, R. G. (1959), *J. Sci. Fd Agric.*, **10**, 604

PIETERS, A. J. (1962), *Proc. Brit. Insecticide and Fungicide Conf.*, 1961, **2**, 461

RICHMOND, D. V. and SOMERS, E. (1962), *Ann. appl. Biol.*, **50**, 33

RICHMOND, D. V. and SOMERS, E. (1963), *Ann. appl. Biol.*, **52**, 327

RICHMOND, D. V. and SOMERS, E. (1966), *Ann. appl. Biol.*, **57**, 231

RICHMOND, D. V., SOMERS, E. and ZARACOVITIS, C. (1964), *Nature, Lond.*, **204**, 1329

ROBBINS, R. C. and KASTELIC, J. (1961), *J. agric. Fd Chem.*, **9**, 256

ROBURN, J. (1961), *J. Sci. Fd Agric.*, **12**, 766

ROSE, G. J. (1963), *Crop Protection*, (2nd ed.) Leonard Hill, London

RUDD JONES, D. (1956), *Outl. on Agric.*, **1**, 111

SCHECHTER, M. S. and HORNSTEIN, I. (1957), *Adv. Pest Control Res.*, **1**, 353

SIJPESTEIJN, K. and KASLANDER, K. (1964), *Outl. on Agric.*, **4**, 119

SIMON, E. W. (1953), *Biol. Rev.*, **28**, 453

SOMERS, E. (1962), *Sci. Progr.*, **50**, 218

SOMERS, E. (1966), *Proc. 18th Symposium Colston Res. Soc.*, **18**, 299

SPRAGUE, R. (1949), *Proc. Wash. St. hort. Ass.*, **45**, 47

STOLMAN, A. and STEWART, C. P. (1960), *Toxicology: Mechanisms and Analytical Methods*, Vol. 1, (Ed. Stewart, C. P. and Stolman, A.) Academic Press, New York (p. 206)

STRICKLAND, A. H. (1966), *J. appl. Ecol.*, **3,** 3, (Supplement—'Pesticides in the Environment and their Effects on Wildlife')

THORN, G. D. and LUDWIG, R. A. (1962), *The Dithiocarbamates and Related Compounds,* Elsevier Publ. Co., New York

VAN DER KERK, G. J. M. (1959), *Plant Pathology : Problems and Progress,* Univ. Wisconsin Press (p. 280)

VAN DER KERK, G. J. M. (1963), *Wld Rev. Pest Control,* **2,** (3), 29

WAIN, R. L. (1959), 'Some Chemical Aspects of Plant Disease Control', *Lect. Monogr. Rep. R. Inst. Chem.,* No. 3

WAIN, R. L. (1960), *Jl. R. agric. Soc.,* **121,** 117

WATERHOUSE, D. F. (1958), *Adv. Pest Control Res.,* **2,** 207

WEDDING, R. T. and KENDRICK, J. B. (1959), *Phytopathology,* **49,** 557

WEED, R. M., MCCALLAN, S. E. A. and MILLER, L. P. (1953), *Contrib. Boyce Thompson Inst.,* **17,** 299

WEST, B. and WOLF, F. T. (1955), *J. gen. Microbiol.,* **12,** 396

WOODCOCK, D. (1959), *Plant Pathology : Problems and Progress* (Ed. Holton, C. S. *et al.*) Univ. Wisconsin Press (pp. 267, 270, 274)

YARWOOD, C. E. (1951), *Proc. 2nd Internatn. Congr. Crop Protn.,* p. 500

9

HERBICIDES

Unlike insects and fungi, weeds only seriously reduce yield or quality of produce when they compete with the crop for available light, nutrients or water and when such factors as the nature of soil and farming techniques do not in themselves seriously limit food production. In many parts of the world, weeds may fare little better than crop plants and, where labour is cheap, they may in any case be readily eliminated by hand. But in advanced farming communities, where crops are grown on good soil and over vast areas, the financial loss due to weeds (or to the necessity for their control) may be prodigious. Shaw (1963) estimated that the energy expended for weed control each year, in the United States of America alone, was equivalent to that which would be needed to remove a ridge of soil fifty feet high and a mile wide, stretching all the way from New York to San Francisco.

Since several comprehensive accounts already exist (Audus, 1964; Crafts and Robbins, 1962; Crafts, 1961), this chapter will be confined mainly to considerations of general importance in weed control. After classifying herbicides according to their uses and their chemical structure, some of the factors determining their persistence on or in plants and in the soil are discussed. In addition, very brief summaries of the properties, uses and mode of action of several groups of herbicides are included, together with references to sources of more detailed information.

NON-SELECTIVE AND SELECTIVE HERBICIDES

Non-selective weed control involves the elimination of all the plants growing on a given piece of land. Because the poison does not need to differentiate between one type of plant and another, non-selective control is usually simple to accomplish, except when the weeds are well established and deep rooted. If the herbicide is chosen carefully and the dose calculated with care, the length of time the material remains in the soil can be predicted within certain limits. Inorganic substances such as sodium chlorate and sulphuric acid, as well as a wide range of organic poisons, have been employed non-selectively.

A minor difficulty becomes apparent at this point, necessitating a word of caution. Almost any herbicide, when used in large enough amount, loses its selectivity, hence it would not be correct to imagine that non-selective action always involves the use of intrinsically non-selective chemicals. An intrinsically non-selective material may here be defined as one which would kill most kinds of plants if they were dipped into, or sprayed with, a solution of a concentration level just above that which killed the most sensitive species present. Similarly, as will be seen shortly, it does not follow that intrinsically non-selective herbicides cannot be used selectively under field conditions, for, in practice, a variety of other factors determines how much of an applied dose *actually comes into contact* with plants of different kinds.

Compounds employed for non-selective weed control vary greatly in their properties and in the way they can be applied; some are therefore more valuable in particular circumstances than others. Some intrinsically non-selective compounds, such as simazine and certain urea derivatives, have a long term sterilising effect on soil, while others such as aminotriazole, trichloroacetic acid and sodium chlorate, are, at suitable concentrations, of relatively low persistence in soil. Some herbicides, such as copper salts and diquat salts, destroy the foliage to which they are applied, but do not necessarily reach or destroy subterranean growth, while others, such as simazine and trichloroacetic acid, are applied to the soil to kill fibrous roots, runners and germinating seeds.

Most agricultural weed problems, however, require the destruction of weeds without simultaneous damage to the crop plants amongst which they are growing. The biological similarity between the crop and the weeds growing in it is greater than that between crop and insect pests, or even that between crop and pathogens, and presents a correspondingly more difficult problem. Biochemical differences can seldom be exploited to achieve selectivity, since many types of weeds usually grow amongst one crop; moreover, the detailed biochemistry of different species of plants is seldom known. There is, in fact, only one well known case (involving the presence or absence of a β-oxidase), in which a difference in biochemistry probably lies behind the apparently selective action. More usually, selectivity depends upon less subtle attributes. Sometimes, morphological, chronological or ecological factors of various types can be exploited (Fig. 9.1). Thus dicotyledonous plants often have the sensitive meristematic tissue vulnerably exposed (sometimes located at the centre of a rosette of leaves) whereas monocotyledons often have narrow upright leaves which

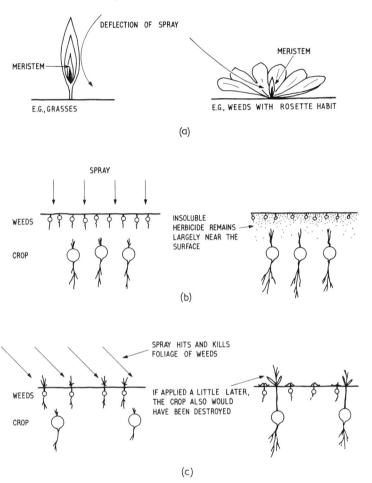

Fig. 9.1. Some distribution factors determining selectivity of herbicides:
(a) Morphological factors (e.g., foliage application)
(b) Ecological factors (e.g., residual pre-emergence treatment)
(c) Chronological factors (e.g., contact pre-emergence treatment)

retain little of the spray and which sheath the meristem. Some weeds are shallower-rooted and grow more rapidly than the crop plants, thus emerging before the crop and becoming a specific target for a spray (e.g. of diquat, sulphuric acid, or hydrocarbon oils) which would, shortly afterwards, be equally lethal to both weeds and the crop. In other cases a placement technique is employed which ensures that only the weeds come into contact with a significant dose of the (non-selective) herbicide.

Again, a soil-acting herbicide of low solubility may sometimes destroy those competitive weeds which arise from seeds germinating near the surface, whereas the crop, though equally sensitive, is protected by the fact that its seeds are sown deeper in the soil and are thus spatially separated from the herbicide. In this respect, it should be observed that a chemical is seldom washed down as one concentrated layer, but instead becomes more and more dilute as some, but only some, penetrates deeper into the soil. The selective toxicity of herbicides has been discussed in more detail by Ennis (1964) and by Holly (1964).

SELECTIVITY BETWEEN PLANTS AND ANIMALS

Many of the most frequently used selective herbicides, including MCPA, 2,4-D and propham, are also selective in a quite different sense, in that they are relatively toxic to most plants yet relatively innocuous to animals. There are, however, certain exceptions. The substituted dinitrophenols, for example, which are used for the control of weeds in cereals, are extremely toxic to higher animals.

Those herbicides which attack biochemical systems of peculiar importance to plants may (unless they possess some alternative mode of action) have remarkably high LD_{50}s for animals. On the other hand, these compounds cannot be expected to show great selectivity between different types of plants unless some factor other than biochemical action is also involved. Thus photosynthetic poisons such as the carbamates, urea compounds and triazines, all of which are soil-acting, are of low selectivity unless placement technique, depth of the root system of the crop, or some similar factor, intervenes. Diquat dibromide, which, unlike the substances mentioned above, is used as a foliage spray, is similarly a non-specific inhibitor of photosynthesis. It can destroy any foliage with which it comes into contact, although suitable timing or placement can often lead to selective action. The LD_{50}s of herbicides have been reported by Edson, Sanderson and Noakes (1966) and a few selected examples are provided in Table 9.1.

It will be clear from what has been said above that, 'selectivity' being a relative property, the use of this term can be misleading unless the context is defined clearly. A compound showing high selectivity between plants and animals may possess low selectivity between different plants, or between plants and micro-organisms. Similarly, as was evident in earlier chapters, insecticides which show great selectivity between insects and higher animals may show little or no selectivity between insect pests and beneficial arthropods.

Table 9.1 THE AQUEOUS SOLUBILITIES AND ACUTE TOXICITIES OF SOME HERBICIDES

Substance	Toxicity to rat, mg/kg body weight		Aqueous solubility
	Oral LD$_{50}$	Dermal LD$_{50}$	
DNOC	25*	200*	130 ppm. Salts more soluble
DNBP	50	135*	1000 ppm. Salts more soluble
Paraquat	157	—	Very soluble
PCP	280	150*	20 ppm. Na salt very soluble
Diquat	400	—	Very soluble
2,4-D	375	1500	620 ppm. Triethanolamine salt very soluble
Barban	600	> 1600	Low
MCPB	680	1000	44 ppm. Na salt moderately soluble
2,4-DB	700	800	46 ppm. Na salt moderately soluble
MCPA	700*	> 1000	825 ppm. Na salt very soluble
Mecoprop	650 (mice)	—	620 ppm. Na salt very soluble
	930 (rat)	—	
Propham	1000*	—	Between 32 and 250 ppm
Aminotriazole	1100*	> 10,000	28g/100ml/25°C
Chlorate-Na	1200*	—	79g/100ml/0°C
Monuron	3500	> 2500	230 ppm
Maleic hydrazide	3800	> 4000	6000 ppm. Salts soluble
Chlorpropham	3800*	—	Between 80 and 108 ppm
Simazine	5000	—	5 ppm. (In methanol, 400 ppm)
Trichloroacetate-Na	5000	—	The acid and its Na, NH$_4$ salts, very soluble
Dalapon-Na	6600*	—	Sodium salt very soluble

Table compiled from data collected by Edson, Sanderson and Noakes (1966) and from information given in the *Weed Control Handbook* (1968).

*signifies that the lowest of several recorded values has been given here.

> signifies that the highest dose tested was less than the LD$_{50}$.

CLASSIFICATION OF HERBICIDES

A useful scheme of classification is based upon the most usual method of application of a substance, and upon whether or not the substance is translocated from the place where it makes contact with the plant. It should, however, be stressed that classification is not sharp; sprays customarily applied to foliage may occasionally be applied to the soil, while some substances are toxic both when they act through the leaves and when they act through the roots. Moreover, since the distinction between contact and systemic action depends ultimately, amongst other things, upon solubility relationships which are themselves not absolute (for nothing is 'insoluble'), no clear cut distinction is, in fact, to be expected. Thus, after root application of a sparingly soluble substance, translocation can often be demonstrated using a radio-isotope technique where some less sensitive method of analysis would have suggested an exclusively local action. Furthermore, although substances of similar chemical type usually behave in a similar manner, it is often possible to modify the chemical structure to fit the substance for application by a different route. Thus the phenoxycarboxylic acid herbicides are nearly always applied to leaves, but derivatives can be made which are non-toxic to foliage yet, after undergoing certain alterations in the soil, gain entry to weeds through their roots.

The following classification gives some examples and uses of herbicides:

FOLIAGE APPLICATION

Contact poisons
1. Most *inorganic herbicides,* including H_2SO_4, $CuSO_4$
2. *Pentachlorophenol*
   (Added to oils for general weed control; also a pre-harvest desiccant for legumes)
3. Substituted *dinitrophenols,* e.g. DNOC, dinoseb
   (Control of dicotyledons in cereals; some are safe on legumes)
4. Mineral *oils*
   (Selective weed control in Umbelliferae; also for non-selective pre-emergence weed control)

Systemic (translocated) poisons
1. *Phenoxycarboxylic acids,* e.g. 2,4-D, MCPA, mecoprop, MCPB
   (The most used and valuable herbicides for weed control in cereals and some other crops)
2. *Chlorinated carboxylic acids,* e.g. dalapon
   (Low persistence; used to control couch and similar grasses in arable land)
3. *Triazoles,* e.g. aminotriazole
   (Non-persistent and of low selectivity. Can also enter through roots. General weed control in fallow land; susceptible crops can often be sown within a few weeks)
4. *Quaternary ammonium salts,* e.g. diquat, paraquat
   (Under field conditions, only enter through foliage. Destroy foliage but, as translocation is limited, subterranean tissue of perennials may survive).

SOIL APPLICATION

Contact poisons

1. Many *soil fumigants,* e.g. CS_2, CH_3Br
2. *Chlorinated carboxylic acids,* e.g. TCA
   (Trichloroacetic acid, unlike dalapon, is mainly applied to the soil. Used in conjunction with cultivation techniques to destroy couch grass).
3. *Ioxynil*
   (Used to control mayweed; available only in mixtures with certain carboxylic acid herbicides).

Systemic (translocated) poisons

1. Modified *phenoxycarboxylic acids,* e.g. 2,4-DES
   (Inactive on foliage, but changed to active acids in soil)
2. Substituted *ureas*, e.g. fenuron, monuron, diuron, lenacil, linuron
   (Highly persistent and of low selectivity. At low dosage, control annual weeds in some perennial crops)
3. Substituted *carbamates,* e.g. propham, chlorpropham, barban, di-allate, tri-allate.
   (Of low selectivity; applied to soil to destroy seedling weeds; in-effective against established plants. One member, barban, a foliage spray for the control of wild oats in cereals)
4. *Triazines,* e.g. simazine, atrazine, desmetryne, ametryne
   (Extremely persistent, of low selectivity. At low dosage, control annual weeds in tolerant crops such as maize and also in some crops with deep root systems).

The extent to which compounds of these various types are employed in different countries, or regions within a country, naturally depends upon the nature of the principal crop grown in the locality, as well as upon the economic and ecological factors mentioned earlier. Table 9.2 illustrates the probable total herbicide usage in Great Britain for the period 1965–7. It will be observed from the table that, with the exception of cereals and sugar beet, less than half the total area planted with a particular crop was being sprayed with herbicide at that time.

UPTAKE, DISTRIBUTION AND PERSISTENCE OF HERBICIDES

Any highly stable material, or the decomposition products of a less stable material, may remain on or in a plant after spraying. The chemical

Table 9.2 HERBICIDE USAGE IN THE UNITED KINGDOM DURING THE PERIOD 1965–7
(APPROXIMATE FIGURES COMPILED FROM SEVERAL SOURCES)

Crop	% Total planted area treated with herbicide	Principal chemicals applied
Grass	8	Mainly MCPA, 2,4-D
Cereals	90	About 35% of total was a single chemical such as MCPA or 2,4-D; The remainder consisted of mixtures containing both a plant growth regulator and a contact poison (e.g. Ioxynil)
Sugar beet	90	Mainly pyrazon, some lenacil
Potatoes	20	43% was paraquat, 13% a mixture of paraquat and linuron, 22% linuron used alone, 10% dinoseb, 6% ametryne, 4% MCPA
Brassicae	25	Desmetryne
Root crops	14	Pyrazon
Peas	45	Dinoseb
(Horticultural crops)		
Top fruit	3	Diquat, paraquat
Soft fruit	50	Diquat, paraquat
Brassicae	30	Desmetryne
Carrots	30	Urea derivatives
Beans	30	Simazine, dinoseb

characteristics determining uptake, distribution and persistence of herbicides can often be predicted in general terms by assuming that the upper part of a plant is hydrophobic by virtue of its waxy cuticle, whereas the root is essentially hydrophilic since one of its functions is the absorption of water. Thus, if a toxic substance which is applied to the foliage has a measure of oil solubility, it may well penetrate into the leaves. If, in addition, it possesses adequate solubility in water, it may then be transported in either the xylem or phloem. On the other hand, if it is insoluble in both water and oil, it may tend to remain on the surface of the plant near the point of application, so acting as a contact poison. Naturally, these generalisations represent a great over-simplification, for an oil-insoluble substance may be changed after spraying to one capable of penetrating the cuticle; inorganic copper compounds, for example, are probably changed into complexes which penetrate the cuticle (compare pp. 164, 204). Again, corrosive or caustic substances may kill the cells near the point of contact, thus gaining access in successive steps to deeper layers of tissue. Sulphuric acid is probably an example of such a substance. Very frequently, salts of weak acids (or of weak bases) are used as herbicides. Such materials are hydrolysed to a greater or lesser extent, with the formation of the only slightly ionised, and hence often lipid-soluble, parent substances. In addition, the carrier medium sometimes affects the absorption of the poison (p. 33).

Conversely, because the root absorbs water, there is a possibility that a water-soluble substance may enter the plant dissolved in the water that is to be transpired. It is well known, however, that the ionic content of plants differs greatly, both quantitatively and qualitatively, from that of the soil water. This implies a selective uptake of 'natural' ions, and there is reason to believe that selective uptake (or rejection) of 'foreign' ions may also occur. Once within the root, the substance may, as in the case of arsenites, remain in the root cells in the vicinity of the point of entry, so acting as a contact poison. In other cases, there may be little binding to the cellular components of the roots, with the result that the ions or molecules are rapidly transported upwards in the transpiration stream. It is useful, perhaps, to visualise the plant, which has negative fixed sites on some components of its cells, as a selective ion-exchange column (though again, of course, the situation is actually more complex than this), which allows some ions to escape upwards with ease whilst others are firmly bound near the point of entry.

Covalent solutes may similarly be taken up by roots in a selective manner, but many covalent compounds are of low aqueous solubility. Since lipid affinity usually rises as aqueous solubility falls, many of the more complex herbicides probably enter the external or structural lipid of root cells and, having entered, are bound differentially to cellular components. Thus, according to Crafts (1964) of six herbicides tested, 2,4-D was the first to enter the plant, but the last to reach the leaves, whereas the extremely insoluble simazine apparently not only penetrated quite rapidly but also appeared in large quantities in the shoot. Clearly, in addition to solubility in transpiration water, other factors have to be taken into consideration, including the amount of water transpired, the alternative means of entry into root tissue, and the extent of fixation and transformation of the toxic substance after entry.

In soil, stable substances insoluble in water will tend to persist longest, and hence have the best chance of coming into contact with plant roots. Neither stable water-soluble substances, nor unstable insoluble materials, normally persist long in soil. Again, however, it must be remembered that physical adsorption of the toxicant on organic matter (e.g., urea derivatives) or upon soil particles (e.g., bipyridylium compounds), as well as chemical precipitation by soil constituents and non-destructive microbiological or chemical alteration, may render the situation more complex. It is therefore essential not to assume that the properties of the applied substance *in vitro* are necessarily those which determine the persistence of the applied substance in soil or, indeed, in plants.

The varying chemical stability and physical properties of different herbicides are such as to provide a wide range of persistence in soil. Care must therefore be exercised in the choice of herbicide for any specific purpose. The use of a herbicide of too low persistence may result in the unnecessary work and extra cost of multiple application, whereas the use of one which is too persistent could prove financially disastrous by putting land out of commission for a season or more. Fig. 9.2 illustrates, on a logarithmic time-scale, the variability of persistence of some herbicides·

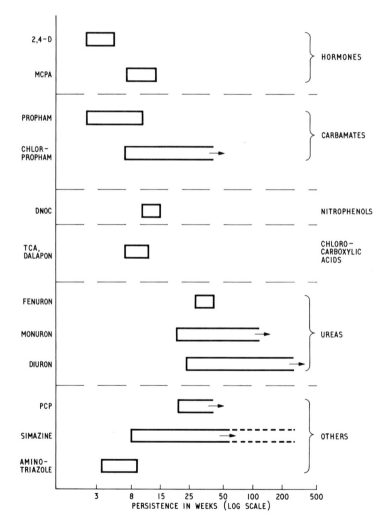

Fig. 9.2. Residues of herbicides in soil. Persistence depends not only on the herbicide but upon soil type and rainfall ; the rectangles indicate minimal and maximal persistence under different conditions.

218

it will be seen that some persist for only a few weeks, while others may still be present in toxic amounts after several years.

The problems relating to the choice and use of herbicides are complex because, as Fig. 9.2. shows, any one herbicide may persist for different lengths of time—and differ greatly in its toxicity to weeds—in different types of soil. Thus, the carbamate and urea herbicides are far less toxic to weeds in a heavy organic soil than they are in a light soil. Even 2,4-D has been observed to be about eight times as effective, in terms of the amount having unit effect, in a light soil than it is in a black acid clay. Corresponding concentration ratios of 43 and 80 have been observed for monuron and pentachlorophenol (Hartley, 1964). The times of persistence of carbamate and urea herbicides also vary in different soils, the persistence being longest in an organic clay soil.

In addition, the effectiveness of many herbicides, especially the more insoluble ones now often used for pre-emergence treatment, depends greatly on the uncontrollable factor of the level of rainfall within the few weeks immediately after application. The amount of rain determines the extent to which a substance is washed down in the soil, and this in turn not only influences persistence but also the toxicity to both weeds and crop. If the rainfall is light, wash-down may be so slight that the substance may fail to reach even shallow-rooted weeds; if the rainfall is excessive, even very insoluble substances may be washed down to the level of the germinating crop and so become phytotoxic. Using monuron, Hassall and Jewell (1956) observed (for a limited but practically important range of rainfall) that, as the rainfall in unit time in different experiments doubled, so the amount of herbicide having a given toxic effect was roughly halved.

Finally, it should perhaps be pointed out that pre-emergence treatments are of two kinds, and the substances used for them should have very different properties. Pre-emergence *contact* sprays are essentially foliage sprays, for they are applied pre-emergence to the crop but post-emergence to the bulk of the weeds. This type of treatment is of particular value for weed control in crops which germinate slowly in comparison to weeds. The chemicals employed (e.g., diquat, mineral oils, pentachlorophenol) generally possess some solubility in lipid; they are of low persistence and so provide little long term protection. On the other hand, pre-emergence *residual* sprays are essentially soil-acting herbicides, usually of high persistence (e.g., simazine, monuron). They are applied any time after the sowing of the crop, and hence may well be sprayed on to a bare piece of land, though some of the weeds may be in the seedling stage at the time of spraying. Ideally, such compounds should be highly selective (although, in fact, none of the compounds currently used for this purpose fulfils this condition). Alternatively, or in addition, they should be sufficiently in-soluble in water or adsorbed on soil colloids to prevent their coming into contact with the deeper-sown crop. Their persistence does, however, ensure continued protection against later-developing weeds for many weeks after application.

PROPERTIES AND USES OF HERBICIDES

PHENOXYCARBOXYLIC ACID DERIVATIVES

In terms of tonnage applied annually, this group of herbicides is used more extensively than all other groups combined, because its members control weeds in cereal crops—crops which form a very important part of the essential diet of mankind and which are therefore grown in vast areas of monoculture. Survey data quoted by Bullen (1964) show that in 1960, 77 to 95% of grain crops in four arable areas of Britain were sprayed, nearly always with MCPA (Fig. 9.3, R = CH$_3$). This compound is safer on spring

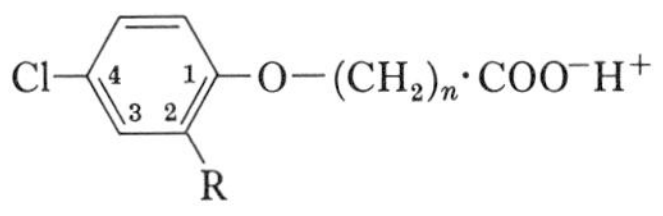

$$Cl-\underset{R}{\overset{4\ \ 1}{\underset{3\ 2}{\bigcirc}}}-O-(CH_2)_n \cdot COO^-H^+$$

Fig. 9.3. General formula of phenoxy carboxylic acids
In 2,4–D and 2,4–DB, R = Cl
In MCPA and MCPB, R = CH$_3$
In the acetic compounds, n = 1
In the butyric compounds, n = 3

oats than is the closely related 2,4-D (Fig. 9.3, R = Cl), and has a more soluble sodium salt. These compounds are of low to moderate acute toxicity to animals (Table 9.1) and are of limited persistence, though com-mon sense precautions and elementary hygiene must necessarily be ob-served during their handling and application. Animals should be excluded from the sprayed area for at least two weeks, not only because of the possible toxic effects of the chemicals themselves, but because naturally poisonous weeds may be rendered more palatable by these and some other herbicides (Ministry of Agriculture, Fisheries and Food, 1968). Phenoxy-carboxylic acids are translocated within plants after entry through the leaves, the movement being mostly in the phloem and in the direction of food distribution. From lower leaves, movement is often downwards, whilst from upper leaves it is towards the growing points of the shoots.

If applied to soil, simple salts of MCPA and 2,4-D are readily washed away or are decomposed by micro-organisms within a few weeks. But it is possible to modify the structure of these compounds so as almost to eliminate foliage penetration yet to increase the chance of entry through roots. To do this, the acid is first converted to the corresponding alcohol, which is then esterified with some suitable acid; 2,4-DES (Fig. 9.4) is an

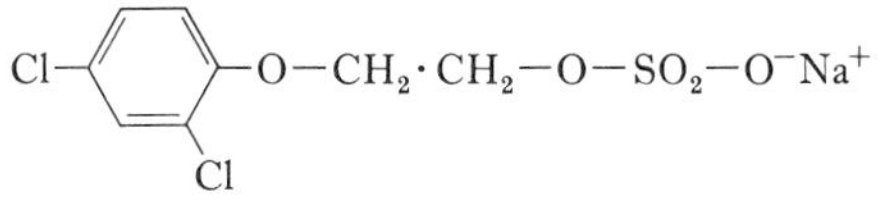

$$Cl-\hspace{-4pt}\langle\rangle\hspace{-4pt}-O-CH_2 \cdot CH_2-O-SO_2-O^-Na^+$$
$$\overset{|}{Cl}$$

Fig. 9.4.   2,4–DES : sodium 2,4–dichloro-phenoxyethyl sulphate

example of such a derivative. Within the soil it undergoes hydrolysis, the alcohol so liberated being oxidised by certain soil bacteria to 2,4-D, which then enters through the roots. This is an interesting example of the participation of micro-organisms in the process of chemical weed control. Such soil-acting derivatives as 2,4-DES are used mainly for weed control in strawberries. They are also used as herbicides in bush fruits, groundnuts, and various other perennial or deeply-sown crops (Holly, 1964).

Some of the alkane carboxylic acid homologues of 2,4-D and MCPA have been used commercially, the most noteworthy being compounds containing a branched chain propionic acid or a straight chain butyric acid. The isopropionic acid derivative, mecoprop (Fig. 9.5), is very similar to

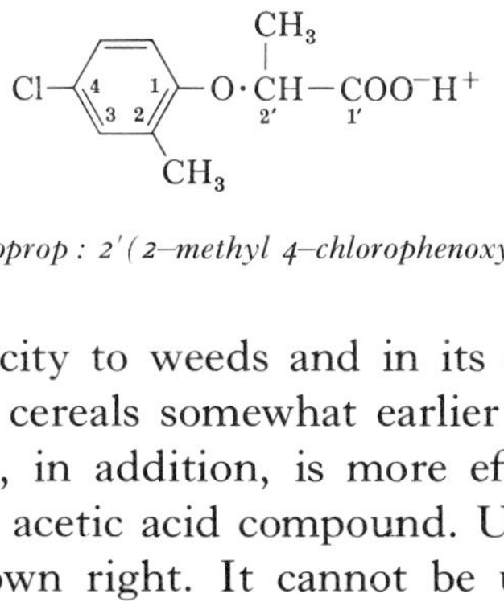

$$Cl-\hspace{-4pt}\langle\rangle\hspace{-4pt}-O \cdot \overset{\overset{\displaystyle CH_3}{|}}{\underset{2'}{CH}}-\underset{1'}{COO^-}H^+$$
$$\overset{|}{CH_3}$$

Fig. 9.5. Mecoprop : 2'(2–methyl 4–chlorophenoxy) propionic acid

MCPA both in its toxicity to weeds and in its safety to animals. It can, however, be applied to cereals somewhat earlier than MCPA (i.e., before the five-leaf stage) and, in addition, is more effective against chickweed and cleavers than is the acetic acid compound. Unlike MCPB (see below), it is a toxicant in its own right. It cannot be used, any more than can MCPA, on leguminous crops or undersown cereals.

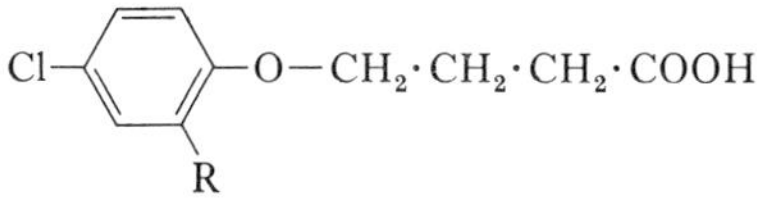

$$Cl-\hspace{-4pt}\langle\rangle\hspace{-4pt}-O-CH_2 \cdot CH_2 \cdot CH_2 \cdot COOH$$
$$\overset{|}{R}$$

Fig. 9.6. Substituted phenoxybutyric acid
In 2,4–DB, R = Cl
In MCPB, R = CH₃

The butyric acid compound (Fig. 9.6), on the other hand, is of low phytotoxicity unless it is converted in the plant to the acetic acid member of the series. The enzyme responsible for this breakdown is a specific β-oxidase, and, like the reactions concerned in the oxidation of fats, the degradation involves the splitting off of two carbon atoms at a time. Only those plants possessing this specific enzyme (why or how such an enzyme could be present at all is intriguing), will therefore be vulnerable to the butyric acid homologue. Several types of legumes lack the enzyme, so 2,4-DB and MCPB are used widely for weed control in certain leguminous crops and in undersown cereals, where the acetic and iso-propionic acid derivatives would be as non-selective and injurious to legumes as they are to most other dicotyledonous plants.

Trichlorophenoxyacetic acid, 2,4,5-T, is far more toxic to foliage and more persistent in soil than either MCPA or 2,4-D. Formulated as a (covalent) ester and usually mixed with an ester of 2,4-D, it is dissolved in oil and marketed as a brushwood killer. The persistence of 2,4,5-T in soil can be attributed in part to the reluctance with which micro-organisms attack it. In this respect it is of interest that, with 2,4-D and some other phenoxycarboxylic acid herbicides, a phenomenon termed 'enrichment' occurs—if soil organisms are exposed to a second and subsequent applications of these compounds they are able to proliferate, and hence to break the substances down more rapidly than they could on the first occasion. This effect presumably occurs as a result of some sort of metabolic adaptation. 'Enrichment' seldom occurs readily, however, when soil organisms are exposed to consecutive applications of 2,4,5-T.

The phenoxycarboxylic acid herbicides are, in general, safe and very valuable materials but nevertheless they present one or two problems. First, because of their high toxicity to most dicotyledonous plants, it is essential to avoid spray drift to nearby fields. This can be done by the correct use of machinery (type of nozzle, beam height and spray pressure can often be adjusted), and by applying these materials when the weather is favourable. The danger of vapour drift is only serious when certain esters are used, but spray drift can occur for any type of active ingredient and is most hazardous when the application is made at low volume.

Another unsatisfactory aspect of these chemicals is that their mode of action remains obscure. This does not imply that responses on the part of plants are difficult to observe, but rather that they are so varied that it has not been possible to disentangle cause from effect. A major factor is probably the effect of phenoxycarboxylic acid herbicides upon the metabolism of pectin methyl esters, materials which are significant to the growth of plants but not to the growth of animals. On the other hand,

McGowan (1963) has shown that their action has certain of the attributes of physical toxicants.

The physiology and biochemistry of the natural and synthetic plant growth regulators have been discussed in detail by Audus (1959), by Fawcett (1961), and by several authors in a symposium edited by Audus (1964). Wort (1962) has described the varied and apparently beneficial effects on crop plants of sub-lethal doses of 2,4-D and similar substances. For further information about the chemical structure of substances in this group, and the relation of structure to toxicity, reference should be made to the accounts by Wain (1958) and Martin (1964).

SUBSTITUTED DINITROPHENOLS

Dinitrophenol and phenoxycarboxylic acid herbicides are alike in that they are derived from weak acids. Maximal selectivity is obtained for compounds in both groups by formulating them in such a way that their ionisation is high. This generalisation—that high ionisation favours selectivity—is usually explained by the somewhat over-simplified assumption that the rate of entry of covalent molecules through lipophilic barriers possessing fixed negative sites is greater than the rate of entry of the corresponding anions. A consequence of such an assumption is that minor differences between such barriers in weeds and crop plants can best be

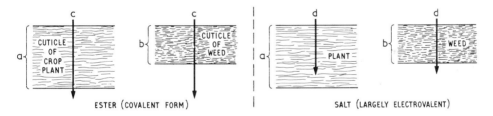

ESTER (COVALENT FORM)   SALT (LARGELY ELECTROVALENT)

Fig. 9.7. Diagram illustrating how selectivity of threshold concentrations may depend on the penetrability of a barrier: (a), (b) Relative penetrability (not necessarily thickness) of cuticle of crop plant and weed; (c) Length of arrow represents ease of penetration of a given concentration of poison, when in the covalent form. Cuticles of both weeds and crop penetrated; (d) Length of arrow represents ease of penetration of the same concentration of poison, when largely in the electrovalent form. Only the weed cuticle is penetrated

exploited when some constraint (such as lipid-insolubility, or electrical repulsion) exists which impedes penetration (Fig. 9.7).

For both groups of compounds, ionisation may be chosen or adjusted to suit the purpose of the spray. One way of doing this is to change the pH of the solution which is sprayed; another is to apply suitable derivatives.

Weakly acidic substances may be used as the almost un-ionised free acids, or in the form of un-ionised esters. Alternatively, salts may be used, the ionisation of which, under specified conditions, may be pre-selected by choice of a base of appropriate strength. This possibility of modifying either the toxicant or its carrier medium is of particular importance for dinitrophenol compounds because, in addition to their use as herbicides, they are used as insecticides to control over-wintering eggs on fruit trees. Dormant trees have a high resistance to the poison, and it is customary to achieve maximal toxicity by applying the free acid dissolved in oil. Such a formulation, even when the oil is emulsified in water, would destroy all vegetation if it were applied to foliage in the summer. It is worthy of note that the cyclohexyl member of the series has molluscicidal properties (Muller, 1962) and that dinocap (p. 187) is a fungicidal member of the group.

The degree of selectivity between crop and weeds is determined not only by molecular architecture but also by those physical properties, especially ionisation, which are inseparably correlated with structure. Ionisation depends on structure, of course, since the nature of the substituent group (Fig. 9.8, R) determines the dissociation constant, and, as

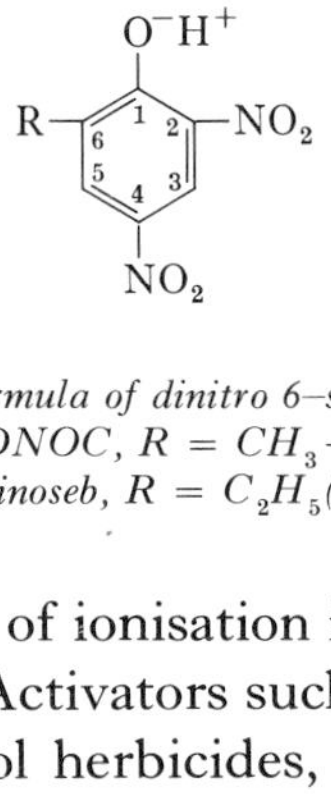

Fig. 9.8. General formula of dinitro 6–substituted phenols
In DNOC, $R = CH_3-$
In dinoseb, $R = C_2H_5(CH_3)CH-$

was seen on page 48, the degree of ionisation is determined by this constant and by the pH of the medium. Activators such as sodium bisulphate, which are often added to dinitrophenol herbicides, make a spray more toxic but less selective. They do this by decreasing ionisation since they increase the acidity of the solution.

The two most common selective herbicides of the group are DNOC (Fig. 9.8, $R = CH_3-$) and dinoseb (Fig. 9.8, $R = C_2H_5(CH_3)CH-$). They are intensely yellow, forming orange salts with alkalies. Both compounds attack a wide range of annual weeds, but whereas DNOC is employed primarily for weed control in cereals, dinoseb is used chiefly for weed control in peas, seedling lucerne and undersown cereals. Both are normally applied as high-volume sprays, for even at 80 gallons per acre their salts are usually too insoluble to be fully dissolved in the spray tank water. Neither compound is as effective at low temperatures (below 55°C) as on warm days. Both are non-selective at high concentrations, especially when formulated in oil. It is of interest that Bruinsma (1962) observed that when winter rye was grown in a weed-free environment, application of a suitable dose of DNOC resulted in a 10% increase in yield. He attributed this to stronger vegetative growth and to a prolonged period of generative development consequent upon spraying.

The problems associated with the use of dinitrophenol pesticides are almost the reverse of those encountered with organochlorine compounds. Though dinitrophenols are insoluble in water in their covalent form, their tendency to ionise to form salts soluble in water reduces the risk of storage in lipid body tissue. Moreover, the presence of nitro- and acidic groups in the molecule provides points of weakness which enable detoxication mechanisms to operate in both animals and plants. Dinitrophenols are therefore contact poisons, which are able to penetrate to their site of action either by diffusion of non-ionised molecules in lipids, or by aqueous diffusion of ions. As a result, they are able to enter mammals with almost the same ease as they enter insects and plants. Concentrates of DNOC and dinoseb are therefore extremely dangerous to all forms of life, and their use is subject to certain Ministry regulations (Ministry of Agriculture, Fisheries and Food, 1968). This universal toxicity relates to the fact that at appropriate concentrations, dinitrophenols uncouple oxidation from phosphorylation; and while respiration proceeds because the cytochromes continue electron transport at the inner mitochondrial membrane, associated phosphorylation no longer occurs. The biological energy-producing system races in an attempt to rectify the deficit, with the result that over a

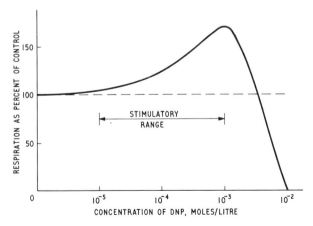

Fig. 9.9. Effect on respiration of different concentrations of dinitrophenol, DNP

suitable range of concentrations of the poison, the oxygen consumption actually rises (Fig. 9.9). The situation is analogous to a car kept at constant speed, balancing a slipping clutch by depressing the accelerator pedal. In mammals, rapid breathing, flushing and sweating are typical symptoms of acute poisoning. The best general review of the properties and uses of substituted dinitrophenols is probably still that of Simon (1953). The precise mechanism whereby dinitrophenol (DNP) and its homologues uncouple oxidation from phosphorylation is still uncertain, though DNP is known to affect the rate of exchange of inorganic phosphate with the terminal phosphate of ATP. Some aspects of this important problem have been discussed by Lehninger (1959) and by Davies (1961).

According to Boggs (1964), the best method of separating and identifying the various dinitrophenols is one involving paper chromatography, but gas chromatography can also be used.

HYDROCARBON OILS

Various types of oils are being used not only as herbicides but also as ovicides, insecticides and as spray supplements. Tar oils and highly un-saturated petroleum oils are extremely phytotoxic and are therefore non-selective herbicides. They can be used to control eggs of mites and insects over-wintering on trees during the period of dormancy.

Unsaturated hydrocarbons can be removed from crude petroleum by treating it with sulphuric acid. Products of suitable boiling point may then be used in the presence of foliage. Some are used as carriers for other pesticides—'fortified oils' are obtained by dissolving such materials as DNOC or pentachlorophenol in diesel oils and then emulsifying in water. Similarly, oils have been used as carriers for dithiocarbamate and other fungicides. In all these cases, the oil no doubt not only carries the main toxicant passively into lipid surfaces but also contributes to the total toxic effect. When oils are used as spreading and adhering agents, their action depends on their physical solubility in the lipid of the sprayed surface, whether it be the cuticle of an insect or the leaf of a weed. Oils which have been suitably refined are employed as selective herbicides, since umbelliferous crops, including carrots, parsnips, parsley and celery, possess a tolerance to them. Oils of lower grades may be used as pre-emergence contact poisons (p. 211).

When umbelliferous crops are sprayed selectively with oils, application must be carefully timed, for in addition to possible phytotoxic action if oils are applied too soon, tainting may occur if they are applied too late, especially when oils of poorer grade are being employed. Tainting is particularly noticeable, in crops such as carrots, if oils of lower grade are applied at the time that the storage material is being actively deposited in the tap root.

Hydrocarbon oils, especially the paraffins, are largely or exclusively physical poisons for when a homologous series of aliphatic hydrocarbons is tested, it is found that each member of the series exerts an equal physiological effect when present at about the same relative saturation (toxic concentration/saturation concentration) while the isotoxic external concentrations may be very different. It has long been recognised that the concentration of a poison which has a given effect at the site of action within the organism bears no simple relation to the concentration in the external medium, yet measurements of toxicity such as LD_{50}s (Chapter 1) are measurements of amounts of toxicant present in some external phase. Clearly, the complicating factor of phase distribution has been superimposed upon the intrinsic toxicity of the substance (in more complex cases still, metabolism and excretion may add further uncertainty). The use of relative saturation as a measure of toxicity removes the phase distribution factor—at least for closely related compounds of a sort which are metabolised sufficiently slowly for a near-equilibrium condition or a steady state to be achieved.

Compounds such as hydrocarbons and alkyl chlorides fulfil the requirements for 'physical toxicity' mentioned above. To illustrate the value of the concept of relative saturation and its use in disentangling intrinsic toxicity from phase distribution, Table 9.3 records the concentrations

Table 9.3 ISONARCOTIC CONCENTRATIONS AND RELATIVE
SATURATIONS OF SOME ALKANES, APPLIED AS VAPOURS TO
MICE (BADGER, 1946)

Substance	P_t mm Hg	P_o mm Hg	P_t/P_o
Pentane	85	794	0·11
Hexane	30	240	0·13
Heptane	12	81	0·15
Octane	6	28	0·20

of four hydrocarbons needed to induce an equal degree of narcosis in mice—narcosis, being reversible, is a more reliable and sensitive index of toxicity than, say, herbicidal action, but the conclusions are equally valid for herbicidal action. The concentrations are expressed as toxic vapour pressures, P_t, and hence relative saturation of the external medium can be expressed as P_t/P_o, where P_o is the saturation vapour pressure of the homologue concerned.

The principal point to note is that while octane appears to be about fourteen times as toxic as pentane when the external isotoxic concentrations are considered, nevertheless, when seen from the point of view of the *internal* phase, pentane is nearly twice as toxic as octane, because it acts at about one-tenth saturation instead of one-fifth. It should be added that, for thermodynamic reasons described by Ferguson (1939), and with certain provisos, the relative saturations of internal and external phases are necessarily the same once equilibrium is reached. Results such as those shown in Table 9.3 have been obtained for hydrocarbons used against organisms of many types and in experiments employing a wide range of criteria of isotoxic action, including lethal effects; they have been obtained with alkyl chlorides (Ferguson, 1951; Hassall, 1953), alcohols (Brink and Posternak, 1948) and even with inert gases and unreactive gases (Ferguson and Hawkins, 1949).

The thermodynamic significance of relative saturation and the reason why its use in specified circumstances can eliminate the contribution of phase distribution has been discussed by Ferguson (1939) and Hassall (1957); reference has also been made earlier in this book (pp. 59, 73, 182). Physical poisons may have a variety of effects, according to the nature of the living material being tested and the level of poison being applied. As well as affecting the nervous system of animals so as to induce anaesthesia or narcosis, they can affect photosynthesis, disrupt mitosis and alter the permeability of cell membranes. At high concentrations, and when applied for long periods of time, they induce irreversible effects which lead to death and for this reason some of them are used widely not only as herbicides but also as insecticides and ovicides.

CARBAMIC ACID, UREA AND TRIAZINE DERIVATIVES

Most herbicides based on phenoxyacetic acid and dinitrophenol are used to control broad-leaved weeds growing in a monocotyledonous crop or on grassland. They are valueless against monocotyledonous weeds, and cannot normally be employed to control a mixture of weeds growing in a broad-leaved crop.

The aryl carbamic esters, introduced in 1946, were heralded as a possible solution to the first of these problems—the control of monocotyledonous weeds. Unfortunately, the early promise was not fulfilled, for although seedling grasses succumb, they proved to be of little value against established plants. However, detailed investigations of the properties of chlor-propham (Fig. 9.10), have revealed that several crops are resistant to it when it is applied to soil. It is now employed for weed control in bulbs, rhubarb, strawberries, sugar beet and peas. Thus carbamate esters have, in fact, contributed to a partial solution of the second problem—the

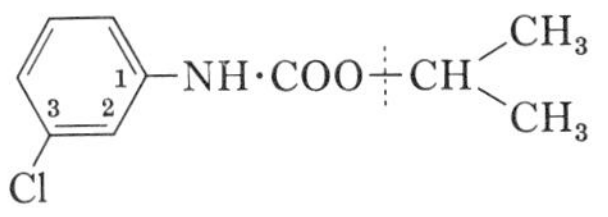

Fig. 9.10. Chlorpropham : isopropyl 3–chlorophenyl carbamate
(Propham itself contains no chlorine)

selective control of seedling or annual weeds growing in any suitable resistant crop. Chlorpropham controls chickweed, but is otherwise seldom of value against established weeds. A more complex carbamate, barban (Fig. 9.11), has been used to control wild oats (Holmes and Pfeffer, 1962).

More recently, various thiolcarbamic acid esters have been investigated, especially in relation to their possible use for controlling wild oats in wheat and barley (Parker, 1963). Di-allate (2,3-dichloroallyl di-isopropyl thiolcarbamate) and tri-allate are two well known examples. Mixtures of

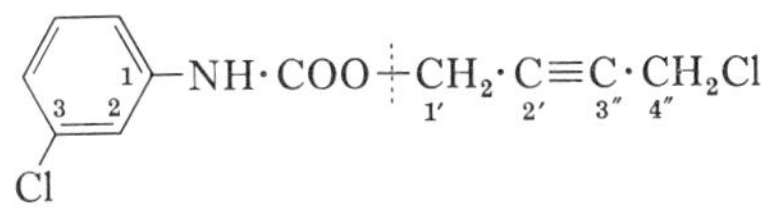

Fig. 9.11. Barban : 4″–chloro–2′ butynyl (3–chlorophenyl) carbamate

such esters were found by Sullivan, Abrams and Wood (1963) to be superior to the individual substances for weed control in sugar beet. One of the few biochemical studies on these thiols was made by Ashton (1963), who con-cluded that they only affect photosynthesis, respiration and oxidative phosphorylation when present in somewhat high concentrations, but that smaller amounts markedly inhibit uptake of phosphate. According to Rothwell and Wain (1963), esters of the related dithiocarbamic acid act as plant growth regulators.

Several *aryl-substituted ureas* have been marketed as herbicides, the best known being fenuron, monuron, diuron (Fig. 9.12) and linuron (Table 9.2). Linuron is (3,4-dichlorophenyl-N-methoxy-N-methylurea. As non-selective weedkillers these materials are excellent, but in most crops they have proved unreliable as pre-emergence herbicides under British conditions, for they show low selectivity between crop and weeds. More-over, results have been variable from year to year, as is so often the case

229

when both persistence and apparent selectivity depend upon environmental factors such as depth of root system, soil type and level of rainfall
(Harris and Warren, 1964; Hartley, 1964; Roberts and Wilson, 1962).

When employed selectively, the principal use of aryl-substituted urea is
to control annual weeds in naturally resistant crops and in certain deeply-
sown crops. In addition to fenuron and its chlorinated analogues, several

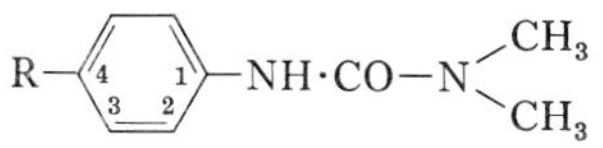

$$R-\text{C}_6H_4-NH\cdot CO-N\begin{array}{c}CH_3\\CH_3\end{array}$$

Fig. 9.12. General formula of monuron family of urea herbicides
In fenuron, R = H
In monuron, R = Cl
In diuron, R = Cl and a second chlorine is in position 3

other urea derivatives have been tested as herbicides. Thus, Scheuerer
and Fischer (1962) investigated the use of cyclo-aliphatic ureas for weed
control in tuber and root crops, while various tetra-substituted ureas have
been used to control Johnson and quack grass. Urea compounds are normally regarded as exclusively soil-acting herbicides, and it is of interest
that McWhorter (1963) found that the toxicity of monuron to crab grass,
when applied as a post-emergence spray to foliage, was greatly enhanced
by the inclusion of a non-ionic surfactant.

Among the fenuron analogues, solubility in water decreases with increasing chlorination, with the result that persistence in soil follows the
order:

$$\text{fenuron} < \text{monuron} < \text{diuron}$$

Under conditions where maximal contact between chemical and plant is
established by the use of water cultures, Hassall (1961) showed that the
concentrations of variously substituted alkyl and aryl ureas having the
same effect on the growth of seedling peas were inversely correlated with
solubility in water—i.e., the substances became more phytotoxic as their
solubility in water decreased to a limiting value of a few ppm.

Although some differences may exist between them, the modes of action
of carbamate and urea herbicides may be considered together; it is probable
that the triazines (discussed below) behave very similarly. Both carbamate
and urea herbicides have a powerful effect on the photo-reduction reaction
of photosynthesis (Good, 1962; Moreland and Hill, 1963). On the other
hand, no enzyme has been found which is particularly sensitive to either
group of compounds. In view of the nature of their mode of action, they

would not be expected to be very toxic to mammals, and the acute toxic dose, is, in fact, high. Nevertheless, these compounds illustrate the need for caution in the use of pesticides, for their low solubility in water, coupled with their high chemical stability, leads to persistence in soil with concomitant hazard to soil micro-organisms (though this seems very temporary), to seedling crops of future seasons, and possibly also to animals. Much of this danger arises from the fact that, in addition to their effect on photosynthesis, members of each group have been shown to affect mitosis. Indeed, a little inconsistently perhaps, the inhibition of mitosis is often regarded as the principal toxic effect of the carbamates. Hassall (1961) pointed out that carbamic acid and urea derivatives caused several apparently unrelated toxic effects in different circumstances, and suggested that in each case the toxicity might be due, not so much to a direct effect upon particular enzymes, but to the distortion of an organising lipoprotein membrane in relation to which complex chains of cellular reactions occur. According to this interpretation, the observed response would depend on which of these cellular processes was most crucial in the tissue under investigation.

Herbicidal triazine derivatives in many ways resemble the urea and carbamate weedkillers. The commonest is simazine (Fig. 9.13); the chemistry and herbicidal properties of this and other triazines have been reviewed by Gysin and Knüsli (1960). The solubility in water of simazine and most of its analogues is very low. It is of low toxicity to plants when applied to the foliage but it is absorbed by roots. In soil, its persistence is governed by the same factors as those which determine the persistence of carbamates and urea derivatives. Volatility may, however, limit persistence in certain soils (Kearney, Sheets and Smith, 1964). Micro-organisms may

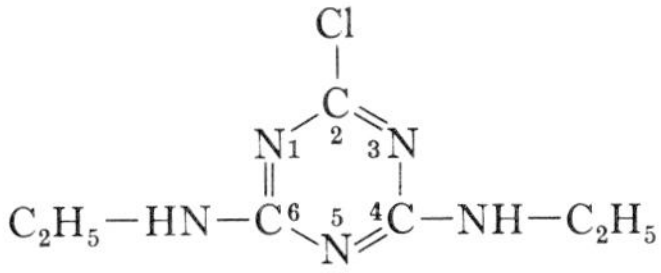

$$
\begin{array}{c}
\text{Cl} \\
| \\
\text{C} \\
\diagup\diagdown \\
\text{N}1\ \ 2\ \ 3\text{N} \\
\| \qquad | \\
\text{C}_2\text{H}_5-\text{HN}-\text{C}\ 6\ \ 5\ \ 4\text{C}-\text{NH}-\text{C}_2\text{H}_5 \\
\diagdown\diagup \\
\text{N}
\end{array}
$$

Fig. 9.13. Simazine : 2–chloro–4,6–bis (ethylamino)–
1,3,5–triazine

also accelerate its decomposition, for Holly and Roberts (1963) and Talbert and Fletchall (1964) have reported that it disappears from certain types of soils more rapidly than might have been anticipated.

Pharmacological studies indicate that most triazines, including simazine, are remarkably inert. Thus Gysin and Knüsli (1960) reported that all the rats in one test survived a dose of simazine of 2·5 g per kg body weight administered six times a week for four weeks. This inertness is probably a function of the low solubility of the substances in both water and oil, rather than a feature of the triazine ring, for analogues less insoluble in either type of solvent were found to be more toxic to mammals. As in the preceding groups of herbicides, the primary biological action on plants appears to be the inhibition of photo-reduction (Good, 1962; Kerr and Wain, 1964; Brian, 1965). Ries, Larsen and Kenworthy (1963) have reported that sub-lethal doses of simazine appear to affect the nitrogen metabolism of plants, sometimes to the advantage of fruit trees.

The principal use of simazine as a selective herbicide appears to be the control of weeds in maize, many strains of which are tolerant to simazine. It is of interest that Anderson (1964) observed that strains of maize which were resistant to the corn borer and to stalk rot were also resistant to simazine, a correlation which he attributed to some favourable metabolic factor. Simazine is also being used to control weeds in such shrubs as blackcurrants, and in tree crops. Certain other plants with deep root systems, such as beans, may also be treated with it, because its low solubility ensures that it does not normally wash down to the region of the developing crop, but great caution is necessary when it is used in this manner. Other triazines are used for weed control in potatoes (ametryne and prometryne), in maize (atrazine), in sprouts, cabbage and kale (desmetryne) and in carrots, parsley and celery (prometryne).

One of the best general reviews of the chemistry and biological uses of the triazines is that of Gysin and Knüsli (1960). Analytical techniques involving thin layer and gas chromatography have been described by Stammbach, Kilchher, Friedrich, Larsen and Szekely (1964).

CHLORINATED CARBOXYLIC ACIDS

A powerful, rapidly acting herbicide possessing low chemical stability and high solubility in water might be expected, if applied to the soil, to attack the subterranean ramifying growth of established grasses and then to disappear from the soil before a crop was planted. Where such a method is possible it has advantages over the use of persistent materials of the type discussed above—there is far less risk to crop, livestock or man— but it clearly gives no permanent protection against weed re-infestation. A similar result can sometimes be achieved by foliage application if the herbicide is subsequently translocated downwards.

Dalapon, the sodium salt of 2,2-dichloropropionic acid (Fig. 9.14), is translocated when applied to foliage but it can also enter roots. In either case, the application is most effective if carried out when the weeds are growing actively. Dalapon decomposes slowly in plant tissue, but generally disappears from soil within 20 to 40 days of application. Variations in the rate of decomposition in soil are due to environmental influences which affect micro-organisms participating in its decomposition (Kearney, Harris, Kaufman and Sheets, 1965). Very little is known about the mechanism of

$$\overset{3}{C}H_3-\overset{2}{C}Cl_2-\overset{1}{C}OO^-Na^+$$

Fig. 9.14. Dalapon: sodium 2,2–dichloropropionate. (In TCA, the 3–methyl group is replaced by a chlorine atom)

its toxic action and nothing is known about why it appears to be more toxic to grasses than to other plants.

The main agricultural use of dalapon and of the related trichloroacetic acid, TCA, is for the control of couch grass and other established grasses, but, as with many of the newer herbicides, several specialised uses have been discovered, amongst them the selective control of grasses in lucerne, blackcurrants and apples, and the control of sedges and other water weeds. TCA, unlike dalapon, is poorly translocated when sprayed on to foliage, but gains ready access to plants through the roots when applied to the soil. It has been employed to control wild oats in peas and sugar beet. Its use is usually combined with cultivation techniques.

When dalapon is absorbed by roots, it first collects in the growing tissues and then, as these mature, is re-translocated to other parts of the plant which are still growing actively (Smith and Dyer, 1961). Several workers have reported that it is, at most, loosely bound within the plant, for it can be readily leached from the tissue by extraction with water. No well defined breakdown products have ever been found. When dalapon is applied to leaves, it penetrates best at low pH, when the dissociation is least. Surfactants can increase its effectiveness (Foy, 1963). McIntyre (1962) has studied its translocation at different transpiration rates, at different light intensities, and at different environmental humidities. He observed that when the transpiration rate of couch grass was decreased, the amount of dalapon translocated to the roots and tillers increased.

SUBSTITUTED TRIAZOLES

Aminotriazole (Fig. 9.15) is the commonest of several triazole derivatives introduced principally for the control of perennial weeds such as couch

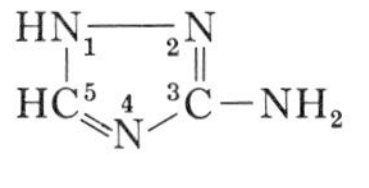

$$\overset{\quad}{HN}\underset{1}{\overset{\quad}{\text{——}}}\underset{2}{N}$$

Fig. 9.15. Aminotriazole (amitrole): 3–amino–1,2,4–triazole

grass, though in some countries it is also used as a cotton defoliant. For control of grasses, it has been found to be more effective in the presence of ammonium thiocyanate. It shows little selectivity and is mostly employed for the control of weeds in land which is uncultivated but in which a crop is to be planted within a few weeks of application.

The phytotoxicity of aminotriazole was at first considered to be related indirectly to a fall in catalase activity. Other work has, however, suggested that it interferes with the synthesis of purines (Sund, Putala and Little, 1960) or with histidine metabolism (Crafts, 1961). The symptoms of its action include chlorosis and retardation of growth. These and other aspects of its action have been described by Schweitzer and Rogers (1964). Wills, Davis and Funderburk (1963) have observed that aminotriazole reduces transpiration and causes stomata to close even in the presence of light.

Aminotriazole is strongly absorbed by soil particles, its phytotoxicity being roughly proportional to the amount readily recoverable from any particular type of soil. Riepma (1962), who studied its breakdown in different soils and at two temperatures, demonstrated that breakdown occurred on account of microbial action, and that increase of temperature up to 30°C accelerated decomposition. Aminotriazole resembles the carbamate, urea and triazine derivatives in that heavy organic soils adsorb it most readily, but unlike these other soil-acting herbicides, it usually only persists for a few weeks after application. This low persistence is in part explained by the action of soil bacteria, but is also due to the fact that it is soluble in water, chemically reactive and amphoteric. It is generally believed to disappear rapidly from plants and to present no hazard to man or animals except for a few days after application. Onley and Storrherr (1963) however, have demonstrated the presence of aminotriazole or its degradation products in cranberry plants twelve months after its application to cranberry bogs, even though the application was at only half the recommended dosage.

Metabolic studies have indicated that aminotriazole is able to form complexes with sugars (see Crafts, 1961) and with amino acids (Massini, 1963). According to the latter author, aminotriazolyl-alanine is a major metabolic product, is stable, and is translocated in both phloem and xylem. Other aspects of the metabolism and translocation of aminotriazole have been reviewed by Brian (1964).

Finally, it should be pointed out that 'hybrids' of triazoles with organophosphorus compounds have aroused considerable interest as potential insecticides, acaricides and fungicides. Bos (1960), in a series of papers, has described fungicidal and acaricidal compounds containing the triazole ring joined to bis(dimethylamido) phosphoryl chloride. The latter is related to the insecticide schradan. Elings (1962) described the use of a 'hybrid' to control a powdery mildew and Meltzer (1961) reported the testing of aphicidal and acaricidal 'hybrids' which were of low contact toxicity to house flies and bees.

QUATERNARY AMMONIUM OR BIPYRIDYLIUM COMPOUNDS

Herbicides based upon this structure were first introduced in 1958 and possess some unique features, both in regard to their field use and their physiological effect upon plants. The best known examples are diquat (Fig. 9.16) and paraquat (Fig. 9.17). They are absorbed by foliage, which

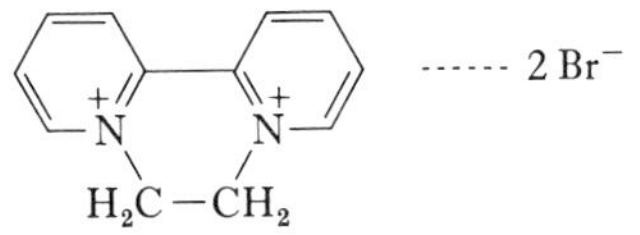

Fig. 9.16. Diquat dibromide: ethylene bipyridylium dibromide

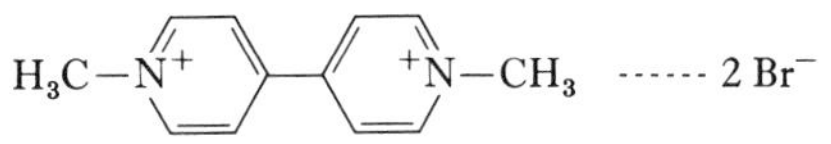

Fig. 9.17. Paraquat dichloride: dimethyl bipyridylium dichloride

they desiccate within three or four days. They do not normally enter through roots since they are rapidly inactivated following sorption on to soil particles (Harris and Warren, 1964).

Robson and Procter (1963) have described the uses of bipyridylium compounds, which include contact pre-emergence treatment for many crops, including carrots, kale, swedes and turnips. Jeater (1964), who described their use in rubber plantations, concluded that where grass weeds predominated, paraquat was usually superior to diquat. In certain circumstances it is possible, and perhaps even desirable, to employ them as an alternative to ploughing (Hood, 1965). Similarly, a Canadian wheat trial demonstrated that yields following chemical treatment, which left the stubble dead but standing, were 20% higher than when conventional cultivation techniques were used—probably because the stubble protected the soil from wind erosion and from excessive surface evaporation (Anon, 1968). Bipyridylium compounds are also used for the destruction of potato haulms and for the pre-harvest desiccation of legumes grown for seed (but not for eating), and paraquat has been recommended as a possible aid to grassland renewal—*Nardus,* one of the least valuable of upland grasses, is killed by paraquat (Allen, 1967). These and other uses have been summarised and illustrated by Springett (1965). Mixed with simazine or diuron they are also employed as non-selective herbicides (Wheeler, 1962).

A striking feature of the bipyridylium compounds is that they act exclusively by foliage contact under normal field conditions. They pass readily through the leaves and their movement within the plant has been studied extensively. If a drop of solution containing one of these compounds is placed upon a leaf exposed to daylight, the damage is very localised. Nevertheless, if the same treatment is carried out in darkness and then, some while later, the plant is placed in daylight, the whole plant is killed. Baldwin (1963) has provided a partial explanation for these observations; he demonstrated that, in darkness, the herbicide does not move from the treated leaf, but that it becomes distributed throughout the plant when the plant is moved into sunlight.

No definite biochemical degradation products have been discovered in plants, but Calderbank (1966) reported that photochemical decomposition products can be detected on the surface of plants in sunlight. Deposits of diquat decompose in sunlight much more rapidly than those of paraquat, but in neither case are decomposition products of high mammalial toxicity, nor are they translocated to other parts of the plant. Aqueous solutions of paraquat are not degraded by light.

When bipyridylium compounds are inactivated by soil particles, the initial cause of inactivation is physical adsorption at the negative sites of clay minerals. According to Knight and Tomlinson (1967), the capacities of soils to reduce the concentrations in soil solutions to a negligible level are less than the cation exchange capacities of the soils in question, but are nevertheless very large in comparison to the application rates employed in the field. Moreover, the affinity of clay minerals for bipyridylium cations is greater than their affinity for inorganic cations, so that little danger exists that fertilisers or lime will displace them. Unlike the carbamate and urea herbicides, little strong sorption on soil organic matter appears to occur, for removal of organic matter by treatment with hydrogen peroxide does not greatly affect the capacity of the soil to adsorb paraquat. Microbial decomposition occurs as a secondary inactivation process some time after initial adsorption on clay particles.

Boon (1964) has discussed a number of physical and chemical factors which may contribute towards, or be involved in, the toxic action of bipyridylium herbicides. It would appear that, in all probability, these materials disrupt the light reaction of photosynthesis, but that they do so by a mechanism quite different from that of urea compounds, carbamic acid esters and triazine derivatives (all of which seem to act in a rather similar way). Nevertheless, very little is known about precisely how the bipyridylium compounds function, though it seems that the formation of free radicals is an essential step in the manifestation of their biological action.

The bipyridylium compounds possess moderately large LD_{50}s (Table 9.1) and, so far as is known, their use in the field has not been responsible for any deaths. Being ionic, they are poorly absorbed from the gut and, in normal circumstances, the traces which enter the body are rapidly and completely metabolised. Recently, however, a disturbing delayed action toxic effect has been reported (Barnes, 1968). When paraquat is swallowed accidentally in *large amounts,* few symptoms are apparent for several days, but later a non-cancerous proliferation of lung cells leads to respiratory failure and death. This proliferation appears to continue long after all traces of paraquat have disappeared from the body. It seems likely that the substance brings about an irreversible change in some cellular system which has a fairly long term regulatory effect and which, in addition, is only slowly repaired by natural replacement processes. At *low dosage,* the body appears to cope adequately with the poison and no damage has been observed. Analogous but different delayed action responses (which are not chronic responses of the sort discussed in chapter 1) have been obtained with experimental organophosphates and certain methyl mercury compounds. It is therefore appropriate that this book should end, as it began, with a note of caution regarding the handling and storage of toxic materials of all kinds. New and hitherto unsuspected hazards have an unpleasant habit of emerging from time to time and the safe use of pesticides depends ultimately upon the care and vigilance of all concerned in their manufacture, screening and use.

REFERENCES

ALLEN, H. P. (1967), *Outl. Agric.,* **5,** 149
ANDERSON, R. N. (1964), *Weeds,* **12,** 60
ASHTON, F. M. (1963), *Weeds,* **11,** 295
AUDUS, L. J. (1959), *Plant Growth Substances.* (2nd ed.) Leonard Hill, London
AUDUS, L. J. (Ed.) (1964), *Physiology and Biochemistry of Herbicides,* Academic Press, Ltd., London
BADGER, G. M. (1946), *Nature, Lond.,* **158,** 585
BALDWIN, B. C. (1963), *Nature, Lond.,* **198,** 872
BARNES, J. M. (1968), *New Sci.,* **38,** 619
BOGGS, H. M. (1964), *J. Ass. off. agric. Chem.,* **47,** 346
BOON, W. R. (1964), *Outl. Agric.,* **4,** 163
BOS, B. G. VAN DEN (1960), *Recl. Trav. chim. Pays-Bas Belg.,* **79,** 807, 836, 1129
BRIAN, R. C. (1964), *Weed Res.,* **4,** 105
BRIAN, R. C. (1965), *Chemy. Ind.,* p. 1955

BRINK, F. and POSTERNAK, J. M. (1948), *J. cell. comp. Physiol.*, **32**, 211

BRUINSMA, J. (1962), *Weed Res.*, **2**, 73

BULLEN, E. R. (1964), *Outl. Agric.*, **4**, 64

CALDERBANK, A. (1966), *Outl. Agric.*, **5**, 55

CRAFTS, A. S. (1961), *Chemistry and Mode of Action of Herbicides*, Interscience Publ., London

CRAFTS, A. S. (1964), *Physiology and Biochemistry of Herbicides*, (Ed. Audus, L. J.) Academic Press Ltd., London (see p. 75)

CRAFTS, A. S. and ROBBINS, W. W. (1962), *Weed Control*, McGraw Hill, Inc., London

DAVIES, D. D. (1961), *Intermediary Metabolism in Plants*, Cambridge Univ. Press

EDSON, E. F., SANDERSON, D. M. and NOAKES, D. N. (1966), *Wld Rev. Pest Control*, **5**, 143

ELINGS, H. (1962), *Proc. Brit. Insecticide and Fungicide Conf.*, 1961, **2**, 451

ENNIS, W. (1964), *Weed Res.*, **4**, 93

FAWCETT, C. H. (1961), *A. Rev. Pl. Physiol.*, **12**, 345

FERGUSON, J. (1939), *Proc. R. Soc.*, **127(B)**, 387

FERGUSON, J. (1951) *Mechanisme de la Narcose*, 26th Colloques Internationaux du Centre National de la Recherche Scientifique, p. 25

FERGUSON, J. and HAWKINS, S. W. (1949), *Nature, Lond.*, **164**, 963

FOY, C. L. (1963), *Hilgardia*, **35**, 125

GOOD, N. E. (1962), *Wld Rev. Pest Control*, **1**, 19

GYSIN, H. and KNÜSLI, E. (1960), *Adv. Pest Control Res.* **3**, 289

HARRIS, C. I. and WARREN, G. F. (1964), *Weeds*, **12**, 120

HARTLEY, G. S. (1964), *Physiology and Biochemistry of Herbicides*, (Ed. Audus, L. J.) Academic Press, London (see p. 150)

HASSALL, K. A. (1953), *Ann. appl. Biol.*, **40**, 688

HASSALL, K. A. (1957), *J. Sci. Fd Agric.*, **7**, 415

HASSALL, K. A. (1961), *J. exp. Bot.*, **12**, 47

HASSALL, K. A. and JEWELL, C. A. (1956), *Rpts. 3rd Brit. Weed Control Conf.*, p. 663

HOLLY, K. (1964), *Biochemistry and Physiology of Herbicides*, (Ed. Audus, L. J.) Academic Press, London (see p. 423)

HOLLY, K. and ROBERTS, H. A. (1963), *Weed Res.*, **3**, 1

HOLMES, H. and PFEFFER, R. (1962), *Weed Res.*, **2**, 110

HOOD, A. E. M. (1965), *Outl. Agric.*, **4**, 286

JEATER, R. (1964), *Weed Res.*, **4**, 133

KEARNEY, P. C., HARRIS, C. I., KAUFMAN, D. D. and SHEETS, T. J. (1965), *Adv. Pest Control Res.*, **6**, 1

KEARNEY, P. C., SHEETS, T. J. and SMITH, J. W. (1964), *Weeds*, **12**, 83

KERR, M. W. and WAIN, R. L. (1964), *Ann. appl. Biol.*, **54**, 447

KNIGHT, B. A. G. and TOMLINSON, T. E. (1967), *Soil Sci.*, **18**, 233

LEHNINGER, A. L. (1959), *Symp. molec. Biol.* (Ed. Zirkle, R. E.) (see p. 122)

MCGOWAN, J. C. (1963), *Nature, Lond.*, **200**, 1317

MCINTYRE, G. I. (1962), *Weed Res.*, **2**, 165

MCWHORTER, C. (1963), *Weeds*, **11**, 265

MARTIN, H. (1964), *Scientific Principles of Crop Protection*, (5th ed.) Edward Arnold, London

MASSINI, P. (1963), *Acta bot. neerl.*, **12**, 64

MELTZER, J. (1961), *Meded LandbHoogesch. OpzoekStns. Gent.*, **26**, 1429

Ministry of Agriculture, Fisheries and Food (1968), *List of Approved Products for Farmers and Growers*, (A yearly publication)

MORELAND, D. E. and HILL, K. L. (1963), *Weeds*, **11**, 284

MULLER, R. L. (1962), *Wld Rev. Pest Control*, **1**, (2), 11

ONLEY, J. H. and STORRHERR, R. W. (1963), *J. Ass. off. agric. Chem.*, **46**, 996

PARKER, C. (1963), *Weed Res.*, **3**, 259

RIEPMA, P. (1962), *Weed Res.*, **2**, 41

RIES, S. K., LARSEN, R. P. and KENWORTHY, A. L. (1963), *Weeds*, **11**, 270

ROBERTS, H. A. and WILSON, B. J. (1962), *Weed Res.*, **2**, 60

ROBSON, J. W. and PROCTER, G. C. (1963), *Wld Crops*, **15**, 264

ROTHWELL, K. and WAIN, R. L. (1963), *Ann. appl. Biol.*, **51**, 161

SCHEURER, G. and FISCHER, A. (1962), *Weed Res.*, **2**, 130

SCHWEITZER, E. E. and ROGERS, B. J. (1964), *Weeds*, **12**, 7

SHAW, W. (1963), *Natn. agric. Chem. Ass. News*, (2), 14

SIMON, E. W. (1953), *Biol. Rev.*, **28**, 453

SMITH, G. N. and DYER, D. L. (1961), *J. agric. Fd Chem.*, **9,** 155

SPRINGETT, R. H. (1965), *Outl. Agric.*, **4,** 226

STAMMBACH, K., KILCHHER, H., FRIEDRICH, K., LARSEN, M. and SZEKELY, G. (1964), *Weed Res.*, **4,** 64

SULLIVAN, E. F., ABRAMS, R. L. and WOOD, R. R. (1963), *Weeds*, **11,** 258

SUND, K. A., PUTALA, E. C. and LITTLE, H. N. (1960), *J. agric. Fd Chem.*, **8,** 210

TALBERT, R. E. and FLETCHALL, O. H. (1964), *Weeds*, **12,** 33

WAIN, R. L. (1958), *Adv. Pest Control Res.*, **2,** 263

Weed Control Handbook (1968), Vols 1 and 2, (5th Ed.). Edited by Fryer, J. D. and Evans, S. A. and issued by the British Crop Protection Council. Blackwell Scientific Publications, Oxford

WHEELER, A. F. J. (1962), *J. Sci. Fd Agric.*, **13,** 103

WILLS, G. D., DAVIS, D. E. and FUNDERBURK, H. H. (1963), *Weeds*, **11,** 253

WORT, D. J. (1962), *Wld Rev. Pest Control*, **1,** (4), 6

INDEX